Rowan the Strange

Julie Hearn

OXFORD
UNIVERSITY PRESS

OXFORD
UNIVERSITY PRESS

Great Clarendon Street, Oxford OX2 6DP

Oxford University Press is a department of the University of Oxford.
It furthers the University's objective of excellence in research, scholarship,
and education by publishing worldwide in

Oxford New York

Auckland Cape Town Dar es Salaam Hong Kong Karachi
Kuala Lumpur Madrid Melbourne Mexico City Nairobi
New Delhi Shanghai Taipei Toronto

With offices in

Argentina Austria Brazil Chile Czech Republic France Greece
Guatemala Hungary Italy Japan Poland Portugal Singapore
South Korea Switzerland Thailand Turkey Ukraine Vietnam

Oxford is a registered trade mark of Oxford University Press
in the UK and in certain other countries

First published 2009
This educational edition first published 2011

British Library Cataloguing in Publication Data

Data available

ISBN: 978-0-19-912946-1

1 3 5 7 9 10 8 6 4 2

Printed in China by Printplus

Paper used in the production of this book is a natural,
recyclable product made from wood grown in sustainable forests.
The manufacturing process conforms to the environmental
regulations of the country of origin.

For my cousin, Harry Dixon

'I don't want to become any better. I should like to remain in this stage where I feel just like a little child. Please don't give me any more of those treatments. It disturbs my whole life.'

Unidentified lunatic, circa 1938

CONTENTS

THE VAN WITH THE BLUE CROSS

On the day war broke out Rowan's grandmother turned up outside his house, in a white van with a blue cross on it, and told him to get in.

'I can't,' Rowan pleaded, shrinking lower on the doorstep where he'd been sitting as still as a boot-scraper, watching the sky. 'What if those sirens go off again? What if Spitalfields gets bombed? I need to be here.'

'Rowan,' his grandmother replied, 'if Spitalfields gets bombed—which it won't, trust me—you're best off being somewhere else, aren't you? Come on. I need you.'

Inside the house, Sunday dinner was cooking and Rowan's little sister was playing the piano. The smell of Bisto . . . the sound of the 'Moonlight Sonata' spilling from an open window . . . so very normal, Rowan thought; so very *safe*, even though his mother was probably cursing the gravy for going all lumpy in the pan and ten-year-old Laurel was hitting so many wrong notes that the sonata made you wince.

Only . . . there was something else; some small, niggling

thing that, on any other day, might have seemed to him as bearable as the lumpy gravy and his sister's poor playing, but which right now . . .

Rowan shifted on the step. His grandmother was getting impatient, pressing her right foot up and down so that the van sounded impatient too, and raring to go. If he went with her now—immediately, without thinking twice—the Small Niggling Thing might disappear. Then again, it might actually get worse, looming larger and larger, like an escaping genie, the further they got from the house until . . .

'Nana,' Rowan said, in growing alarm, 'was Beethoven German or Dutch?'

'German,' his grandmother replied, raising her voice above the thrumming of the van. 'I believe. Now, are you coming with me or not?'

Rowan stood up. His heart was pounding, out of rhythm, and the sweat was forming, as it always did at moments like these, in a wet band around his hairline and two slicks under his arms.

'Rowan?'

'Just a minute, Nana. I have to . . . I need . . . '

'Oh, Ro . . . there isn't *time*. Just shout down to your mother that you're coming with me and that it's important. Where are . . . ? Oh, for goodness' sake, pet . . . ' She switched off the engine and got out of the van. 'Well, *I'll* tell her then. Just hurry up, my darling. Don't take all day.'

She thinks—hopes—I need the lav . . . Rowan tore into the house, his heart bumping harder as he passed gas masks hanging, like ugly bonnets, from pegs in the hall. And in his agitation, as the 'Moonlight Sonata' limped and thumped towards its third movement, he *was* tempted to head straight on, to the sanctuary of white tiles, running water, and a locked door. But what Laurel was doing was too distressing, too dangerous, to be ignored. Nor could it be drowned out, or made safe, by the flushing of a lavatory or the turning on of a tap.

She had to stop. He had to stop her. Immediately. Right now.

The drawing room door was shut. A barricade. A bad omen. For a moment or two—long enough for his grandmother to come in and go grumbling down to the kitchen—Rowan simply stood and sweated. Then he kicked open the door.

'Go away, Ro.' His sister's voice was firm above a clash of chords. 'I'm practising.'

The September sunshine was on her like a spotlight. She looked sweet, sitting there on the antique piano stool, her head bent in concentration, the sun gilding her hair. But Rowan saw no sweetness. To him the sun was a searchlight and his sister's bright red hair looked to be on fire. To him it was all danger, danger, danger.

'Stop playing that,' he ordered. *'Stop it, Laurel.'*

His sister shrugged and carried on. *A-flat major*, she thought, grinning at the image that popped into her head of a stout military man squashed flat by a tank. This final movement of the 'Moonlight Sonata' was a stormy thing, full of sadness and rage. Beethoven had been known to break hammers and strings playing it.

'Go *away*, Ro,' she said again, without turning round, and the notes she struck were the harshest yet.

Rowan stood his ground. His head had a whirlpool in

it. His heart felt as if it was trying to burst, like a rat, through the bones of his chest. 'I said STOP IT!' he yelled, loud enough to sear his throat.

Grimly Laurel played on, pounding the keys with all her might. She didn't care any more about keeping time but was doing her best to follow the melody because she sensed it was the tune itself, rather than her playing of it, that was driving her brother nuts. And she wanted to get the better of him. To teach him a lesson. Because he was Ro-the-Strange, a brother to be ashamed of, and because right now, with the country gone to war, she could do without his craziness making everything worse.

'Children—PLEASE!'

Dimly Rowan heard a clang of pans, like tin heads being banged together, as his mother called angrily for peace. In a minute his father would come hurrying down from his studio, not furious or shouting but distracted, obviously, and disappointed, too, which for some reason Rowan always found harder to bear from him than any great loss of temper.

Imagining, already, the look on his father's face, Rowan made a big effort to hold himself together. To not mind so horribly much that German music was filling his ears, the hall, and the street. To stop believing that the longer it went on the more likely it was that the first of Hitler's bombs to fall over England would land smack-bang on this house.

It's all right, he tried telling himself. *This is just our Lol practising some music, like she always does on Sundays, before we have our roast. It doesn't mean anything. Nothing bad is going to happen.*

But it was no good. As always, the bit of him that was panic-stricken was too far gone to be reasoned with. Like a dark twin, or a Russian doll—himself, but not—that part had its own logic; its own way of seeing things. And right now, with the 'Moonlight Sonata' playing on and on and on, it was terrified. It was seeing rubble. It was seeing arms and legs poking gorily from the ruins; a piano bombed to splinters. It was chanting *'stop the bitch'*, over and over and, as usual, it was loud.

Nothing bad . . . *nothing* . . . . But his mind was a sieve . . . a net . . . a strainer of thoughts, with reason, like water, rushing straight through all the holes.

'For*tissimo*!' young Laurel called out boldly, just to show him who was winning this particular battle of wills. 'Ar*peggios*.'

Rowan didn't understand. It was just more noise, and foreign noise at that, upsetting the balance of things further still. Lurching forward, like someone pushed, he set off across the room. His sister, intent on finishing the third movement, determined not to stop until the very last note had sounded, and died away, neither heard nor sensed him coming until he was right there behind her, his breath hot on her neck.

'Get—' was all she had time to say before the piano lid slammed down, breaking three of her fingers, like twigs.

'I didn't mean to do it, Nana. I don't know what came over me.'

They—Rowan and his nana—were hurtling towards the West End in the van with the blue cross on it.

Hurtling along, and swerving round corners, like bank robbers evading the law.

'Rowan,' his grandmother said to him, 'there are no excuses. Not this time. These wild outbursts, they've got to stop, pet. If you were a dog they'd've had you put down back there. Immediately. No reprieve. "We thought the world of him," they would have said. "But he was too unpredictable; too dangerous to have around."'

Appalled, Rowan hung his head.

'I don't mean to be harsh, my darling.' The van shot, heedlessly, over a junction. 'But you can't carry on like this.'

'I can't help it,' Rowan said. 'It just happens. I get a thought and it . . . it *grows*. I try and stop it, Nana, but I never can.'

'How?' his grandmother asked him. 'How do you try and stop it, Rowan?'

Rowan thought hard, biting his lower lip as he struggled to remember. It was too difficult, though, like trying to recall what it had been like to be a baby. All he knew was that sometimes, right out of the blue, his mind had a mind of its own.

'Well, whatever you're doing,' his grandmother said, eventually, 'it's not working is it, pet? It's having no effect whatsoever. You might as well be whistling in the wind for all the effect it's having.'

Whistling in the wind. Rowan allowed himself to be entertained by the idea of that. The next time it blew a gale, he decided, he would step outside and whistle a tune, just to see how much of himself he could hear.

'Is Laurel going to be all right?' he asked, humbly. 'Will she still be able to play the piano?'

'I can't tell you,' his grandmother replied. 'We'll know more, I imagine, when she and your father get back from the hospital. Now . . . I know you're sorry, so let's let the matter drop, shall we, and concentrate on where we're going? All right?'

'All right.'

His nana, Rowan knew, was on a mission. A life or death mission. Only, thanks to him, she was running late and driving ten times worse than usual (which up until now he hadn't actually thought possible). In the great scheme of things, this, far more than the earlier business, was what ought to be scaring him witless: being zoomed across London by a wild-haired eighty-three year old who couldn't tell a stop sign from a lollipop and kept bouncing off the kerbs.

Surprisingly, though, Rowan felt perfectly safe being jounced around in the van. He trusted his nana behind the wheel, despite her great age and complete disregard for the highway laws. He admired her nerve. And anyway, the van had a blue cross on it, which meant that other people were supposed to get out of their way sharpish, like for a fire engine or a parade.

They were approaching Hyde Park Corner—always a tricky moment.

'Look!' Rowan's grandmother said, suddenly. 'Up there in the sky! Our boys haven't wasted any time, have they? They look like elephants, don't you think?'

Rowan looked, and marvelled, at the sight of barrage balloons drifting at the ends of steel cables, high over Buckingham Palace and its surrounding parks. They *did* look a bit like elephants, all baggy and grey in the sunshine and jostling, idly, for space.

'What . . . ?' he began.

'To stop the enemy coming in for a low level attack,' his grandmother explained. 'Although, if you ask me . . . Oh, *heck*.'

A policeman was blowing his whistle, and waving wildly at their van.

'I think he wants you to pull over,' Rowan said. 'Safely,' he added, as his grandmother braked so sharply that the tyres squealed and the van slewed, like a dodgem, before coming to a halt.

The policeman's face looked heated as he hurried towards them, one hand raised to stop other cars from hitting him, the other resting purposefully on his right hip, as if he might suddenly pull a gun.

'Uh-oh,' said Rowan. 'I think we're in trouble.'

'Nonsense, pet.' His grandmother cranked down her window and stuck her head out. 'Afternoon, officer,' she called out. 'I trust this won't take long. I'm on a life or death mission, and every second counts.'

Police Constable Eddie Dobbs was young, although he looked completely grown-up to Rowan and formidable too in his uniform. He was young and he was tetchy: uncomfortably aware that being on traffic duty, today of all days, was no great shakes and would certainly win him no medals. He had been wondering, for a while, whether he might leave the police force, if things got really nasty, to fight for King and Country. But now that the war had officially started he knew that he would not. He was too big a scaredy-cat.

For several hours, as traffic flowed smoothly all around him, he had been feeling useless. A coward. A shirker of his patriotic duty. And now here was this civilian, and an old boot of a woman at that, as good as telling him to get out of her way.

'And what "life or death" mission would this be then, madam?' he snapped, bending his knees the better to glare into the van.

'The kind in which a life hangs in the balance,' Rowan's grandmother replied, sweetly. 'And it would help, *tremendously*, officer, if you would give me specific directions to the German ambassador's residence in Carlton House Terrace.'

'Would it now,' said PC Dobbs. 'Would it really.'

Rowan, sitting quietly, understood straightaway that his grandmother was making no friends here and might even be getting herself into very hot water indeed.

'Tell him, Nana,' he said. 'About the dog.'

PC Dobbs adjusted his gaze, his eyes sliding over and then away from the pale-faced, dark-haired boy in the passenger seat. 'The dog,' he repeated. 'Yes, do tell me about the dog. No—on second thoughts, don't.'

Behind him, someone hooted. *You're in the way, idiot,* said the hoot. PC Dobbs pressed so close to the side of the van as a car sped by, that he hurt himself.

'You've no business, either of you,' he snapped, 'going anywhere near any German ambassador's residence. It'll be cordoned off like as not. Out of bounds, anyway. In fact, you're to turn right round and go straight back home. Only first . . . ' He held up his traffic-stopping hand as Rowan's grandmother opened her mouth to protest. 'Only *first*, I'm going to search every inch of this van. Yes . . . I can assure you, madam, I am perfectly within my rights.

We're at war against Hitler, in case you hadn't noticed, so any vehicle caught tearing across London, in a mighty strange hurry, like, to reach the German ambassador is going to get searched. Thoroughly. With a very fine-tooth comb.'

'But . . . ' Rowan began, 'you don't . . . ' Someone—he—needed to tell this policeman that the German ambassador was no longer at home in Carlton House Terrace. That he had fled the country days ago, taking everything he owned except his poor little dog who, right now, would be cowering in the darkest place it could find, waiting to be rescued.

Someone—he—ought also to point out that Nana was a lot more ancient than she looked and should be treated gently, like valuable china.

His grandmother, however, placed a hushing hand on his knee. 'It's all right, pet,' she whispered into his hair. 'Leave this to me.'

'But . . . ' If they were forced to turn back, what would become of that helpless little dog? It might die of thirst, or fright. Or someone else—someone cruel—might get to it first.

Rowan took a deep breath, then another. Amazingly . . . incredibly . . . he continued to feel safe. No voice in his head. No niggles. His grandmother had clambered out on to the road. She would deal with this, Rowan told himself. She would explain everything properly, and then they would be on their way.

'Are you the owner of this vehicle, madam?'

The policeman's voice was deeply sarcastic, as if he couldn't imagine Rowan's grandmother owning anything much apart from her clothes, a few bits of jewellery, and her Very Unfortunate Attitude.

'The blue cross!' Rowan cried out. 'Haven't you noticed the blue cross? Don't you know what it means—sir?'

'Pipe down, sonny,' the policeman ordered. 'Just pipe down, sit still, and don't try anything funny.'

Chastened, Rowan turned to look out through the windscreen. His stomach gurgled and he thought, wistfully, about dinner. It would be late, now, and probably not very nice. Would Laurel be able to hold her knife and fork? *I didn't mean it,* he communed, silently, with the sky above Hyde Park. *I didn't mean to hurt my sister.*

The barrage balloons had altered their position. No longer sideways-on they looked menacing now, to Rowan: enemy aliens with enormous behinds. *Don't try anything funny,* he warned them in his head. *I'm watching you and I'm warning you: I have secret powers. Zap! Ker-Pow! Boom! I am Superboy from Planet Krypton and I am here to protect humankind.* When he heard a loud scraping noise, on the outside of the van, he fondly imagined one of the huge balloons flicking its chain at them, warning them off.

Then: 'I can assure you, officer, that won't rub out,' his grandmother said. 'It is a genuine blue cross, and I am a genuine volunteer rescue worker for Our Dumb Friends' League. And if my grandson and I don't make it across the city, to the German ambassador's—'

'Unlock the back of the vehicle, please.'

'If we don't get there soon a poor little dog is going to die. An innocent creature whose—'

'I *said* unlock these doors.'

Rowan winced. This policeman clearly didn't give a ha'penny chew about the German ambassador's dog. Either that or he didn't believe in it. Perhaps he reckoned Rowan and his grandmother were up to no good. Maybe . . . just maybe . . . he thought they might be spies.

'And when I've searched inside,' PC Dobbs was saying, 'I want the bonnet lifted. Then I'm going underneath. With a flashlight.'

We're going to be stuck here all day, Rowan realized. *Even when he doesn't find anything he's going to keep us here for ages, just to be mean.*

'Very well,' he heard his grandmother say, followed by the chink-clunk of her keys as she unlocked the back of the van. Nobody in the world carried as many keys as Rowan's grandmother. She wore them like a medieval weapon, on a chain attached to her belt, and sometimes, if she'd been asleep a long time in her chair, they weighed her down as she tried to get up and her friend Rosa said: 'Honestly, Ivy, if you ever fall into the Thames it'll be curtains for you.'

The back of the van had a lot of dog paraphernalia in it: muzzles and grabbers and old blankets so hairy they looked a lot like creatures themselves. Most of the space, from floor to roof, was taken up by a wire cage, with newspapers laid down to sop up inevitable accidents. The back of the van was smelly. It shrieked 'dog' at you the second the doors swung open. Only a fool, Rowan reassured himself, would suspect the driver of being anything but a collector of stray animals. A bit dotty, perhaps, but certainly no threat to national security.

'What's in that box?' PC Dobbs snapped. 'There, in that corner?'

'Biscuits,' Rowan's grandmother told him. 'Shaped like little bones.'

'And that pile of old rope—what's that for?'

'Those are muzzle-leads of varying sizes. Small for dachsunds, medium for springers, and large for Great Danes and Alsatians.'

'German dogs,' said PC Dobbs. 'Some of those mutts are Jerry breeds, aren't they?' He sounded both disgusted and triumphant.

Rowan's grandmother kept her voice very calm: 'Your point being?' she said.

PC Dobbs didn't rightly know what his point was. All he knew was he had stopped these people, he didn't like these people, and there was no way he was going to let them drive off on their life or death mission, whatever it was, while he himself went back to the lowly task of directing traffic round Hyde Park Corner.

'Step aside,' he ordered Rowan's grandmother. 'I'm going in.'

Spies, thought Rowan, wildly. *He definitely, seriously, honestly believes we are spies, on our way to the German ambassador with top secret information about the war. Maybe he reckons the dog biscuits have codes baked into them, or that the blankets are for hiding under, or that . . .*

When the van doors slammed, and the lock clicked back into place, he assumed the policeman had either been quick-smart about searching the cage, or had taken one good whiff of the hairy blankets and changed his mind. Then the shouting started, and the banging, and by the time his grandmother eased herself back into the driving seat, her eyes bright and her keys jangling, he was in no doubt at all about what she had just done.

'Nana . . . ' he began, as the van's engine roared, the tyres screeched, and they re-joined the traffic on Hyde Park Corner.

'Not a word!' she interrupted, cheerfully. 'We're on a life or death mission, remember, and every second counts.'

'But . . . '

'I know, I know . . . just try to ignore him, pet. It's not for very long, he can't come to any harm, and as soon as we get to Carlton House Terrace we'll let him out. All right?'

In the back of the van, PC Dobbs was threatening all sorts. Court. Fines. Prison. The Full Weight of the Law.

'Let's hope his bark is worse than his bite,' said Rowan's grandmother and, in spite of everything, Rowan chuckled.

THE CHOW WITH THE DICKY HEART

The German ambassador's dog turned out to be a chow—a Chinese breed, as Rowan's grandmother was quick to point out to PC Eddie Dobbs; meek by nature but so very highly strung that their poor little hearts often failed under stress.

When they found it, it was cowering beneath the German ambassador's abandoned dining table and panting so hard that Rowan feared its heart would stop any second.

'You see?' his grandmother said, her voice echoing round the enormous room even though she was keeping it low. 'You see, officer? It looks as if we got here just in time.'

PC Dobbs did not reply. He was beyond speech. Released from the back of the van, with different coloured hairs all over his uniform and his helmet all skew-whiff, his own stress level had been so dangerously high that he would have handcuffed this crazy old bird to the railings and bellowed his anger an inch from her face had a small crowd of bystanders not welcomed her like royalty.

'Hurrah! We knew you'd come.'

'I do hope you're not too late.'

'Trust the Jerries to leave a poor little doggie to starve.'

There had been two senior police officers guarding the entrance to the German ambassador's residence and they had nodded to PC Dobbs as if his being there was all in the line of his duty. Then someone—a man from The Press—had stepped forward and taken a picture, the flash on his camera exploding like a star.

All in all, it had not been quite the right moment for PC Dobbs to lose his temper. So, as one of the senior officers opened the German ambassador's front door, and Rowan and his grandmother went hurrying up the steps, he had summoned what was left of his dignity and gone treading heavily after them.

'God bless you, officer,' a woman in the crowd had called after him, and *It's only a ruddy dog,* he had thought, in amazement; *we've got the Jerries on their way to bomb us all to blazes, and this lot's fretting over a flaming hound?*

Rowan's grandmother had brought a selection of biscuits in her pocket, and the right-sized muzzle for a chow. But: 'I doubt we'll need to restrain her,' she said, her joints twingeing like old bedsprings as she bent to peer under the table. 'She's scared, but not dangerously so, and the muzzle will only frighten her more. No sudden moves though, officer, just to be on the safe side. And keep your truncheon out of sight. Rowan? Here—unclip the muzzle, and be ready with the lead when I say so.'

Rowan took hold of the muzzle-lead and did as he'd been told. His nana was amazing in situations like this.

Once, long ago, she had stroked a wolf—at least that's what she told people—and it had lain at her feet for its tummy to be tickled. Not many people believed that story, but Rowan did, and if his nana could handle a wolf then the German ambassador's chow was going to be a doddle.

'I'd muzzle it all the same,' muttered the policeman, as if reading his mind.

'Shhh,' Rowan whispered. 'We have to stay quiet.' It felt odd, being in this house; odd and a little bit scary even though he was here on a genuine mission and two big strong Englishmen were watching the door.

Ka-boom, he thought, for extra courage. *I am Superboy. I have an iron fist. If the enemy rushes us, from the kitchen, I am ready to defend my people.*

The house really had been abandoned, though, little doubt about that. There were wet rings on the sideboard where bottles or decanters had recently stood, and picture hooks, with nothing underneath, at precise intervals round the walls. Above Rowan's head a chandelier of looped and dusty glass made him think, for some reason, of the Snow Queen's palace—awesome, yet ice-cold—and a sheet had been flung over the enormous dining table, beneath which his grandmother had begun to croon.

Had the German ambassador lived here alone, or with a family? Rowan wondered. It was hard to imagine children in this grand and echoey room, squabbling over their puddings the way he and Laurel usually did, or slipping titbits to the dog. Maybe this was where the German ambassador had entertained important guests. Maybe Hitler had been here for his tea.

'What's happening under there?' said PC Dobbs. And, beneath the table, the chow began to growl: a low but definite rumble.

PC Dobbs took two steps backwards. 'Chinese or not,' he muttered, 'the Jerries have probably trained this—what's it called again?—this mutt to attack to order. Any trigger word in English, like "sit!" or "heel!", and it'll go for the throat, like. Fangs in the jugular quicker than a whistle.' He raised his voice: 'I'd be very very careful under there, madam, if I were you.'

Rowan's grandmother made no reply. She was still crooning: a soft unintelligible lullaby that was supposed to calm the chow right down while letting it know who was boss.

'Well, I don't trust this situation,' said PC Dobbs, belligerently, 'I don't trust it at all.'

Beneath the table, both the crooning and the growling intensified.

And Rowan no longer felt safe.

'Please, sir,' he appealed to PC Dobbs, just loud enough to be heard. 'It's you. It's *your* voice that's upsetting the dog. You have to be quiet, as quiet as a mouse, or my grandmother might get bitten.'

PC Dobbs curled his lip and made a sound like 'pah!'

This time the panic did not creep up on Rowan gradually, the way it usually did. It hit him like an invisible tram. *Bam, ker-pow, smash.*

If he says one more word my nana will die.

The certainty of this filled him one hundred per cent, leaving no room for argument; no room to *breathe.* And as his fists tightened on the lengths of leather and rope in his hands the bit of him that knew what it knew; that was already steeling itself for the dog's leap and the carnage it would cause, said: *'Muzzle him. Go on.'*

PC Dobbs was taller than Rowan; stronger too. Muzzling him would be like trying to lasso a living breathing totem pole; Rowan knew that, somewhere beneath the roaring of the Voice.

Stand on a chair. Take the stupid arsehole by surprise. Hurry up.

As usual, the Voice was insistent. Bullying. All the same, Rowan hesitated, for the policeman might easily yell something, before the muzzle was over his head, and then . . . his nana . . .

Get on with it, splat-brain. Now!

. . . Or the muzzle might not fit a grown man the same way it did a dog. It might slip straight over the man's face, miss the mouth completely, and end up looped around his neck.

Then you'll have to strangle him with it, won't you.

All right then. Good idea.

A chair. He needed a chair. But just reaching for one would be risky. The policeman was bound to ask why. Not the chair, then, or the muzzle either, but something . . . drastic . . . had to be . . . done. To silence the policeman. To keep Nana safe. The fear was so bad he was having trouble keeping still. His face, he knew, was twisting like a fiend's with the effort not to yell or wail. And the voice in his head, that was his and yet not, was sharp and clear and certain:

Kill him! Go on. Hurry up, you dithering moron or the Nana will die. Knife! Knife! Penknife in pocket. Go on! Go on!

'Rowan?'

His right hand was deep in the pocket of his shorts;

fingers trembling around the penknife, easing out the blade.

'Rowan, can you hear me? Look at me. Rowan?'

That's Nana's voice. That's the Nana talking. Does that mean it's all right? Are we safe, now? Am I?

The penknife was a good one. A beauty. His grown-up cousin Tommy John had sent it from America for his last birthday—his thirteenth. It had a mother-of-pearl handle and was sharp enough, so Tommy John had informed him, to gut a fish, whittle a stick, or even to shave his whiskers off one fine day.

To date, being whiskerless, he had made do with sharpening coloured pencils and carving his name on a floorboard under his bed. Until now, despite the increasing wildness of his outbursts, he had never once considered hurting someone with the fish-gutting, stick-whittling, whisker-shaving blade. Why would he? For that would be . . . that would be . . .

Nothing, bloody IDIOT you. Just do the thing. Do it NOW!

'Rowan. What are you doing? Rowan?'

'NO TALKING!' he heard himself scream. 'Shut UP. Shut flaming well up, *SHUT UP . . .* ' And the knife was ready, the blade exposed, and the Voice was crowing: *That's it, go on, stick it! Stick it!* Only . . . this was Nana speaking, not the policeman, so what should he do? With them? With himself?

'No talking ANYONE!' he shrieked, a sob catching in his throat as he clenched his fist around the knife in his pocket and took one, staggering, step towards his nana.

Then: 'Oh—*Rowan . . .* '

He was squatting down, so close to the floor that he

could see a breadcrumb, or a bit of fluff, or something, caught in the fibres of the carpet. He couldn't remember bending his knees or wanting to make himself this small, so what was he doing, crouched as if for a somersault? And why was there blood . . . ?

'Officer—hold on to the dog for a moment, please. And you, sir . . . no, there's no panic, everyone's absolutely fine, but would you kindly fetch my grandson a glass of water from the kitchen?'

'Nana . . . I think . . . I feel . . . 'And then Rowan was panting, worse than the chow, and lying flat on his back while his grandmother lifted his right hand and gently, very gently, prised open his wet and smarting fingers.

When she saw the knife, its blade all bloodied, she quickly turned her body, so that PC Dobbs wouldn't see; snapped the knife shut and hid it deep in her own cardigan pocket.

For a moment, her eyes met Rowan's.

This is the second time today, her look said, plain as anything. *It's not good, pet. I love you, but this is not good.*

I know, his own eyes told her back. *I know, I know, I know.*

'My hand . . . ' he croaked, needing to shift her gaze before all the love and the worry in it made him cry.

'You'll live, you silly sausage,' she told him. And from another of her many pockets she produced a surprisingly clean handkerchief and bound it tightly round his hand. It reddened immediately, in three stripes, but not enough to create an emergency.

'What's he done?' PC Dobbs wanted to know. 'What the blazes was that all about? And how'd he cut himself?

This is a right situation and a half this is . . . Oi! Get . . . leave . . . don't you sniff me there, like, or I'll . . . I'll . . . '

The chow was breathing harder than ever, but in hope and gratitude now. Whatever it was he had just said or done, Rowan told himself, it couldn't have been all that distressing, otherwise the dog's heart would have failed, wouldn't it? At the very least, it would have stayed under the table, out of harm's way.

He tried to stand, but his grandmother pressed him back. 'Take it slowly,' she told him. 'Slowly and calmly.'

'The chow's wagging her tail,' he appealed to her. 'That's good, isn't it?'

He could tell, from his grandmother's face, that his getting the dog's breed right, and the fact that it was a female, had reassured her, a lot, about the state of his mind now that the panic was over. Still, she kept her hand where it was, keeping him down.

A man in uniform—one of the guards from outside—came back from the kitchen with a big glass tumbler of water. 'I'm all right,' Rowan told him. 'Give it to the dog. She's parched.' He was straining to sound normal; to *appear* normal, even though he was stretched out on the floor with sliced fingers, a torn pocket, and large gaps in his mind where recent memory should have been. They were like holes in a roof, those gaps, wide open to the elements; to whatever blew in.

The guard raised his eyebrows, and looked to Rowan's grandmother for a yes or a no. From the corner of his eye Rowan saw his grandmother nod, her hand and most of her attention still very firmly on him. Then they all listened, in silence, to the sound of the chow lapping from the glass.

'She'll need more than that, in a proper bowl,' said Rowan. 'Can I get up, please?'

He wanted to go home now, and be ordinary. He wanted his dinner, lumpy gravy and all, and then to go to his room, to read—to *devour*—the exploits of Superman in the latest comic Tommy John had sent from America. He wanted to forget about the war; forget about his outbursts; forget about everything except the possibility of sleep. He would have to apologize to Laurel first, of course, for the earlier thing, and then accept whatever punishment his parents had agreed upon. Apart from that, he hoped, everyone would just leave him alone.

Without a word, his grandmother removed her hand.

'Thank you,' he said, and stood. As soon as they were alone, he would ask her not to say anything to the rest of the family about this second outburst. After all, she had locked someone up in her van today, and how crazy was that? Incredibly, the kidnapped policeman appeared to have let the matter drop, but all the same . . . If he promised not to tell on her, maybe she would agree not to tell on him. That was only fair, he reckoned.

The guard who had rushed in, and then gone for the water, had persuaded his grandmother to sit down for a minute on one of the German ambassador's abandoned chairs. 'Does he need to go to hospital?' he was saying. 'Do you want someone to take him in?' And he was looking over at Rowan as if it was he, not the chow, who was the animal in the room.

'No.' Rowan's grandmother leant back in the chair as if gathering strength from its upholstery. 'It was an accident. A little bit of broken glass that he picked up off the floor so the dog wouldn't tread on it. The lacerations aren't deep enough to need stitches. He'll be fine.'

The guard opened his mouth, then closed it again and cleared his throat. 'All right,' he said. 'If you're sure.'

'We're sure.' Rowan's grandmother closed her eyes, just for a second, braced herself, and got up.

Good, Rowan thought. *That's a good story about the glass. She can tell that at home. I'll ask her to. I'll get her to promise.* But his grandmother's hands were shaking as she picked the dog lead up off the carpet and, as he watched her take hold of the chow's collar, and saw how the dog, sensing her distress, timidly licked her nose, Rowan knew, for shame, that it would be wrong to bargain with her.

Then: 'I'll drive the van if you want,' said PC Dobbs, gruffly. 'Get the dog to wherever it needs to go. Make sure you and the boy get home all right, before the black-out.' There were hairs and stains on his uniform, still, from his earlier ride in the van. His pride had been injured and his temper was still cooling. And yet . . . the old bird had spirit, he granted her that, and she looked too done in to be in charge of a vehicle. The lad could go in the back this time, with the blankets and the smell and the dog. There was something odd about that lad—something not quite right. None of his business, but still . . .

'Thank you, officer,' Rowan's grandmother said, her voice small and surprised. 'You are a hero.'

I'm not, thought PC Dobbs, grimly, *but it's nice that someone thinks so.*

'WE THOUGHT—HOPED—HE WOULD GROW OUT OF IT'

Dinner was so late now that they would be calling it supper and having it cold. Rowan's grandmother was going back to her own house, for something on toast, but not before having a long talk, behind a closed door, with her daughter and son-in-law.

PC Dobbs was in the kitchen, waiting to drive Rowan's grandmother home, as he'd promised, and Rowan's older sister, Daphne, was making him a cup of tea. Of Laurel there was no sign.

The German ambassador's chow had been safely delivered to the League of Dumb Friends' rescue centre and given a kennel all to itself while it recovered from its trauma. Leaving it behind, Rowan had envied it the privacy and peace of that small, dark space. Once he got home, he knew, there would be only questions, recriminations, and injured looks for him, with no escape until bedtime.

'What's your old man's line of business then?' PC Dobbs shifted, uncomfortably, in a bentwood chair and eyed with suspicion the family's ancient black-leaded range, the enormous cream-painted dresser, and the collection of pots and griddles, candlesticks and meat plates that looked to him as if they'd come out of the Ark.

'He's an artist,' Rowan told him. 'He paints pictures. Big ones.'

His sister wrapped a towel round the handle of the kettle before lifting it from the range. 'Daddy is famous,' she said, happily. 'He exhibited in Paris last year, at the International Surrealist Exhibition, and his *Enigma of Feet and Clouds* is considered a masterpiece. Milk?'

'Please,' said PC Dobbs, faintly.

'And our nana was an artist's model, back in the eighteen seventies. Dante Gabriel Rossetti was absolutely crazy about her and so was another painter who left her two houses in his will—although they both had to be sold when our grandfather died, to pay off his gambling debts . . . So you see, officer, we are a frightfully bohemian lot. Sugar?'

'Y-yes—ar*hem*—two. Please.'

Rowan's stomach growled.

'There's some bread in the crock,' Daphne said to him, 'if you absolutely can't wait.' Her voice had a chill to it, all of a sudden, and she kept her eyes firmly fixed on the teapot.

'I can wait.' It was a lie. He was starving. But Daphne, he could tell, didn't think he deserved to gorge himself on bread and butter after all the trouble he'd caused.

Daphne handed PC Dobbs his cup of tea and began talking about the war. Was it true, she wanted to know, that Londoners would be expected to eat squirrels and crows if food supplies ran low? And that Winchester Cathedral was not to be bombed because Hitler intended to be crowned King of England there? Was it true that dark-coloured cows were having white stripes painted on them in case they wandered onto roads during the black-out? And did he think—could they dare to hope—that it would all be over by Christmas?

PC Dobbs was looking at Daphne as if she had just stepped out of a Hollywood movie and walked straight down the aisle of a cinema to stand by his seat for a chat. He was looking at her, Rowan thought, the way Clark Kent would look at Lois Lane, if he was a real man, not a character in a comic, and could show emotion better.

Daphne was seventeen. She had dark red hair and beautiful skin and was training to be a secretarial assistant. She was sweet-tempered and sang a lot, and Rowan often wished he had been born first, as her, instead of four years later, as himself.

Everyone fell in love with Daphne—young men, small children, old people, everyone. If the Germans captured England, Rowan mused, they were bound to love Daphne too and then she would be able to plead for the rest of the family so that he and Laurel, his parents and his nana would not end up as slaves or prisoners of war.

PC Dobbs was asking Daphne where their shelter was. Their bomb shelter, he meant. 'Down here won't be safe,' he said. 'In case that's all you've got planned. I know it's the cellar, like, and the kettle's handy, and it saves going outdoors in all weathers, but it wouldn't hold up against a direct hit. You're going to need a proper Anderson, all of you.'

Rowan waited, with interest, for Daphne's reply. He'd been wondering about the shelter thing too. His nana and her friend Rosa had an Anderson in their garden. It had been delivered free, because Nana and Rosa were old and not particularly well off, and a neighbour had set it up for them. A raw construction of corrugated iron and sheets of steel, it had been half buried in the ground, with a load of earth heaped on top. There was room inside it for six people (or, in this case, for two elderly ladies, four dogs, and a budgerigar) and there were plans afoot to plant flowers on the top.

There was no garden here, at the house in Spitalfields, just a courtyard full of ivy and ferns where the cat basked and a statue stood and where, according to Rowan's father, an Anderson shelter would be an 'abomination on the eye' even if there had been room for one.

'The church,' Daphne was saying. 'If a warning sounds, we can get to the church in less than a minute.' She turned her back on Rowan and lowered her voice: 'The crypt, you know. It's vast—big enough for the whole neighbourhood.'

'I heard what you just said,' Rowan told her. 'Anyway, you don't have to whisper. What are you whispering for?'

'I'm not,' his sister replied. 'Go and wash your hands. We'll be eating soon.'

Rowan stayed put. 'I'm not scared of the crypt, if that's what you're thinking,' he said. 'I'm not scared of tombs, or of dead people, or ghosts. I'll go down in the crypt if there's an air raid. It won't bother me.'

'Wash your hands, Ro,' Daphne repeated. And PC Dobbs gave him a look that said *do as your sister tells you* which made Rowan scowl because he didn't think Eddie Dobbs had a right to do that.

Still, he went, closing the kitchen door behind him. Listening outside was sneaky, he knew that, and whatever he overheard might distress him, he knew that too. All the same he pressed his right ear to the wood and waited.

It was dark outside the kitchen, with the door shut; dark from the pitch-coloured panelling that covered all the walls, and dark from the giant shadow cast by the staircase. Most of the house was dark like that, apart from the studio at the very top where Rowan's father painted his pictures. There was spooky dark, though, and cosy dark and this ancient, rackety house, where Rowan had been born, had always seemed cosy to him: a place where time stood still and where, up until this morning, and the war, he had felt safer than anywhere else.

'Your brother,' PC Dobbs was saying, *'gets pretty worked up over things, doesn't he? Upset, like.'*

Rowan heard the rattle of china as his sister carried dirty tea things to the sink. *'Yes,'* she replied. *'He does rather. We thought—hoped—he would grow out of it but it seems to be getting worse. He has these panics; strange times when he gets terribly distressed, for no obvious reason, and starts shouting and lashing out.'*

'Hmm. That must be difficult for you—for the whole family.'

'It has been. It is.'

'So he's not being evacuated then? With all the other kiddies?'

'I doubt it. My little sister's going to Weymouth—that's the plan, anyway—but I don't know what we're going to do about Ro. Sending him to live with strangers wouldn't be fair. He can get quite aggressive, you know, and he's growing up; getting bigger and stronger and harder to control. Sometimes,

even though he's my brother . . . well, the truth is, he scares me.'

'You were scared just now, weren't you? When you said to me about the crypt and he got angry.'

'I was a bit. We can never tell, you see, what's going to set him off. It can be anything . . . anything at all . . . This morning he . . . '

'You're eavesdropping. You're a snoop. If I tell you'll be in even more trouble.'

Spinning round, Rowan noticed Laurel sitting halfway up the stairs, peering between the spindles of the banister. Her plaits were hanging down, like bell-pulls. Ordinarily he might have tugged them—not hard and only, really, to annoy—but, ordinarily he wouldn't already have put her into hospital.

And oh . . . if Daphne was scared of him then Laurel must be terrified. No wonder she was keeping her distance.

I don't mean to scare them. I don't mean to scare anyone.

'How are your fingers?' he asked.

Laurel didn't answer, just held up both her hands.

'Oh!' Rowan looked away, down at the floor.

'I won't be able to take my music exam because of you,' Laurel informed him. 'I can't even hold a *pen*. And when I go to the toilet someone's going to have to wipe my bottom.'

'I'm sorry, Lol. Honestly.'

He clenched his right hand, hard; felt the cuts he had made with the penknife open up, like nasty grins. They were throbbing, those cuts, but the pain, at that moment, with his sister watching him as if he was a devil, was not only bearable but welcome.

Was he really sorry? He knew he certainly should be, and if causing himself even more pain, with the penknife or anything else, could have made him so he would have done it.

Briefly—very briefly—he considered banging his head, hard, against the kitchen door. To knock some sense and sorriness into it. To punish himself, violently, before his parents tried, uselessly, to punish him with their disappointment and reasonable words. To show his sisters . . . what?

'I'm sorry, Lol,' he said again. 'Will you still be evacuated? To Weymouth?'

Laurel kept her splinted fingers raised, accusingly, as she pulled a suffering face. 'Shouldn't think so,' she said. 'I expect I'll have to stay here now and get bombed to bits. Then you'll be like a murderer because that will be your fault as well.'

Rowan nodded. That was fair. That was just. That was how he himself would see it, in Laurel's shoes.

The sound of a door opening overhead made them both jump.

'Are you sure you won't stay for something to eat?' they heard their mother say.

'No,' their grandmother replied, her feet creaking on floorboards. 'It's been a long day. And that nice young policeman will be wanting to get going, before the black-out.'

No he won't, Rowan thought. *He'll be wanting to stay right where he is, worshipping Daphne and drinking tea. Even if bombs start falling or his clothes begin to smell, he'll be wanting to stay in our kitchen for ever.*

'Where's Rowan?'

Laurel looked back down at her brother, her expression triumphant as she caught his faraway gaze. Their father sounded grim—really grim. 'Hah, now you're for it,' she hissed through the banisters. 'You're in big trouble now, Ro-the-Strange.'

THE GIRL WITH THE SEAWEED HAIR

As a very little boy, Rowan had truly believed that his father's studio was just a short leap from Heaven. There was a couch in the room, draped in faded brocade, and he had loved nothing better than to lie on that, looking up at the sky through an enormous glass dome that his father said was called a cupola.

For hours he would watch the shifting of clouds and the changing of the light, hoping to see an angel, or even God. Sometimes he would fall fast asleep among the cushions and musty brocades, to be lifted up later and taken down for his tea.

The couch was still there and Rowan could still have lain on it (just) without the springs breaking or his feet sticking off the end. But it was many years since he had watched the sky for celestial beings, and almost as long, it seemed to him, since his father had tolerated his company for more than half an hour, whether or not he was working.

Now, with the daylight fading, it was hard to see

anything much, either through the cupola or down at floor-level, among the paints and the easels and the bottles of brushes and turpentine. All through the rest of the house, heavy wooden shutters had been tightly closed and any chinks stuffed with rags. It was the law now. Everyone had to black out their windows after dusk, so that the enemy wouldn't see lamps glowing, or firelight flickering, and have something to aim their bombs at.

Rowan's mother, who was a journalist, had written so many articles on how to make a blackout blind out of dark sateen and press studs that she jokingly said she could have run off half a dozen in her sleep. Rowan's father, however, wanted nothing to do with such tat. Shutters, he said, were the natural eyelids of their home. Closed, they had been blocking the light for centuries and would continue to do so, with just a few small adjustments, for as long as The Current Situation lasted.

He wouldn't say 'war'. When he tried, the word stuck in his throat like a fishbone. Rowan's grandmother said it was because he had fought in France in 1914 and seen things—terrible things—that part of him kept trying to forget and part of him had wanted to capture in paintings so raw and so heartrending that countries—all countries—would think twice, in the future, about sending their men into battle.

So far as Rowan was aware, no such paintings had ever been completed, not by his father or anyone else. Certainly he had never had his heart rended by one and neither had his nana.

Right now there was just the one large canvas—a 'work in progress'—propped and drying against the far wall of the studio. With the light disappearing it was hard to make out what was on it but Rowan could see cliffs, chalky-white against the blue of a sky, and, in the foreground, the disembodied head of a young girl, her hair like seaweed, all dark and drifting. He would have liked a better look at that girl's head, to see if it was a real person's, or part of a tumbled-down statue, but that would have meant moving away from the spot he had been told to stand still on while his father Had Words.

Instead, he tipped back his head and gazed up through the cupola wondering 'Will there be stars?' There were no shutters to cover the curves of this most magnificent and complicated of windows and no one, as yet, had dared to suggest going over it with blackout paint. It was imperative, Rowan knew, that not a single scrap of light be seen up here after dark, not the tip of father's cigarette, even, or the briefest flare of a match. But . . . would the enemy see the whites of their eyes, he wondered, if they flew in low enough? Or the glimmer of those cliffs in his father's new painting?

'Look at me, Rowan. You need to listen. It's important.'

In the half light it was easy to look without really seeing; to focus on a point just a whisker away from his father's right cheekbone and then to think of other things.

As the enemy approaches Spitalfields, Superboy hears the drone of aircraft and knows there is no time to lose . . .

'I'm sorry,' he said to his father, automatically, and at intervals, while his imagination roamed. 'I'm sorry, Dad.' And then: 'But . . . what? . . . I don't understand?'

'An assessment,' his father repeated, patiently. 'Of your health. Mother and I think it's high time you saw a specialist. Someone who understands these things and will be able to help you to . . . No, it's all right, Ro. Nothing to get upset about, old chap. These fits of yours . . . there are things they can do about them nowadays. Doctors, psychiatrists . . . people trained in this sort of thing. Should have had you checked out sooner, really . . . got it sorted . . . '

Dumbly, Rowan nodded. He wasn't a baby. Wasn't going to blub.

'Where is it, father?' he said. 'This hospital?'

'Kent,' his father told him. 'The grounds are top-notch apparently. Apple trees and so on. Your nana knows of it; says it has a fine reputation. You'll be in good hands, son, and a lot safer too, away from the worst of all the hoo-ha.'

The worst of all the hoo-ha, Rowan knew, meant the same as The Current Situation. He was being evacuated, like Laurel, only not to the same place or as a matter of safety—unless you counted the safety of anyone who happened to be around him when he panicked, which was probably exactly what his parents were most worried about.

'Will I have to stay in bed?' he asked, for that was the first thing he had imagined upon hearing the word 'hospital': rows of beds full of poorly people . . . children with diphtheria . . . men with their heads and legs all bandaged up . . . women with their eyes closed, lying as still as saints. 'I don't feel like staying in bed. I don't need to, do I? I'm not . . . I'm not *sick.*'

His father hesitated. Then: 'Probably not,' he said. 'Not all the time anyway.'

'What about school?' He was in his second year now at

the grammar and it wouldn't do to fall behind; not when the other boys—the ones being evacuated—were still going to be taught, wherever they landed up.

'Well, we'll have to see about that. It depends what the doctors decide. It won't hurt you to miss a bit of school though, will it; give the old brain a rest, eh?'

His brain. That meant his mind—or the part of it, anyway, that triggered the panics and the strangeness and the fear.

'A bit of a rest,' his father continued. 'Lots of fresh air . . . exercise, I expect. If you're a good chap, do as the doctors say, you'll be right as rain in no time.'

The light was really going now. Before long it would be hard getting out of the room without tripping over something.

'What will they do to me?' Rowan wanted to know. 'The doctors at this hospital. How are they going to stop my . . . these . . . "fits"?'

Fits . . . it was a word that didn't seem quite right; not for him, and the way he sometimes was. Dogs, and certain people, had fits that made their mouths foam. Clothes fitted, or not, and if you were 'fit' you were supposed to be healthy. In all those cases 'fit' meant something you could put your finger on. You knew where you were with it. His own strangeness, though, seemed too personal . . . too *complicated*, to be summed up by a word already in such common use, and such a little word at that.

'I don't know for certain, son,' his father was saying. 'There are various treatments nowadays, depending on the diagnosis. A lot of patients are given a drug that makes them sleep very deeply for a while—rests the old brain, apparently; gets it working the way it should.'

Rowan nodded. Sleep. He could certainly do with more of that.

'Everyone's on your side,' his father added. 'The doctors, me, your mother, your sisters . . . we just want you to be happy. Happy and normal. OK?'

'OK.'

'Good chap. Now . . . how about we go downstairs and see what's left for our suppers?'

Rowan nodded again but didn't move.

'Unless you have any more questions,' his father said, warily.

He had lots: *Will Daphne ever smile at me again? Will I need to take my gas mask? How does a doctor examine a person's brain? . . . It's not like looking at your tonsils, is it, or your appendix? . . . They won't use any knives on me, will they? What if the Germans come to Kent, dropping their bombs through the apple trees? What do happy and normal feel like? Will Laurel's fingers be damaged for the rest of her life or just for a couple of weeks? And, oh . . . will I be home for Christmas?*

'Is that seaweed?' he asked instead. 'Over there in your new painting. The girl's hair.'

Surprised, his father turned to look. For several moments he considered the half-finished canvas as if he hadn't set eyes on it before, never mind planned and dreamed and laboured over it.

'Is that how it appears?' he said, eventually.

'Yes. Sorry.'

'No, no.' Rowan's father reached out a finger, as if he might stroke or move the seaweed hair. 'If that's how you see it, son, then that's how it is.'

'I'm sure I'd see it differently in daylight.' Rowan was worried now in case he had said the wrong thing. 'And I expect other people would know straightaway that it's hair. If it is hair, that is. Is it hair, Dad? Is that what it is?'

He was gabbling, he knew he was, but suddenly it was important to know. He wouldn't sleep if he didn't know. It would play on his mind—more than the war, more than the hospital, more than anything else he could imagine.

His father swivelled round, alarmed. 'You know what, old chap,' he said, quickly, 'I *like* the way you're thinking. First thing tomorrow I'm going to paint in a few more fronds—masses of 'em. Might even add a starfish or two, eh? Make her look like a proper little mermaid.'

Rowan felt his pulse rate slow right down. The idea of the starfish appealed to him. 'Just one, though,' he said, as soon as he could speak. 'Just one starfish will be enough.'

'Okey-dokey,' his father replied. 'Just the one starfish it is.' He sounded relieved. *He's humouring me,* Rowan thought. *Jollying me along so that I don't get into a panic. He'll probably come back up here tomorrow and just carry on painting the sky.* It didn't matter though, not really; not now that the panic had stopped, or been averted, before it swallowed him whole. It made Rowan feel sad, that was all, hearing his father talk to him like that, all merry and false like a Father Christmas in a shop.

'Shall we go down, son?'

Rowan nodded. His head felt heavy—heavy and dull, like a donkey's head—and although he hadn't eaten a thing since breakfast he no longer wanted his supper.

How does Nana know about this hospital in Kent? he

wondered, stepping carefully down the wooden stairs. *How can she say if it's any good or not when it's for people, not for dogs? How does she know about the apple trees and the grounds being top-notch?*

If he hadn't been so tired, or so aware that his father didn't want to talk any more that night about hospitals and minds, Rowan might have asked those very questions. But he didn't. He let them go.

THE SUITCASE WITH PLENTY OF ROOM

He went on the Wednesday. No particular fuss was made about him going and, since Laurel was getting ready after all, to be evacuated to Weymouth, it was easy for him to pretend that he really was only leaving because of the war.

First thing Tuesday morning, his mother helped him to pack. The suitcase she lugged into his room and deposited on his bed was the one his father usually took when he went off to art shows in Paris or New York. It looked enormous to Rowan—big enough to curl up and sleep in if he felt like it, with the lid up for a bit of air or down for total privacy.

'Can I take *all* my comics?' he asked his mother. 'And will you send on any others that come?'

'I'll bring them,' his mother replied. 'Personally.'

The comics took up a lot of room, despite the size of the case, and Rowan was surprised, after putting them in, that his mother didn't take half of them straight out again. Her hands, he noticed, were hovering above an open drawer; the one with his winter vests in it. She saw him watching and quickly slid the vest drawer shut. 'I can bring those as well,' she said, 'if necessary.'

Rowan knew exactly what she'd been thinking to herself—*will he still be there, in the hospital, when it's cold enough for a vest*? She hadn't wanted to upset him, he realized, by packing winter clothes; hadn't wanted him fretting over how long he might be gone. And if she, like his father, was just trying to avert a panic, well . . . he supposed he couldn't blame her for that.

'Let's put one in anyway,' he said, kindly. 'It might be a cruel and early winter.' It was the kind of thing his nana would have said and, ordinarily, his mother would have pulled his leg for being such an old-fashioned boy. Instead, she bent over the open suitcase and planted a loud kiss on his right cheek.

'What's that for?' he said, pleased despite the ringing in his ear.

'Because I felt like it,' she replied. 'Now—socks. Let's see if we can find matching pairs, shall we, without any darns in the heel?'

The day passed slowly. There was no school. All over London, children were still being evacuated; great gaggles of them crowding onto station platforms with their luggage and their name tags and no idea at all of precisely where they were going. Around midday, a class from Rowan's old infant school passed right by his house. He was sitting on the top step, watching the sky, when he heard the trudging of small feet and the excited twitter of voices. They were only little, this lot—no more than seven years old—but most of them knew Laurel and a few recognized him.

''Ello, Rowan Scrivener.'

'We're goin' to the country, we are. With cows and tractors.'

'There's Rowan Scrivener. 'Ello, Rowan Scrivener.'

'Where's your sister then? Where's Laurel? She already gone to the country has she?'

And he nodded, then shook his head; smiled and then nodded some more, hoping to convey, without having to speak, something along the lines of *Yes, it's me, Rowan Scrivener. Ro-the-Strange to those in the know. Hello, everyone. The countryside? How nice for you all. Laurel's fine. Everything's wonderful. Goodbye.*

They were so bold these little ones, skipping along with their knobbly knees scrubbed clean for the journey and their gas masks bumping their bottoms. He didn't want to talk to them, or have them asking him things. He just wanted them to go—to skip past and disappear.

One of the teachers stared at him as if she too had a question. Avoiding her glance he looked back at the sky, frowning into the blue as if there was a knotty problem up there that only he could solve.

Then the whole class turned the corner, and his mother called him indoors.

'Is it important?' he shouted down. 'I'm on lookout here, for German planes.'

'We have air raid sirens for that,' she shouted back up. 'They'd give us a warning long before there was anything for you to see. Come down to the kitchen, I've a little job for you.'

It was a long time, Rowan realized, since he'd done any kind of a little job for his mother. He used to like doing stuff for her: sifting flour for cakes, shelling peas, or polishing silver teaspoons until he could see the whole of one of his eyes in them. For at least a year, though—since he'd started at the grammar school—she hadn't asked him to do anything at all except homework. Oh, and to calm down. She, like everyone else, was forever telling him to do that.

'What is it?' he asked, bounding downstairs and into the kitchen. 'Are you making a cake?'

His mother shifted a pile of magazines from one of the bentwood chairs, so that he could sit. 'No,' she said. 'But what a good idea. We haven't had a cake for ages, have we? What would you like, chocolate or plain? We've got eggs . . . I think we've got eggs.'

'It's all right,' Rowan said to her, sitting himself down. 'We don't have to have a cake. It doesn't matter.'

His mother was busy, he could see that. Usually she wrote her articles in the drawing room but if it was cold, or she had a meal to see to, or Laurel was practising the piano, she brought her typewriter down here to the kitchen and worked at the big table.

Today was warm, for September, there was no meal being prepared, so far as Rowan could see or smell, and the piano (he had the grace to wince, thinking about the piano) . . . the piano was going to remain unplayed for quite some time to come.

'Why are you working down here?' he asked.

His mother didn't answer straightaway. For what seemed like a long time she examined his face; reading it, it seemed to him, the way she might read one of her articles in *Woman and Home*: slowly, critically; wondering if it really was all right or if some glitch or error was about to jump out at her. Then: 'I just fancied being cosy,' she said, carefully. 'Like a badger in its den.'

He nodded. 'Safe, you mean,' he said. 'From the bombs.'

His mother blinked. 'Yes,' she admitted. 'I suppose that *is* what I meant. Sorry, pet, I didn't want to scare you. And it's not like I'm thinking we're going to be bombed at any minute because I'm quite sure we won't be. I'm not frightening you, am I? You're all right?'

Rowan didn't answer. From where he was sitting he could just about read what his mother had been working on before she'd pushed the typewriter aside and called him down.

We are the women of England, the women behind the men who are going out to fight and the best way we can help is by being BRAVE and staying BEAUTIFUL. Why not invest in a coat with large pockets to keep your air raid beauty products in? And remember, when HE comes home he will want to kiss the hands that have kept the home running, so keep those hands as smooth as silk with POND'S HAND CREAM

'Don't read that, it's rubbish.'

Rowan smiled. 'Are you going to get a coat with large pockets,' he said, 'to keep air raid beauty products in?'

'Not likely,' his mother replied, with feeling. 'Since when did I wear make-up? I bet Daphne would like something with great big pockets though, just in case there's a raid in the middle of the night, when she hasn't got her face on, and we all have to make a mad dash for it.'

'Daff would need my big suitcase,' said Rowan. 'And that's just for her lipsticks.' (*Not 'all' he was thinking. We won't 'all' be making a mad dash for it, will we, because we won't 'all' be here.*)

His mother laughed. Then she tousled his hair. 'I'm going to miss you,' she said. 'And, Ro . . . I know it's going to be strange for you, being at the hospital. It's bound to be. But if the doctors can stop you having these funny turns it will be worth it, won't it? Just think how much happier you'll be once they've sorted you out.'

Happ-i-er. That was a comparative adjective, Rowan knew that from his Latin lessons at the grammar school. *Happy, happier, happiest.* But how could he be happi*er,* he wondered, when he was rarely ever happy in the first place? He would settle, he decided, for just feeling less awful about himself.

Awful, less awful, least awful. That sounded more like it—more achievable anyway.

'What's this job you want me to do?'

'It's not a job, exactly,' his mother said. 'I'm doing an article on things for children to do in the evenings—"Ten ways to brighten the blackout"—and one of the ideas is to dig out family snaps and paste them onto a tray. Look, here's an old wooden tray, here's our box of snaps, and here's the glue pot. Father has some quick-drying varnish upstairs so you can seal the pictures as soon as they're glued, so . . . what do you think?'

Rowan looked from the tray to the glue pot to the box to his mother and wondered what to say.

'I thought it would take your mind off things,' his mother added, encouragingly. 'And that you might like to take the tray with you, to the hospital, to have your supper off, or keep things on, or whatever. Anyway . . . you can't sit on the doorstep all day, can you, so come on, choose your pictures. Any ones you like. There are scissors in the dresser—the left-hand drawer—if you want to do any trimming or cutting out.'

Rowan still didn't know what to say. He wanted, very much, to return to watching the sky. He wanted to be quiet; as still and as quiet as a nail in a wall. He wanted this day to be over with quickly so that he could go, just go, taking only his clothes and his comics and the problems in his head to the hospital in Kent.

Obediently, though, he lifted the lid of the box in which almost three decades of family photographs were stored, all higgledy piggledy.

'Just be careful not to get glue in your cuts,' his mother said. He had forgotten about those cuts but hearing them mentioned like that made them throb all over again. His nana, he remembered, still had his penknife.

'Is Nana coming over?' he asked, shuffling photographs with his good hand—a beaming baby Laurel; Daphne before she got beautiful; Mother beside a lake; Mother and Father beside a lake; Nana and three dogs beside a lake . . .

'Not today,' his mother replied. 'She's frantically busy at the rescue centre and it would be too difficult for her to get home again after the blackout. But you'll see her first thing tomorrow. She's offered to drive you to the hospital.'

'Oh.' Rowan bit back his disappointment. 'I thought father would be doing that.'

'Father's taking Laurel to Weymouth,' his mother said. 'She can't go on the train with the other children, Ro. Not with her hands the way they are. *I'm* going with you, though. Someone—next of kin—will have to sign some forms and, anyway, I want to see the place for myself.'

'Oh.'

Dismally, Rowan rummaged some more among the snaps. He couldn't choose. Didn't want to. Didn't care about taking pictures of his family away with him. Didn't want their eyes looking up at him through a film of glue and varnish.

'I'm sure there are some recent ones in among that lot—can't you find them?'

'Yes . . . no . . . the old ones are fine. I like them.'

Quickly, he pulled out an assortment of snaps, a mixture of old and new.

'Scissors,' his mother said. 'Over in the drawer.' And he wondered, as he found the scissors, returned to the table and began to cut carefully around his father's head, what his nana had actually said to his parents about the incident with the penknife. Because if it had been the slightest bit dangerous (he honestly couldn't remember) his mother, surely, would not be trusting him now with anything sharp.

What if I were to panic with these scissors in my hand? What if just thinking about it—worrying about it—was enough to make it happen? What if . . . ?

But the panics didn't start that way. They never had. They came without warning, right out of the blue.

Sunday, he knew, had been the worst day ever but since then: not a flicker. The doctors would be able to explain why that was, he told himself. They, in all their cleverness, were bound to understand.

Sticking the cut-out image of his father onto the tray seemed cruel, like pressing a butterfly. The picture he'd chosen dated back a long time, to the last war, by the look of it. His father was too old to fight now which was just as well, Rowan thought, considering how scornful he was being of The Current Situation. He looked good in the picture though. His soldier's uniform suited him and his face was all bright and eager as if he couldn't wait to see some action.

'He's not that much older than you there.' His mother bent over his shoulder and sighed. 'It was taken just before his unit went over to France—a few years before I met him.' Rowan stared, hard, at the shape of his father, searching for common ground. 'I have to say, Ro,' his mother added, 'I'm thanking my lucky stars you're not old enough to join up. I'd be worrying myself sick if you were.'

'Why?' he said, pressing down the picture so that it would stick first time. 'In case I had a panic during training, or while I was flying a Spitfire?'

'No,' she replied. 'In case someone killed you.'

'Oh.'

In the evening, as soon as the shutters were closed, the whole family gathered for supper in the dining room. Usually, unless they were celebrating something special, like somebody's birthday, or a painting being sold, they ate downstairs in the kitchen. 'A treat,' Rowan's mother said, placing the silver candelabra dead centre of the table, 'since we have no way of knowing for sure when we're all going to be together again.'

'Christmas,' Rowan said. 'It will all be sorted out by Christmas. Everyone's saying so.' He meant the war.

'Well, that would be a relief, certainly,' his mother replied, lighting big white candles one by one. She wasn't looking at him, but his father and Daphne both were and he could tell that they were wondering, not about the war, but whether he himself would be all sorted out by Christmas—or ever.

Across the table, Laurel began prattling about Weymouth. Because of her fingers, special arrangements had been made for her to stay with a particular family—a doctor, his wife, and their two small girls.

All the other evacuees from her class, Laurel said, were having to take pot luck. 'They could go to *any*one,' she announced, pausing to suck orange squash, noisily, through a straw. ' . . . they could go to murderers, or to people with lice, or to a house full of nasty rough boys who . . . '

'Laurel . . . ' Rowan heard the warning note in his mother's voice and was grateful for it. He didn't want to fight with his sister, not tonight.

'I'm so glad you're driving me, Daddy,' Laurel added, sweetly, over the top of her drink. 'Only, you'll have to hold my hair out of the way if I get car sick because that's another one of the ten hundred million things I can't do for myself because of what *he*—'

'All right, Laurel . . . ' Rowan's mother passed the gravy, 'eat your supper now. Daphne will help.'

Rowan's father made a start on his potatoes. He looked young in the candlelight, Rowan thought; almost as young as in the snap on the tray. He would have liked his father to look his way, if only for a moment, and to say something optimistic about them all being together again by Christmas.

'Well, Daff,' his father said, instead, 'Mother tells me that the young police constable—the one who brought Rowan and your nana home—is to call on us again, only not in the line of duty this time, eh?'

Daphne blushed. 'He wants to take me dancing. Or to see a film in Leicester Square.'

'Everywhere's closed, pet,' Rowan's mother said. 'Because of the situation. There's nowhere to go.'

Daphne held out a fork to Laurel, with a small piece of sausage on it, and smiled fondly as Laurel opened her mouth like a baby bird. 'PC Dobbs—Eddie—reckons everywhere will be open again by the weekend,' she said. 'He says entertainment is going to be vital for as long as the war—sorry, the current situation—lasts. To keep the nation's spirits up, he says.'

'That's true,' said Rowan's mother. 'I'm writing an article on it. "Ten ways to brighten the blackout". Your policeman could come round here, Daff, and help us do a jigsaw.'

'Moth*er*!' squealed Daphne and they all laughed. Even Rowan smiled, although a sadness had come over him to think of jigsaws being done, and visitors coming and going, and Daphne putting her face on to go dancing . . . all without him knowing because he wasn't going to be here.

And what if the German bombers came? One day while he wasn't on the step, keeping a lookout? Or one night while his mother and father and Daff were fast asleep in their beds? What if the sirens didn't sound in time and . . .

No.

He mustn't dwell on horrible things. It was bad for him.

Just think how much happier you'll be once you're all sorted out. His mother had been right to sound so positive. He would cling to that thought—to that possibility of happiness—and try not to fret.

I am Superboy, he pretended to himself, looking down at the food on his plate. *My mind, like the rest of me, is invincible. It will mend FAST at that hospital and I'll be home in a flash.*

THE STRANGE AND TERRIBLE APPLE PICKERS

'Mother, did we absolutely have to bring those wretched animals?'

'We did, rather, pet. You wouldn't believe how many dogs are being abandoned now that we're at war. They're sharing kennels three to the space of one at the rescue centre, poor loves.'

'Well, don't even think about letting them loose at the hospital. There'll be rules.'

'Stop worrying, Hazel. Rosa will take them for a nice long walk when we get there while you and I see Rowan settled. The grounds are big enough, if I remember rightly, and if anyone objects to *that,* Rosa can take the van and drive 'em all to the nearest beach. YOO-HOO, ROSA. EVERYTHING ALL RIGHT IN THE BACK THERE?'

'All fine, Ive! Tickety-boo!'

They were almost out of London—Rowan, his mother, his nana, his nana's friend Rosa, three mongrels, a labrador, and a Dalmatian puppy. The van with the blue cross seemed, to Rowan, to be groaning on its wheels from all the wagging and leaping and yapping going on in the back. He himself was wedged between his mother and his nana, one cheek of his backside on the passenger seat, the other on the driver's side. Whenever his nana changed gear the stick hit his shins. 'Sorry, pet,' she kept saying, and, 'Are you all right in the middle there?'

It was another beautiful day; easily hot enough, Rowan thought, for a dip in the sea and a sunbathe afterwards. He would have liked to go to a beach, with Rosa and the dogs, and thought about asking if there would be time to do that first. Then he remembered that he didn't have his swimming trunks with him, or a beach towel or a shrimping net, and that this wasn't meant to be a carefree jaunt. Not for him, anyway.

'Don't let those dogs widdle on my suitcase will you?' he called anxiously back to Rosa, for that would be a disaster, particularly if it soaked through, because then his clothes would stink to high heaven and people at the hospital might think it was human wee—his wee—that had done it. And his comics . . . all his comics would be . . .

'Please, Rosa, don't let them . . . '

'What, pet? Can't hear you. *Down*, boy. Settle down . . . No nipping. *No*, you rascal . . . '

Rowan felt his mother take his hand. 'It's all right,' she murmured in his left ear. 'Everything's all right.'

'I'm not panicking,' he said, quickly. 'I just don't want . . . '

'The suitcase will be fine. It's all fine. Look—fields. We'll be seeing apple orchards soon. Kent is the "garden of England", you know . . . '

For a while Rowan allowed himself to be soothed by

his mother's voice and by the idea of blossom and apples and peace. Then he turned to his nana: 'Why are so many people abandoning their dogs,' he asked, 'now that we're at war?' It felt good to be able to say 'war' instead of 'current situation', here in the van with the women.

His nana tutted. 'Selfish so-and-sos,' she declared, smacking the steering wheel as if she wished it was a face. 'Cruel and thoughtless blighters!'

'Mother!'

'Well they are, Hazel. Dumping their dogs at an already over-burdened and under-funded rescue centre rather than have the bother of feeding them through the war, or walking them during the blackout, or getting them to a shelter if there's an air raid. People like that shouldn't be allowed to keep animals. It's criminal what they're doing.'

Rowan listened for a moment to the thumping and yapping in the back of the van—annoyingly loud, despite old Rosa's best efforts to calm the pack down with crooning and scolding and a great many bone-shaped biscuits.

'I can sort of understand, Nana,' he said, 'why people wouldn't want a dog in an air raid shelter. Not if it was the type to bark its head off all night and be a terrible nuisance.'

'A dog can't help its nature,' his nana retorted. 'Some breeds are nervier than others, that's all. No reason, in my opinion, for an owner to dump it on someone else the second there's a national emergency . . . '

She fell silent then; suddenly, like a gramophone record with the needle lifted. Rowan waited, expecting her to carry on. Then: 'Look, Ro,' his mother said, as if the silence was a hole that needed filling, 'look at the orchards.'

Rowan looked. His nana slowed the van right down and looked too.

'YOO-HOO, IVY, ARE WE THERE?' called Rosa, for there were no windows for her to see out of in the back.

'NO,' Rowan's nana called back to her. 'NOT YET.' Then she put her foot down, hard, so that the van sped away and the orchard blurred.

Rowan blinked. Had he imagined it? All those people back there climbing ladders, carrying baskets, pulling fruit from the trees, *but with their gas masks on*? They had looked terrible with their faces all covered like that; terrible and strange, like aliens come down from another planet to plunder the garden of England.

'My, what a sad sight that was,' his mother said. 'I suppose they were practising; getting used to working with their masks on in case there's a gas attack. I heard on the wireless that a lot of people are doing that this week. Although . . . goodness . . . I do hope . . . '

She sniffed the air—tried to do it quickly, without being too obvious. Alarmed, Rowan began sniffing too. Dog. He could smell dog. *But what else?* He sniffed harder, almost snorting like a pig. His nana threw him a warning look. She didn't seem bothered but his mother was clutching his hand so tightly it hurt. She was scared, Rowan could tell; really badly scared.

He licked his lips—*could you taste poisoned gas?*—and sniffed so hard he felt the insides of his nose cave in and out. If there was gas in the air . . . if the Germans had done their worst and released a deadly cloud over

England . . . if it was seeping, right now, through the blue September sky then they were done for. It would froth up their lungs . . . blister their throats . . . Nana would crash the van . . .

'Stop it!' Rowan's grandmother took her left hand off the wheel and gave Rowan a push that went right through him to his mother. 'Rowan! Both of you! Calm down. If there'd been a gas attack we'd know about it, wouldn't we. We'd've heard the sirens. Seen the planes. Ro—Rowan—are you going to behave yourself, or do I have to stop the van?'

'Stop the van.' Rowan's mother made a gagging sound, as if she was going to be sick. 'Here! Right now! Pull over!'

They were entering a village. Through the windscreen, as the van screeched to a halt, Rowan could see front gardens with cabbages and chrysanthemums growing in them. Surely, he thought, struggling for breath, those things should be turning black . . . wilting and dying before his eyes as the gas got to them as well.

His mother stifled a whimper. 'There's nobody about,' she said. 'Not a living soul.'

'It's the countryside,' Rowan's nana snapped. 'What were you expecting, Hazel? A brass band? A welcoming party?'

'I don't know, *I don't know*. It's just too damned quiet. Where are our gas masks? Are they in the back? I can't open my door. *Mother!* We're too close to this blasted hedge. Rosa? ROSA?'

No answer.

'She must have dozed off,' Rowan's nana said.

'What, with all those dogs carrying on?'

'It wouldn't bother her. She's as deaf as a post, don't forget.'

They were speaking quickly, the two women. Gabbling over Rowan's head. And his grandmother was beginning to sound anxious now, because of Rosa not answering even though Rosa was as deaf as a post and could have slept through the end of the whole world.

'What if it's too late?' Rowan's mother half-said, half-whispered. 'What if—'

Then: 'Look!' Rowan interrupted. 'Over there, in that garden. On the cabbages—see them?'

Butterflies. Big white ones. Fluttering around the cabbage leaves on wings as pale and strong as parachute silk. Fluttering and landing and fluttering again in chaotic but careful formation.

'They seem all right, don't they?' Rowan pointed out. 'Not gassed or anything? Unless they're going berserk for a bit before they die, like chickens with their heads cut off. Let's watch and see what happens.'

And so they watched the butterflies. Rowan, his nana, and his mother. And after a while a black cat came out of the garden and idly crossed the road. Slinking past the van, it looked up, disdainfully, at the three pale faces high up behind glass, then it jumped through the hedge Rowan's nana had parked so badly against, and vanished into a field.

Then a woman came cycling round the corner. Spying the van she wobbled a bit before bringing her bicycle to a dusty halt, beside the driver's door.

'Can I help you?' she asked, bending down to peer in. There was a loaf of bread in the bicycle's front basket but no sign of a gas mask, in or out of its box.

Rowan's nana wound down her window.

'We were just wondering,' she said, 'what the latest news is? If there'd been a sudden emergency of any kind?'

The woman drew her head back, sharply, from the open window.

Dog-smell, Rowan thought.

'No emergency that I know of,' she replied, warily. 'And my daughter's had the wireless on all morning. I've just come from there.'

'No . . . um . . . gas alerts?'

'Gas? No. That is . . . I don't think so. The man from the Home Service would have said, wouldn't he. Why? Are you from the Ministry? Do you know something we don't? What is it? Are we in any danger?'

'Not at all, not at all.' Rowan's nana turned away from the open window. 'It seems that *some* of us,'—she looked, accusingly, at Rowan's mother—'have let their imaginations run away with them, that's all.'

'Not me,' said Rowan, offended. 'I was all right until mother got me started. And I'm perfectly fine now, aren't I? I didn't panic. I *helped.* I saw the butterflies.'

In the back one of the animals sighed, heavily, in its sleep. All five dogs were snoozing now, along with old Rosa.

The woman on the bicycle had turned her gaze, suspiciously, to the blue cross on the side of the van. 'So what business do you have in the village then?' she asked. 'Who have you come here to see?'

'No one,' said Rowan's nana. 'We're just passing through.' And because the woman on the bicycle looked totally unconvinced she told her the name of the place they were heading for.

'I know that place,' said the woman. 'There's a lunatic asylum there—big house on a hill, full of murderers and raving idiots. If you're planning a picnic—'

'La, la, la . . . Goodbye.' Rowan's grandmother began winding up her window, cranking the handle so quickly that she almost snapped it off. With luck, she told herself, young Rowan wasn't paying attention. With luck he was still watching the butterflies, or away in a world of his own.

' . . . take the coastal path out of town, I would. Avoid that madhouse like the plague. They say there's a—'

THUMP! From the back of the van came a scuffle and a whine, followed by the sound of sudden scolding. Then:

'YOO-HOO, IVY—ARE WE THERE? CAN WE GET OUT? DESMOND'S GETTING AGITATED AGAIN, POOR CHAP. WE MIGHT NEED TO MUZZLE HIM AT THIS RATE. HIS BOWELS ARE ALL TOPSY TURVY TOO. SORRY ABOUT THE SMELL, EVERYONE!'

You could have heard old Rosa a mile off. You could have heard her back in the apple orchards, or halfway across the English Channel.

'Goodbye,' Rowan's grandmother repeated, smiling gamely through the glass of her window before starting up the van.

The woman with the bicycle was already backing away, her mouth a big 'O' of dismay.

'I'm sorry,' said Rowan's mother, as the van sped out of the village. 'For imagining the worst back there. For being wrong about the gas.'

'Never mind,' Rowan's nana told her, kindly. 'All's well that ends well. Now then, Ro, how about a game of I Spy? Come on, I'll start us off. I spy with my little eye something beginning with "H".'

'Hitler.'

'Don't be daft.'

'Horizon.'

'Clever, but no.'

'Hedge.'

'Yes. Your go.'

Cloud. Windscreen. Mother. Roadside. Cornfield. Branches. Fingernail. Ditch. Then it was Rowan's turn again and he could have said 'h' for 'hill' or 'h' for 'house'; considered both of those possibilities as the hill with the house on it came into view . . .

They're hoping I didn't hear what the woman on the bicycle said back there. They're hoping I wasn't listening properly, or that I didn't understand.

'Two words this time,' he announced, as the van drew closer to the house on the hill, 'something beginning with an L and then an A.'

'Lots of apples,' his mother called out.

'Wrong,' he said, although there were apple trees, certainly, beside the road and what appeared to be a great many windfalls in heaps upon the ground.

'Little ants?' his nana guessed. 'Not that I can see any, but your eyes are younger than mine.'

'Nope.'

A large bird rose up from a tree and flew across their line of vision, in a skitter of feathers and feet.

'Lost albatross,' said Rowan's mother.

'You're just being silly now,' he said. 'That was a pigeon. A wood pigeon. Obviously.'

'Well then, we give up,' his nana said. 'Anyway, look—that's the hospital. We're almost there. I might just need to . . . no, it's all right, someone's opening the gates for us. How very kind. WE'RE HERE, ROSA. WE'VE ARRIVED.'

'Lunatic asylum,' said Rowan, bleakly, as the gates clanged shut behind them. 'I spy with my little eye . . . a lunatic asylum, that's what.'

'DO YOU HEAR VOICES, ROWAN? IN YOUR HEAD?'

Admissions Report
Strictly confidential

Date: *September 6th, 1939*

Name of patient: *Rowan Maurice Scrivener (male)*

Date of birth: *12th July 1926*

Referral status: *Private/ family*

Behaviour/incident(s) prompting this referral:
Patient has a history of extreme emotional reactions to minor problems. Recently he has displayed more acute symptoms of paranoid delusion, with aggressive tendencies. Incidents immediately prior to referral include: attacking a younger sibling

causing injury (non-fatal) and an attempt (thwarted) to cause indiscriminate injury with a knife.

Previous committals
(name of institution, year, duration):

None

Attending consultants:

W. Richard Thomas, MD, FRCP, DPM

S. Winterbourne MD

A. Stanley-Hopkins MD

Also in attendance:

Nurse M. J. Bradley
Sarah J. Springfield (junior nursing assistant)

Presenting symtoms:

Pychological:

Emotional:

Physical:

Family history/probability of inherited mental illness:

Diagnosis:

* * *

'So, young man—how are we feeling today?'

Rowan looked up at the row of faces—man, man, man, woman, girl—and the row of faces looked back at him. The girl was some kind of a nurse; Rowan could tell that from her uniform. She looked about the same age as Daphne, and almost as pretty, and Rowan wasn't sure he liked her being there. It was a man asking the questions though; a man with silvery hair and pale, clever eyes. He was older than the others and seemed to be in charge.

'*Rowan!*' His mother nudged him in the ribs.

'I'm feeling all right,' he said, quickly. 'Very well, actually.'

'He's been fine since Sunday,' his mother said. 'No panics at all.' She sounded triumphant as if going three days without wanting to hurt someone was a thing to be proud of.

She had told Rowan, before entering this room, that the woman on the bicycle had been wrong to talk about the hospital and its patients the way she had; that she was an ignorant country bumpkin with a turnip for a brain.

'I see,' Rowan had said, although the words 'lunatic' and 'asylum' were still dancing before his eyes.

The man who had asked, just now, how he was feeling glanced down at a piece of paper in front of him on a long, wide desk. There were things written on the paper, some of it typed and some done with a fountain pen, but it was upside down so Rowan couldn't read it.

'So, Maurice—Rowan, I mean—tell me what you remember about the incident with the knife.'

A cut glass vase, dead centre of the desk, had dahlias

in it. The flowers were huge, great globes of yellow, maroon, and orange, but had been so hastily arranged that Rowan could see the tight loops of gardeners' string still holding the stems together. They looked uncomfortable, those flowers, but Rowan kept his eyes on them while he struggled to remember something—anything—that might be useful.

'I never meant to hurt anyone,' he said, eventually. 'And I didn't, did I? Well, myself, a bit, but that's all. It was nothing serious, was it?'

Nobody answered. The flowers seemed to throb, he was staring so fixedly at them, and he could sense his mother and his nana holding their tongues; biting back words of reassurance, or excuses on his behalf, because the very important people were here to help him, and they could only do that if he helped them first, by being completely honest.

And so: 'I don't remember,' he admitted. 'I never do. It's like . . . it's like I'm not really there. When I'm panicking, I mean. I don't know. It's hard to explain.'

'Voices,' someone—one of the younger men—said. 'Do you hear voices, Rowan? In your head?'

The man who seemed to be in charge butted in: 'Or just the one voice, perhaps? Giving you orders? Telling you what to do?'

And Rowan looked up from the flowers to regard these men with awe. How very clever they were. And how grateful he was for that cleverness because they were right. He didn't need to tax his memory, or even conveniently panic, right then and there, to be sure, on some deep and knowing level, that they had got that spot on.

'That's it,' he said, his voice high-pitched with surprise and relief. 'There *is* a voice . . . there's always a voice.'

The men behind the desk exchanged meaningful glances.

'What?' said Rowan's mother. 'What does that signify then?'

'Just a minute, Mrs . . . um . . . Scrivener.' The man with the piece of paper in front of him picked up an expensive-looking fountain pen, unscrewed the top, and began to write:

Definite signs of delusional dementia, he noted, next to the typewritten word '`Psychological:`'.

'And it's always the same voice,' Rowan continued, amazed—elated, almost—as a memory surfaced, the way an odd dream sometimes did, rising up through the layers of ordinary thought keeping it tamped down and forgotten. 'A voice sort of like my own only meaner—really mean. I don't like it, when I hear it. I try and stop it. I told Nana just the other day that I always try and stop it, but I can't. It takes me over. And just lately it's been getting worse. Nastier . . . '

He was gabbling, the words falling over themselves as he tried to explain; tried to help these very important people understand his strangeness so that they would be able to stop it. Turn it off. Nip it in the bud. And part of the reason he was gabbling was it felt so good to be discussing his panics openly, in a grown-up way, instead of living quietly—shamefully—with the worry of them.

And the people behind the desk were nodding, as if they had met this strangeness before—had met it, got to know it, and come to understand how awful it could be. The young nurse actually threw him a smile; a sweet smile, not a sneer. Even his mother and his nana were listening respectfully, for once, to what he had to say.

'Sorry,' he said, wiping his eyes with the back of one hand.

Highly strung, the man with the fountain pen noted next to the typewritten word `'Emotional:'`. *Patient's behaviour deviates wildly from the norm of adolescent conduct.*

'Thank you,' he said, with a nod in Rowan's direction. 'For your co-operation. All extremely helpful.'

Then the woman behind the desk stood up. 'Come with me now,' she said to Rowan, 'there's a good boy.'

Startled, Rowan looked from the woman to his mother and then to his nana, both of them sitting very still to his left and to his right.

Was that it then? Was this goodbye?

'You'll see your family again,' the man in charge said, briskly, 'but for now you must do exactly as Nurse Bradley tells you.'

Rowan felt his mother shift in her seat. The man's tone had irritated her, he could tell, so he stood up quickly before she could say anything to embarrass him and followed the woman—Nurse Bradley—out of the room. As they left the younger nurse stood up and left as well, shadowing Rowan so closely that he felt her breath in his hair.

'Where are they taking him?' Rowan's mother wasn't happy. She wanted to follow her son but it was like being back at school, knowing you weren't supposed to leave a room without permission.

'We need to examine him, physically,' the man with the pen said. 'It's a routine part of the admissions procedure, so please don't get upset. Now . . . ' He glanced briefly, again, at the piece of paper on the desk, 'Is there any history in the family of extreme anxiety? Sudden changes in mood? Anything at all like that?'

'Yes.'

Rowan's grandmother sat up straighter in her chair, her face both troubled and proud. 'My late husband, Maurice Mull-Dare,' she said, 'suffered very badly with his nerves. He got quite poorly with them in nineteen thirteen and came here to convalesce. It's why I suggested bringing Rowan to you. I understand there are cures now. Things you can do to heal the mind. Rowan's young. We don't want him suffering all his life, the way my husband did.'

The fountain pen's nib began moving very fast, next to the typewritten words **`'Family History/probability of inherited mental illness:'`**.

'Did your husband hear voices?'

'Not to my knowledge. Although . . . well . . . once he did, yes, but only that once. He was a good man, doctor, just prey to his nerves. And Rowan is a good boy, he just needs . . . '

'Your husband—did he ever harm anyone?'

'Not a fly! I told you, he was a good man.'

'Or himself? Did he ever try to harm himself?'

At that, Rowan's grandmother flinched, as if something had just nipped her, or flown into her eye. Had this doctor been a dog she would have called him a bad boy and taken away his pen.

'I don't wish to appear rude,' she said to him, icily, 'but we do seem to be straying, rather, from the point. My husband died sixteen years ago—of natural causes, I hasten to add—so I suggest we return our attention to the here and now and consider what can be done to help my grandson.'

The man with the pen didn't so much as blink before pressing on:

'This is important, Mrs . . . um . . . Mull-Dare. It might even be crucial to an accurate assessment of your grandson's state of mind. I must ask you again: did your husband try to harm himself? Is that why he was admitted to this hospital in . . . when was it . . . nineteen thirteen?'

Rowan's mother, quiet up until now, put a restraining hand on her mother's knee and said:

'My father had a nervous breakdown. He lost a great deal of money, gambling on a horse, and the worry made him ill. He came here, as my mother has just told you, to rest for a while. But as for having tried to "harm" himself . . . you're suggesting he attempted suicide, aren't you. Well? Aren't you?'

The man with the pen inclined his head in agreement—such a small and grudging gesture that Rowan's mother could have risen up and slapped him.

'Well you're wrong,' she cried out. 'How dare you! My father would never have done such a terrible thing. You've just insulted his memory. You owe us an apology.'

All three of the men behind the desk continued to look at Rowan's grandmother. Waiting. For the truth. 'It is for your grandson's sake,' one of them reminded her, 'that we need an honest answer. There may be a connection, you see.'

For a few moments there was silence. The men, it

seemed, had all the time in the world to wait and would remain there, behind that enormous desk, until it grew dark, or their wives or their mothers came searching for them. Then:

'I do not believe,' Rowan's grandmother said, her voice beginning to shake, 'that this is necessary. Nor do I accept what you seem to be implying . . . that because, yes, my husband did try to take his own life—once, many many years ago—Rowan is bound to do the same. That it is somehow inevitable . . . '

She paused then, and took a deep, shuddering, breath.

'I'm sorry, Hazel,' she said, as soon as she could. 'I never meant for you to know. There was no need for you to know.'

For a moment Rowan's mother remained utterly still and totally silent. Then: 'It's all right,' she said, reaching for the older woman's hand. 'Don't get upset. There's no point in getting upset, is there, after all this time?' Yet her mind was whirling . . . spooling back through her childhood for clues . . . wondering, even though she knew it was morbid: *What did he use? A knife? A rope? Poison? Who stopped him? Who saved him?*

She remembered, then, coming home from school one day to find the door to her father's study locked and everyone—her mother, the servants—shocked and secretive. She remembered being told that her father had gone away to rest for a while, and how she had never been brought here—not even once—to visit him. He had returned to them eventually, thinner and sadder, and she had spent the rest of his life, it seemed, working hard to make him smile.

'How does this affect my son?' she asked, stiffly.

'Congenitally,' the man with the pen replied, pronouncing the word slowly and clearly as if to an idiot child. It wasn't a sexual word, Rowan's mother knew that, but still her face turned flaming red because it was clear to her that this awful man had expected her to think so.

Rowan's grandmother tutted, completely confused by it all. 'What *are* you suggesting?' she demanded, crossly. 'How on earth can a person's private parts . . . '

'He means "inherited",' Rowan's mother interrupted her, more harshly than she meant. 'He's telling us that Rowan's condition was passed down to him, through father's side of the family like—I don't know—like eye colour, or the shape of a nose.'

'Pah!' Rowan's grandmother was having none of it. 'My husband, gentlemen, had red hair and green eyes,' she said. 'When he was happy he lit up a room and when he was sad it was like living with his ghost. Our Rowan is not like him, in either looks or personality, and the panics that he has are totally unlike the days—weeks—of quiet despair my husband was prey to. So I do not see how . . . I really cannot understand . . . '

'You told us that your husband heard voices,' one of the younger doctors cut in, gently. 'Just the once, you said. Am I right, Mrs Mull-Dare, in thinking that this "once" was just before he tried to kill himself? Did a voice in his head tell him that was what he should do?'

Somewhere outside, from a long way off, came the sound of a dog barking. Rowan's grandmother lifted her head to listen. The sound, faint though it was, seemed to both calm and deflate her.

'Yes,' she said. 'It did.'

'Thank you.'

The fountain pen spluttered a little, beside the word **'Diagnosis:'.**

'I'm beginning to think,' Rowan's mother said then, 'that we should take my son home; that this might not, after all, be the best environment for him right now. Mother?'

'Whatever you want, Hazel. It's your decision, pet.'

'Then that's what we'll do. We'll take him back with us to London. Get a second opinion.'

The splatter of ink was minuscule, like a spray of fairy blood. The man wielding the pen blotted it, carefully, before continuing to write:

Schizophrenia.

Had Rowan been there, and able to see that word, he would have thought it rather a good one. Better than 'fit' anyway. And the more he'd thought about it the better a thirteen-letter name, making no immediate sense, would have seemed, as a title for his strangeness.

Schiz-o-phre-nia.

The door opened. Nurse Bradley came in, looking pleased.

'Where's my son?' Rowan's mother turned sharply as the door clicked shut. 'Where is he? What have you done with him?'

'Mrs Scrivener,' said the man who had spoken gently to Rowan's grandmother. 'Don't worry. Rowan is being kept occupied—shown around—while we complete his assessment.'

The man with the pen peered expectantly at Nurse Bradley. 'Well?' he said.

Nurse Bradley nodded at him. 'He's thin,' she replied. 'But in extremely good health.'

Rowan's mother shivered. For some reason she was being reminded of a witch; of the one in 'Hansel and Gretel' who put children in a cage and fed them sugar buns and gingerbread until they were fat enough to be cooked and eaten.

'We're taking Rowan home,' she said. 'Whatever your "assessment" of him is, he's coming back with us.'

Nurse Bradley raised her eyebrows, *oh is he now?* before looking to the men for an official response.

Rowan's mother felt her pulse quicken. She had sounded so determined, speaking up like that, but, really, she was all at sea. *What to do for the best? For everyone's sake, not just Rowan's?* Her mother's hand in hers had felt as frail as a poorly child's. Laurel had gone to live with strangers. The house in Spitalfields had no air raid shelter and any day now the Germans might arrive, with their bombs and their poisonous gas. And as if all that wasn't enough, memories of her own father had just been altered for ever—altered shockingly, as if someone had drawn devil horns, or a Hitler moustache, on the one and only photograph she had left of him.

'Taking Rowan home would be a mistake,' insisted the man with the pen. 'He is showing classic symptoms of paranoid schizophrenia which, without treatment, will only get worse. To put it bluntly, Mrs Scrivener, your son is a ticking time bomb. Take him away from here and the next "panic" he has could prove fatal. He could actually kill someone—a stranger . . . your mother . . . himself. He won't know he's doing it and nor will he care. He'll be obeying the voice—the voice in his head. Do you want that on your conscience?'

'No.' It came out as a whisper. *We are the women of England,* she reminded herself. *The best way we can help is by being BRAVE and staying BEAUTIFUL.* Had she really written that?

Rowan's grandmother leaned forward, holding tight to her handbag as if the familiar, well-worn touch of it might give her extra strength. 'This "suitable treatment",' she said. 'What form will it take?'

A ripple of something—excitement, anticipation—caused each man to fidget a little; to smooth his hair or adjust his tie. The one with the pen flexed his free hand the way a concert pianist or a boxer might.

'Nothing's set in stone,' he lied. 'Not yet.'

'I understand that you give them something nowadays to put them to sleep,' Rowan's grandmother persisted. 'That sleeping deeply, under medical supervision, soothes the brain and heals the part that causes strange . . . unacceptable . . . behaviour.'

The man with the pen eyed her, warily. She was surprisingly sharp, this old duck.

'Insulin therapy. That is one option, yes,' he agreed.

Rowan's grandmother nodded, but the lines on her face deepened as she said: 'You'd wake him up, though, wouldn't you, if he slept too long? You wouldn't forget? And this drug—I've forgotten the name already—he wouldn't start to crave it, would he? He wouldn't come home wanting to sleep all the time and needing more and more of that drug to—'

'Mrs Mull-Dare,' the gentle doctor interrupted, 'we

understand your concerns but, really, you are jumping way too far ahead. The most important thing to agree upon right now, is the need—the very urgent need—for Rowan to benefit as quickly as possible from the very latest research into the schizophrenic mind. We'll let him settle in—get comfortable—before starting to treat him. But rest assured, doctors at this hospital are world leaders in the field of delusional insanity. Young Rowan, we can promise you, will be in safe and healing hands.'

It was all too much to take in. Rowan's mother and his nana heard the words 'settle in' and 'get comfortable' and felt a little better. Then the words 'delusional insanity' clanged in their ears and their faces fell again. 'Safe' was a pleasant enough word though, and so was 'promise'.

'Can we visit him?' his nana wanted to know.'Often?'

'Of course.'

'He'll want his comics,' fretted his mother. 'And more clothes maybe. His vests, if it turns cold . . . '

'Naturally.'

'I'm worried it might get difficult though. The travelling down from London, I mean. Because of the situation—the war. Anything could happen.'

'Mrs Scrivener,' said the man with the pen, 'let's take this one day at a time, shall we?'

'All right. Yes, you're right. Of course you're right. One day at a time.'

Outside, the barking began again; closer this time and a great deal louder.

'Are those *dogs* I can hear?' Nurse Bradley wrinkled

her nose as if the sound had a smell to it. 'Surely to goodness it can't be?'

'We should leave soon,' murmured Rowan's grandmother. 'Rosa will be getting tired. And we need to get home before the blackout.'

'There are a few papers to sign,' said the man with the pen. 'Then you are both free to go. You may say your farewells if you wish, but I would advise you to simply slip away. An emotional leave-taking can play havoc with the balance of a patient's mind. At best it leaves them tearful, at worst—well, full-blown psychotic episodes have been known to occur.'

'Then we'll go,' Rowan's mother said at once. 'Of course, we'll go; we'll go straightaway. But please let Rowan know that it was on your say-so that we left so abruptly and that we'll be back to visit him soon.'

'Of course.'

'And tell him—tell him that we love him very much. It will embarrass him to death—you know how boys are—but tell him anyway.'

'I will indeed.'

'So what is it I need to sign?'

The man with the pen beckoned her forward. He had the form ready on the desk—not the one he'd been writing on but another one, with Rowan's full name already on it, and sections of the Lunacy Act of 1890 set out in faultless italics.

Rowan's mother had to borrow the pen. *Is this solid gold?* she wondered. *It feels heavy enough. He must be very wealthy, this man, to own a solid gold pen.*

Gold or not, expensive or not, the pen did its job. *Hazel*

Louise Scrivener. There it was, her usual signature, practised so many times during the weeks before her marriage that she could have papered a room with it. Since then she had signed so many things—Christmas cards, money orders, letters to her editors, sick notes for the children's schools—but never before had she watched the ink dry with such a terrible sense of foreboding.

Tear it up, go on!

For a few dizzying seconds she wondered if she too had a strange voice in her head—a voice that was going to take control and make her do something crazy. But even as she pictured herself stabbing the man in front of her with the nib of his own pen, or smashing the vase of dahlias over his smart, smug head, she knew it was just her imagination at work. Nothing worse.

And so she turned away from the desk, picked up her gloves and her handbag and then offered a supportive arm to her mother, ready to go.

'Look after him,' was the last thing she said. 'Look after my son, and make him well again.'

'We will do all we can,' said the man in charge, putting the top back on his pen with a jubilant snap. 'Everything humanly possible. You have my word on that.'

THE SPONGE LIKE A HANDFUL OF TWIGS

Re-organization of Hospital wards *(male wing)*

Memorandum to all senior staff

September 6th, 1939

Ward One: New admissions and cases awaiting assessment (no change)

Ward Two: industrious and low-risk patients to whom extra liberty can be allowed (no change)

Ward Three: chronic dements and the helpless feebles (no change)

Ward Four: noisy and disruptive patients (no change)

Ward Five: **IMMEDIATE CHANGE OF USE.**

Formerly epileptics, suicide risks, and general paralytics. Now a recovery and observation unit for male and female test-cases (category A). Epileptics, suicide risks, and general paralytics to be integrated into the infirmary.

Rowan's cocoa had skin on the top. It stuck to his top lip and dripped all down the front of his pyjamas. Quickly he licked round his mouth. *Yuck*. It was too early to be in bed, but he wasn't about to complain. At least he was alone here—alone in the bed, anyway—and could think things over in peace.

Usually, before going to sleep, he liked to read his comics. 'I want that light out by ten,' his mother always said, but she hardly ever checked and sometimes he would read the same Superman stories over and over again, closing his eyes from time to time to imagine himself part of the action—Superboy pitting himself against conmen, spies, bullies, or bank robbers, *wham, ker-pow, splat*! It was only pretend, but it made him feel better—happier—and sometimes, when he eventually got to sleep, he would continue the adventures in his dreams and for a while they seemed blissfully real.

There were no bedside lamps here in Ward One though, only the sickly glow of overhead bulbs providing enough light for a patient to be seen if he got out of bed and went wandering off, but nowhere near enough to read by.

Of the ten iron bedsteads set at precise intervals all the way down the room only three, including Rowan's own, had someone in them. The other two patients were grown men. One kept turning over, making his bedsprings creak, and Rowan hoped he would stop soon before the sound became really annoying.

There were curtains dividing each bed from its neighbour but they were made out of some flimsy white stuff that you could see through. There were no pictures on the walls, no rugs on the floor, and only a small chest of drawers beside each bed in which to store clothes and other possessions.

It was all very sparse but Rowan didn't mind. It was a hospital, after all, not a home. And anyway most of his clothes, all of his Superman comics, and the tray with his family's faces on it were still packed away in his suitcase. Nurse Bradley had told him that he wouldn't be on this ward for very long, so there was no point in getting comfy.

The cocoa was all gone. It had tasted odd but a nurse had told him to drink every drop. 'We can't waste fresh milk, can we?' she had said. 'Not now there's a war on.'

The war. Rowan had clean forgotten, for a while, about the war. And now, as he set his empty cup down upon his empty chest of drawers, it seemed as distant to him as last week's weather. Over by the door sat a man in white. He wasn't a guard exactly but he was there, Rowan knew, to keep an eye on Ward One; to make sure nobody went berserk during the middle of the night.

Slipping lower beneath his sheet and blanket, Rowan

found that he was glad of the man's presence. It took the pressure off him to stay awake himself, watching for trouble through the see-through curtains the way he had watched for German bombers in the sky above his house.

Sleepy . . . he was really very, very sleepy . . .

Turning onto his right side he thought he saw the pretty young nurse come in with a book, or a clipboard, which she gave to the man in white before walking straight out again.

It might not have been her, he could have got that wrong, half asleep in the semi-darkness, but just the possibility of it made him blush. For she had seen him naked—earlier, while he was being examined—and the embarrassment of that was just as awful to look back on as it had been at the time.

'Now don't be coy,' Nurse Bradley had said, snapping her fingers for him to hurry out of his underpants. 'We've seen it all before, haven't we, Sarah Jane?'

'We most certainly have,' the girl had replied. 'In all states and shapes and sizes.'

Sarah Jane. It hadn't helped Rowan at all, to hear her name spoken out loud. It had made her seem less professional somehow, more like an ordinary everyday girl ogling his private parts as he had stood, naked and shivering, while Nurse Bradley fetched her stethoscope.

'If you promise to be a good boy I'll breathe on it first, make it nice and warm,' Nurse Bradley had said. And Rowan had flinched and covered himself quickly with both hands, before realizing to his even greater shame that she hadn't meant him, she'd meant the stethoscope.

Swelling, spots, and vermin, that's what they'd been looking for. And he had felt like a horse at a market, or a fruit being tested for ripeness, as Nurse Bradley had prodded and listened, squeezed and tapped, combed and flicked before finally declaring him sound of body and free of lice.

The girl, Sarah Jane, had remained where she was, standing still and watching. It was part of her training, Rowan had realized, as he listened to Nurse Bradley explaining things to her, but all the same . . .

His underpants had looked such sorry things, draped across a hard wooden chair, and one of his knees, as he bent quickly to put them on again, had clicked like an old man's.

Sound of body. That was something to be grateful for he supposed, when your mind was in deep trouble. And he made himself be glad, as the sedative in his cocoa took him nearer to sleep, that no swelling, spot, or trace of vermin had been detected on his person. That his skin and hair, at least, were nothing to be ashamed of.

He thought he saw his curtains move, as his eyes began to close. There was nobody there though . . . nothing to worry about . . . just a draught, making the curtains billow a little, towards his bed. *Ghost curtains,* he thought, dreamily. *If curtains could die, and then come back to haunt you, that is what they would look like. All pale and transparent and floaty. I don't mind those curtains. It's like being in a tent. They can haunt me if they want to . . . I don't . . .*

'Rowan. Rowan Scrivener. Wake up, son. Bath time. Shake a leg.'

It seemed like only minutes since he had fallen fast asleep. 'Go away,' he almost said. 'It's too early.' But Ward

One was full of sunlight and activity and the man who had woken him up did not look like a person you argued with. Not here. Not in a street. Not anywhere on this earth. He was wearing a white tunic and trousers, like the man who had been on night duty, but he wasn't the same man. He was bigger.

The bathroom was at the end of the ward, with the bath separated from the lavatory by a tiled wall you could see over, like a hedge.

'Hurry up,' the big man said, as Rowan went to use the toilet.

Rowan expected him to leave then, but he didn't. Instead, he waited by the bathtub, whistling through his teeth, while Rowan did his best to pretend he wasn't there.

If the toilet flushes first time he'll go away.

The toilet flushed first time. The man stopped whistling and pointed at the bath. 'In,' he said. 'And jump to it, will you? I haven't got all day.'

The bath water wasn't filthy, exactly, nor was it unbearably cold, but something about the feel of it—the sudsy film that stuck to his skin as he slid in—told Rowan that he wasn't the first person to sit in it.

'I can get washed by myself, sir,' he said. 'Thank you.'

But the man was already lathering a sponge, or what looked like a sponge, only rougher. The soap smelled awful, like medicine, or something Rowan's mother might use to clean a sink.

'Honestly, I can . . . *Ow!'*

It was like being rubbed down with sandpaper, or a handful of twigs. It was as if he was a statue or one of Laurel's dolls. His chest . . . his back . . . his arms . . . the back of his neck . . . *Not my face,* he thought, wildly, *don't scrub my* . . . 'Eyes shut.' The man's hand was like a beast; a warm clammy beast covering Rowan's mouth, his nose, his eyes . . . a five-tentacled swamp creature drooling spit and foul-smelling bubbles as it slid this way and that and . . .

'Hold your breath.'

One big hand was on his forehead now, pushing him under. And he barely had time to gasp for air before the bathwater closed over his face and the swamp creature attacked his scalp.

'Now stand.'

The big hand was tugging at one of his arms, so he didn't have much choice. But he kept his eyes tight shut as he staggered to his feet, water streaming from his hair and dripping off his nose.

A statue. Yes. Superboy has turned himself into a boy of stone, to repel the evil swamp creature.

'Turn around.'

The scratchy sponge scoured the backs of his calves . . . his thighs . . . his buttocks. He almost yelped as it went thrusting between his legs but the moment passed so he breathed out instead, with relief.

'Back round again.'

Shins . . . knees . . . inner thighs . . .

Statues don't feel anything. Statues don't care.

Later he would ask himself which had been the worst: being inspected between the legs by Nurse Bradley, being looked at there by the young nurse, Sarah Jane, or being cupped, lathered, and rinsed by the big man's hand.

Looked at, he would decide. For some reason, being

looked at by the girl had shamed him far more than any prod or touch.

'Right. Out you get.'

He was given a towel which he held in front of himself as if uncertain what it was for.

'Dry yourself off then, soft lad,' said the man. 'Or do I have to do that for you as well?'

No good arguing that he hadn't asked to be bathed like a baby in the first place, or that he was only hesitating now in case he wasn't supposed to dry himself, just as he hadn't been allowed to wash his own skin, clear though it was of swellings, spots, and vermin.

Quickly—gratefully—he rubbed himself down. His clothes were on the floor, over by the doorway (no door, he noted, just a space, a very *wide* space, allowing whoever was on ward duty a clear view of both the bath and the toilet).

'This one's done!' the big man called through the space. 'You can take him away.' He hadn't pulled the bath plug. And as Rowan was led back down the ward, by yet another man in white, he saw that one of the adult patients was still in his bed. Wide awake. Staring at the ceiling. Waiting his turn to be washed.

'I FORESEE NO COMPLICATIONS WITH HIM. REALLY, NONE AT ALL'

Had Rowan been invited to predict how the rest of that day would go his list would have gone something like this:

1. Breakfast
2. A nice long talk with the doctors
3. Lunch
4. A rest, or a walk in the fresh air
5. Another talk with the doctors
6. Supper
7. Read comics for a bit
8. Bed

If asked what he would *like* to happen the list would have been much the same, only with more time for reading, and the proviso that nobody got to see him naked any more.

He would also have liked to be smiled at again by the young nurse, Sarah Jane. But that was a private hope, not something to be shared.

He would have got 'Bed' right but that's about all.

'Good morning, Rowan. This is Doctor von Metzer. He is going to be in charge of your treatment. Pop up onto the bed and lie down for us, there's a good chap. Comfy? Excellent.'

The nice long talk hadn't happened. Surely that was a good sign, Rowan told himself, for it meant that these doctors weren't groping in the dark, weighing up different options. They knew precisely what to do about the panics, without the need for endless chit-chat, and they were getting on with it right away.

I'll be home for Christmas then, definitely. For bonfire night, even.

The man who had asked him to get up onto the bed was the same one who had sat behind the big desk the day before and written things down with an expensive pen. Rowan felt reassured, seeing him again. But Doctor von Metzer? It sounded like a German name and that worried him, a lot.

'What are you going to do?' he asked, raising himself up on his elbows. 'Are you going to put me to sleep?' There were lots of doctors gathered round the foot of the bed—five . . . no, six . . . and most were gazing expectantly at the one with the German-sounding name.

'You are not to worry, young man,' von Metzer said. 'You are lucky, yes? Lucky to be in the right place at the right time with this new and very wonderful treatment available to you. Already, in other parts of Europe, it has given many patients great relief from delusions of the mind. From the voices you are hearing, yes?'

Rowan's stomach gurgled; from hunger partly (he had been told he couldn't eat anything until after the treatment) but also from fear. The doctor's accent was like the bathroom sponge, abrasive and unpleasant. His hair stuck up, as if he had never heard of brilliantine, and there was a small speck of something on the front of his tunic which Rowan sincerely hoped was nothing more gory than a little bit of breakfast. He was looking, not at Rowan, but at a chart he had taken from the end of the bed.

'Very good,' he murmured in his German-sounding voice. 'Very good indeed. Really, this should be a most straightforward procedure.'

'Possible complications?' one of the other doctors asked—not one of the hospital staff but a man who had travelled all the way from Newcastle to witness, first hand, this exciting new procedure.

Von Metzer replaced the chart, straightening it on its hook like a beautiful painting. 'Based on the case studies in Italy,' he replied, 'vertebral compression, fractures, peripheral nerve palsy, circulatory insufficiency, tooth damage, minor skin burns and prolonged apnoea. But this patient is young and physically sound. I foresee no complications with him. Really, none at all.'

Rowan's elbows were beginning to ache but he wasn't going to lie flat again; not until somebody explained to him precisely what prolonged ap-whatsit meant. He had trusted, implicitly, that his treatment would not be too scary: a study of his head, maybe, with one of those new machines that photographed your insides, followed by a course of medicine or pills to help him sleep while his mind healed and the Voice died a permanent death.

He had been hoping, actually, to see a picture of his brain, imagining the problem area showing up as clear as a scratch and some clever doctor saying, *'Aha! There's the culprit. Well, don't you worry, young feller-me-lad, we'll soon have that sorted.'* At worst, he had pictured an operation—the whipping out of the faulty bit, all very quick and simple, and not too painful either because they had stuff nowadays that knocked you out while you were being cut open and tampered with.

But fractures and tooth damage? Skin burns and prolonged whatever-it-was? That didn't sound simple or painless, not by a long chalk.

'I'd like to know . . . ' he began, but then stopped.

Doctor von Metzer had come round to lean against the edge of the bed and he was holding something up. Something Rowan instantly recognized. 'What are you doing with that?' he said. 'It was in my suitcase, with my comics. What have you done with my—'

'You must trust me, yes?' von Metzer replied. 'In a minute I will explain exactly what is to happen to you and all will be clear. But one thing to realize now, Rowan, is that after each treatment it will be necessary to test your memory. You are understanding me?'

'Yes. But my—'

'And this personal item of yours is very fine for that test. So . . . the people pictured here, they are members of your family, yes?'

'Yes.'

'This one, the lady with the dogs. Who is she, please?'

'That's my na—my grandmother.'

'The mother of your father?'

'No, the mother of my mother.'

'And the dogs. Name them, please.'

Rowan frowned. 'It's an old photograph,' he said. 'I never knew those dogs. But the ones my grandmother has now are called Greta, Marlene, Clark, and Errol . . . After Hollywood film stars,' he added, 'in case you were wondering.'

One of the doctors in the background turned a chuckle into a cough. Von Metzer nodded, gravely. 'Marlene Dietrich is a big favourite with me,' he said. 'In *The Blue Angel* she was superb. In *Shanghai Express* also. On Greta Garbo I am not so keen. This man here—who is he, please?'

'That's my father,' Rowan told him. 'When he was young.'

'Ah yes. He fought in the last war, I am assuming.'

'Yes.' And Rowan felt the sweat breaking on his forehead as he looked at the picture of his young soldier-father—so hopeful, so unknowing—with von Metzer's finger aimed directly at his face.

'And this young woman?'

'That's Daff—Daphne—my sister.' He had picked out and stuck down a recent snap of Daphne. She was posing among ferns, in the courtyard behind their house; standing on tiptoe with a pretend bow and arrow like a statue of Cupid, the little god of love. Her hair was all lit up by the morning light and her face the almost exact shape of a heart.

'She is very beautiful, your sister. She could be in the movies, yes? Like Marlene Dietrich.'

Don't touch her, Rowan thought, as the sweat began to prickle beneath his arms and in his hair.

'And this lady?'

The pointing finger moved several inches up and to the left along the tray. It was a very clean finger and very pink, like an uncooked sausage.

If he touches your mother, said the Voice. *If his filthy Jerry finger lands on the mother's face she will feel it like a red-hot brand. Even miles away, even at her typewriter down in the kitchen, she will feel it eating into her flesh, and be scarred for the rest of her life.*

All the doctors were waiting for a reply. They couldn't hear the Voice even though it seemed, to Rowan, to be booming from both of his ears and echoing down his nostrils it was that loud.

Grab the tray. Make a run for it. BITE the sodding Nazi bastard if you have to. Kick him in the man-nuts. What are you waiting for? Do it NOW!

'My comics . . . ?'

He'll have burnt your bloody comics. Or shredded them. Or tied them up with string and sent them off to Hitler in time for a happy Christmas. He's the enemy. Get us out of here.

'Your comics are safe in your suitcase, Rowan, so do not worry, please. Look again at this photograph. Is she an aunt? Or a neighbour? Your godmother, maybe?'

Grabbing the tray was easy. Von Metzer was holding it loosely, with only one hand, and not expecting to be tackled by a test-case. Jumping from the bed, with six grown men gathered round, proved trickier. Running from the room, impossible.

'I'LL KILL YOU! I'LL KILL YOU!'

He was clutching the tray like a shield, his family's faces turned for safety to his chest. Somebody grabbed his arms . . . pushed him back onto the bed and held him down. He lashed out, hard, with both his bare feet; caught someone in the stomach and was glad.

'YOU NAZI SCUM! I'LL KILL YOU!'

'Doctor Atwood—the straps.'

The tray was tussled away, and Rowan felt thick bands of something—leather . . . rope . . . he couldn't see what . . . tighten across the tops of his thighs and then his chest and then . . . oh, Lord . . . his forehead, as he was buckled, tightly, to the bed.

'DON'T TOUCH MY MOTHER, YOU JERRY SWINE. OR MY SISTERS EITHER. YOU KEEP YOUR FILTHY HANDS AWAY FROM THEM!'

Should've gouged his piggy eyes out. Too late now . . . Should've got him where it hurts, right between the legs. Too bloody late now. Idiot.

He began to pant, gathering breath.

'Now bring the apparatus round,' ordered von Metzer. 'Quickly!'

One of the younger men raised his hand to speak, realized he wasn't at school any more, for goodness' sake and blushed.

'Yes? What is it? Speak up, Doctor . . . ?'

'Collins, sir. Terence Collins. Medical student, first year. I was just wondering . . . shouldn't we wait a bit? Observe the whole delusional episode before starting the treatment?'

'I agree.' It was the owner of the expensive pen speaking—the hospital's director, W. Richard Thomas MD, FRCP, DPM. 'It would be extremely useful, research-wise, to let the crisis run its natural course. The patient's ramblings about his mother are of particular interest, I'm sure, to those of us who are familiar with Freud's theories on the development of schizophrenia.'

Two of the other doctors expressed, through nods and murmurs, their own eagerness to wait, watch, and make notes, should Rowan start ranting again.

Doctor von Metzer said nothing at all while he dragged a contraption shaped like a giant radio, with copper wires trailing from it, across the room to the head of the bed. He said nothing, either, while attaching electrodes just above Rowan's temples or while pushing, with practised ease, a solid wodge of rubber into Rowan's gaping mouth.

Then: 'Gentlemen,' he said, 'I have no time, as you know, for the theories of Sigmund Freud. No disrespect, you understand, as I believe Doctor Freud is now a very sick man, but to blame schizophrenia on a patient's long-ago dealings with his mother is, please excuse me, complete excrement. Now . . . You invited me here, Doctor Thomas, to apply the very latest *medical* treatment to the schizophrenic brain in the hope it will lead to a long-awaited cure. We are all keen for the glory of that, are we not, gentlemen? For papers published in our names? For a Nobel Prize one day?'

Oh yes . . . the gentlemen's expressions all said. *The glory . . . the publications . . . the Nobel Prize . . . yes please to all of those.*

'So, then . . . ' von Metzer placed one hand, paternally, on the leather strap across Rowan's head. 'Let me have no more talk, please, about this patient's mother. It will be enough, in a few hours' time, that he still recognizes her face. Now, are we ready, gentlemen?'

The young doctors shuffled their feet, chastised. He was right, they thought. Talk, as a therapy, was old hat compared to this. And old Freud, it was rumoured, could no longer even speak. Cancer of the mouth. A nasty business.

'Yes,' they answered, humbly. 'Of course.'

'Doctor Thomas?'

The director nodded, curtly. He had agreed to these trials, after all, for the greater good of the hospital, not to mention his own bank balance and reputation, should the treatment work, please God.

'Go ahead,' he said.

And Doctor von Metzer flicked a switch, sending one hundred and ten volts of electricity in a barbed-wire arc through Rowan's brain.

'SHOULDN'T HE BE FULLY CONSCIOUS BY NOW?'

Birdsong. He recognized that: a twittering somewhere to his left. And cold breath—no, a breeze—coming from the same direction, bothering his left arm.

He hurt. He ached. His head felt like Humpty Dumpty, put back together again but badly; and just above his eye sockets: two raw spots pulsing like dreadful music, and hurting worst of all. Had the bird been pecking at him there? It sounded close enough to peck at him, had it a mind to.

'Rowan?'

He kept his eyes tight shut. It seemed the safest thing to do. And what kind of bird was that, anyway, making such a din?

'Lost albatross.'

He didn't know why those two particular words came to mind, only that they made him smile, despite the cracked feeling between his ears and the pain like a couple of woodpecker wounds on either side of his skull.

Woodpecker wounds? Well, yes . . . woodpeckers were a species of bird, he knew that from somewhere, and they pecked like the very devil. *Rat-a-tat-tat,* like knocking on doors. *Let me in, let me in.*

'Rowan? Can you hear me, Rowan?'

Confused, he pretended not to hear a thing.

Blackbird, hummingbird, yellowhammer, jay, goldfinch, cuckoo, skylark, owl. He could, he discovered, picture each one of those birds quite clearly . . . its colours, its wingspan, the little tiny tracks it left in sand or snow . . . Somewhere, at some time, he must have seen a book . . . a book of ABCs, with a bird for every letter . . . small watercoloured pictures . . . every detail perfect.

Linnet, magpie, vulture, dove.

The magpie had a nasty nature and was one for sorrow, two for joy. Vultures ripped your innards out, if you died all alone in the desert with no one around to bury your body or give a ha'penny chew about you. Perhaps a vulture had come for him and made a start on his head. *Where in the world though, and how come?* He tried for more words: 'Robin Redbreast'. Those were two, to be going on with. And then 'Christmas', which had something to do with robins, and which, he had an anxious feeling, he really ought to know a lot more about.

'Rowan?'

He kept his eyes closed but managed, this time, a small aching nod. Because the voice was kind and the word it had said meant something after all.

I spy with my little eye, something beginning with 'R'.

Rowan. A tree. A tree with red berries—a feast for all kinds of birds, particularly thrushes. He felt smug, knowing so much about the rowan tree. But the effort of knowing strained the cracks in his head until he feared they might split, like trouser seams. Under no circumstances was he going to open his eyes. Not yet. Sleep was better—safer—when you had so much on your mind to do with trees and birds but not a clue about who or where you were.

They should close the thing though. The window. To keep the bird out, and the breath . . . no . . . the breeze.

'Rowan? Can you hear me?'

'Leave him be for now, Nurse—ah, Springfield. Sarah Jane Springfield, yes? He has gone back to sleep. It is good, for now, that he does this.'

'I'm sorry, Doctor von Metzer. I was quite certain he was coming round; that's why I rang for you. And his head moved a moment ago, I'm sure of it. Shouldn't he be fully conscious by now? I mean . . . it's been hours. Is this . . . is this normal?'

'There is no "normal", Nurse Springfield. Each patient is different, yes?'

'Oh, I know. I know they are. Should I loosen his straps, perhaps? He might take fright otherwise, like Dorothea did when she came round that first time.'

'No. Leave the straps until we see how he is behaving. They are for our protection too, don't forget, should Master Rowan's first wish upon waking be to bite off our noses or fight us with his fists. Am I right in saying so, Dorothea?'

Smiling, just a little, von Metzer turned away from Rowan to the one other patient on the ward—a person who, at first glance, could have been male or female, adult or child, and who was watching everything keenly, over the fold of a sheet.

'He won't fight,' this person said. 'I'm telling you. I know. He'll be pathetically good and say everything you want him to—that's if you haven't killed him by mistake, or turned him into a helpless feeble.'

'We haven't killed anyone, Dorothea,' von Metzer replied. 'And when Rowan is awake you will have a companion, yes? Someone of nearly your own age who is sharing the same problems.'

'You're my only problem,' the person in the bed observed, smoothly. 'You and little Miss Clacton-on-Sea there. Are you aware she spends more time putting lipstick on and flirting with men in the corridor than she does watching over your patients? Hardly surprising, to be fair. Her guardian angel was a prostitute, you know, before she passed over; a terrible old tart who died of an unmentionable disease. She's with us now as it happens—over there beside that chair—and she's getting on my nerves.'

Doctor von Metzer nodded, as if he quite understood. He didn't look at the chair though. 'Well, Dorothea,' he said, 'we will perhaps see what we can do, tomorrow, to calm your nerves some more.'

Behind him, Nurse Sarah Jane Springfield scowled. She hadn't looked at the chair either—knew enough, even this early on in her training, not to give currency to a mental patient's ramblings. But this patient was pushing her luck, tittle-tattling to a senior doctor the way she just had. She was pushing her luck to the limit.

Furtively she wiped her mouth completely clean of its film star scarlet. It was a good job, she thought, that this new German doctor wasn't on the ball. That he hadn't the first idea about the things that went on in this hospital to ease the boredom of watching loonies sleep or listening to them weep and fart. With luck, he would think Dorothea had made it all up, about patients not being watched properly. With luck he would think it was just more of her crazy baloney, like the stuff about guardian angels.

I'm going to spit in your cocoa tonight, you little cow, she thought.

'Just look at her face,' chortled the girl in the bed. 'Miss Clacton-on-Sea is out to get me, doctor, did you know that? She'll be spitting in my cocoa tonight.'

And *Oh, God,* thought Sarah Jane, turning as pale as the sheets. *How did she guess?*

It was another five hours before Rowan opened his eyes.

'About time too,' he heard someone say. And then: 'Don't bother making a run for it. Firstly, you won't feel like walking for at least another week; secondly, they've got you tied to the bed like a cowboy in a film. Do you need to throw up? Aim for the nurse's shoes after she's undone your straps. I always do. OI! HEY! MISS CLACTON-ON-SEA! DOCTOR VON'S LATEST VICTIM IS COMING TO HIS SENSES—OR WHAT'S LEFT OF THEM. TIME TO PRETEND YOU KNOW WHAT YOU'RE DOING.'

And then there was the sound of people running . . . footsteps slap-slapping on linoleum . . . a man's voice saying, 'Welcome back, young man. You are feeling a bit peculiar, yes? It is normal. Trust me.'

Then a girl's face came swimming into view. Blue eyes. Pink cheeks. Wavy blonde hair pinned back beneath a starched white cap. *Pretty,* Rowan thought. *I like you.*

'Tell me your name,' the man said to him. 'And then I will undo the straps.'

It seemed a fair exchange. But why had he been tied down in the first place? Was this a trick? The man sounded foreign and there was a problem with that . . . somewhere . . .

'Head . . . hurts,' he rasped, closing his eyes. 'And thirsty . . . need a drink.'

Someone undid a buckle, raised his tortured head, placed some kind of spout in his mouth and then held him gently while he sucked water down his throat. He hoped it was the pretty girl holding him and kept his eyes firmly closed, the better to pretend that it was.

'His memory's fried,' said the voice on his right. 'At least I could tell you *my* name after *my* first treatment. Mine *and* my angel's. At least *I*—'

'Dorothea,' said the man, setting the cup of water down. 'Have some kindness, please. Some good feeling, yes, towards a fellow patient. Now . . . ' He began to undo the strap across Rowan's chest. 'You are in the hospital, young man, and everything is good. We make you more comfortable and then maybe you will remember your name. Can you open your eyes? Very good. Now . . . will you sit up? Excellent. Your head is sore, yes? It will ease. Trust me. So tell us, please, who you are. What is your name?'

'Fried,' muttered the voice of Dorothea after a moment or two's silence. 'I knew it. I told you so . . . '

Turning his head, Rowan discovered, wasn't easy. It felt odd—not just ear-splittingly painful but really, really odd as if someone had taken his mind out and replaced it with cogs and nails and rag doll stuffing with just a few thoughts thrown in to make him feel human.

Not fried though. It didn't feel fried. And anyway, how would you fry a head? He was going to ask the person in the next bed what she had meant by that, exactly, but the second he saw her he changed his mind.

Slowly, carefully, he turned away. A ball on a stalk, that's what his head felt like; heavy, well-kicked, and likely, at any moment, to topple clean off his neck. The man who had undone the straps, and got him sitting up against his pillows, took hold of both his hands and peered, anxiously, into his face.

What? Oh yes . . . My name. Where's it gone? What did I do with it?

'Oh dear. Shall I call for the director?'

That's the pretty one talking. She sounds worried.

'No. Observe his eyes. He is thinking. He is needing a little more time, that is all.'

'But remembering their own names isn't usually difficult, is it? Surely, Doctor von Metzer, he could have told us that by now?'

Hang on—I know her. I've seen her before and she's seen me. She's seen ALL of me. I remember now . . . Sarah Jane, that's who she is. Sarah Jane, the nurse.

His own name though . . . what was it? The word 'Kent' popped into his head to match the word 'hospital' and then the word 'tray' to match 'mother' and 'Nana' and 'dogs'. It was like rummaging through a box in an attic, this effort to recall . . . or a suitcase . . . a big suitcase with lots of room in it for all kinds of things. 'Comics' . . . the word itself meant nothing very much, but he had a feeling he rather liked whatever it was so he groped around in his head, for a few more clues, and then . . . *Yes!*

He'd got it. He'd remembered who he was.

At first, he considered keeping the information strictly to himself. After all, it didn't always do to give too much away—he remembered that much, at least, about the world and its ways. Also, something about the doctor-man's way of talking was still making him uneasy.

And yet . . . wasn't this doctor trying to help him? Wasn't that what doctors did? He had given him a treatment . . . that was it . . . done something to his head to stop him getting all upset and wanting to hurt people. Not criminals, or enemies of the State but ordinary people; people who had done nothing, really, to deserve the whirling weight of his anger.

In a while—the words were tumbling thick and fast now—this very same doctor would fetch the tray with pictures of Nana and Laurel and the rest of the Scrivener family stuck to it and would ask him to say who everyone was. He would pass that test, he already knew, with ease.

Asking him his own name was just another way, he realized, of making sure that he hadn't lost his memory; that it hadn't been 'fried' during the treatment like that . . . that . . . person had just said.

And so, Rowan decided to come clean.

'Superboy,' he said, proudly, to the doctor and the nurse. 'I am Superboy from Planet Krypton.'

He thought they would be pleased. Delighted. He

thought they would smile and praise him for remembering his true identity. But the doctor said nothing, nor did he smile, and the nurse, Sarah Jane, raised a hand to her mouth and gasped.

It was the girl Rowan hadn't wanted to look at who broke the silence first. Her laughter was high-pitched and it echoed around Ward Five and out into the corridor like the cry of a tropical bird.

'Oh, that's priceless, that is,' she shrieked, wiping tears of mirth from her bruised eyes. 'That's made my day. I think I'm going to like you after all, Superboy from Planet Krypton. I think you and I are going to be friends.'

'WHATEVER KIND OF DEVIL DO YOU TAKE ME FOR?'

'Let me get this straight.' The hospital's director put down his golden pen, rose from his desk, and began pacing up and down. 'He's awake. All his vital signs are normal. He can walk, he can talk, he remembers an impressive number of facts, including the names of his grandmother's wretched dogs, and he ate a hearty breakfast. But—and what a very big "but" it is, Doctor von Metzer—he genuinely believes he is Superman?'

'Superboy,' von Metzer corrected him, quietly. 'He believes he is Superboy.'

'And have you told him he's not, or are you leaving that to us?'

Von Metzer did not reply. Instead, he reached into his battered leather bag, took out a batch of comics, and placed them on the director's desk.

'And if you seriously think I have either the time or the inclination to—'

'No. You misunderstand. These comics belong to

Rowan Scrivener. He brought them with him, from his home, and although he has no conscious memory of them I believe they are precious to him. I have read one and it appears that the hero is two people: Clark Kent, who is a dull fellow, and Superman who. . . '

'I've heard of Superman,' the director chipped in. 'I know what Superman is. And I see what you're driving at, doctor. Not that the publishers of . . . what is it?' (He stopped beside the desk, picked up one of the comics, frowned at it and put it down.) ' . . . *Action Comics* would thank us for labelling their latest creation a paranoid schizophrenic. The question is, what are we to do about Rowan Scrivener? The last thing I need is his family turning up—that difficult mother in particular—to find the boy barmier now than he was when he came in.'

Doctor von Metzer leaned back in his chair and smiled—a faint and rueful smile but one that he would have been wiser to suppress.

'This is no laughing matter, sir,' the director scolded. 'Not for me. I have the reputation of my hospital to consider.'

Von Metzer tensed. He could not afford to annoy this man, not if he wished to remain here, continuing his research. 'I was not laughing,' he said, solemnly. 'I was smiling with relief that Rowan Scrivener's problem is maybe not so bad And I was wondering what you would be saying to the difficult mother, had the electric shock left her son unable to speak at all. For there is always that possibility, doctor, as you know. That element of risk, yes, with a treatment so new that it remains, still, in the nature of an experiment.'

The director turned his back, paced some more, stopped and looked out at the sky. Apart from the visitors' lounge this, his office, was the only room in the hospital without bars at the windows and it was good to see the view—a reminder that he himself was sane, and free, and in charge of this place.

'I would have told Mrs Scrivener the truth,' he said. 'That Rowan's condition deteriorated unexpectedly. A sudden seizure of the brain. Nothing we could do. It would have been a lot easier, believe me, doctor, than presenting her with a son who now thinks he can fly.'

Not fly, exactly, von Metzer thought before daring to ask: 'But for the boy's mind to have been damaged beyond repair . . . his relatives would accept such a thing? Without question? Without some sort of inquiry?'

'Doctor von Metzer,' the director replied, 'nine times out of ten a patient's rapid, and irreversible, deterioration is the best thing that could happen. The families will never admit it, not even to themselves, but it is.'

Outside the sky was clear and blue. An earlier broadcast on the wireless had reported no imminent danger to Britain's shores and, in any case, the hospital was far enough away from all air bases, ports, and major cities to be considered a relatively safe haven. For now.

A group of patients—five men—straggled past on their way to dig up potatoes. Low-risks, all of them, entrusted with the tasks of sweeping, or gardening, or spooning food into the mouths of helpless feebles. One of the men pointed towards the office window and waved, excitedly, the way a child might upon catching sight of its father. A male nurse lowered the man's arm and moved him on, nodding an apology towards the director for any interruption to his thoughts.

In his chair beside the desk—a visitor's chair—von Metzer was trying very hard to convince himself that he had misunderstood what the director had just said. That line in particular, about a patient's 'rapid deterioration' being a good thing . . . he had heard similar sentiments before, back in his homeland, and knew, for shame, where they could lead. He had never thought to hear such dangerous talk in England.

'Are you truly telling to me,' he said, 'that you . . . that Rowan Scrivener's family . . . are hoping all the time for the electric shocks to fail? So that this young boy becomes a vegetable person, with no hopes of going home? Is that what you are saying? You are wishing him to stay here for the rest of his life? With his family paying big fortunes for that privilege?'

He had hoped to sound neutral but the words came out tight with alarm and disgust.

'Not at all.' The director turned, sharply, away from the window. 'I'm not *advocating* failure, Doctor von Metzer. Whatever kind of devil do you take me for? I want the boy cured and away from here just as much as you do, and so does his family. All I'm saying is we're in more of a pickle with this Superboy nonsense than if he had woken up with a black tunnel through his brain and no memory left at all.

'Because if he'd done *that*, doctor, the family would have accepted it as God's will, or a random act of nature. And you and I would not be facing all kinds of awkward questions about bodged or unethical practices, should the boy decide to mention, over tea and cakes one day, that he's been zapped from ear to ear with a massive electrical charge!'

'There was no bodging,' von Metzer replied, with less disgust in his voice this time but roughly the same amount of alarm. 'And you told me, doctor, did you not, that there is permission from the family, for giving Rowan Scrivener electric shocks to the head.'

'Well . . . yes. They gave their consent. In a manner of speaking.'

Von Metzer's expression hardened.

'This manner of speaking,' he said. 'It involved use of the words "electroconvulsive therapy", yes?'

'Well, no. Not exactly. But they wanted us to do everything possible—everything.'

'So did you tell them, doctor, in any "manner of speaking" that a new treatment would be tried on their son—a treatment with . . . what is the word . . . much controversy, yes, and some risks?'

'Not at the time, no.' The director flipped open his pocket watch. He was properly irritated, now. 'The mother was having second thoughts,' he said, consulting the watch with the air of a man who should have been somewhere else ten minutes ago. 'She was talking about taking the boy home, which, as you'll appreciate, would have proved disastrous by and by, given the nature of his condition. And anyway . . . ' His eyes brightened as he hit upon a winning argument: 'And anyway . . . what if she had asked to meet *you*—the specialist in charge of the treatment?'

Von Metzer shrugged, perplexed.

'Well, think about it, man. It's obvious. When we invited you here, to run the trials, your medical credentials were far more important to us than your nationality. And we didn't give a stuff about your politics—didn't even ask. Only now, with things the way they are, what Englishwoman is going to want a Jerry tinkering around with her little darling's head?'

There was silence then, although the word 'Jerry' seemed to echo in it for a very long time. And in the space of that silence, Doctor von Metzer kept his eyes fixed on a bunch of flowers wilting in a cut-glass vase. He didn't know the name for those flowers, only that they were gasping for water and that their stems were in a strait-jacket made out of green string.

He was waiting for an apology.

He didn't get one.

Never mind, he told himself. *What is it that they say in this country? Sticks and stones may break my bones but names can never hurt me. Let them call me what they will. It is not important. The trials . . . my research into electroconvulsive therapy . . . that is all that matters and I cannot allow anything, or anyone, here to weaken my faith in this exciting new treatment—or, indeed, in my own ability to administer shocks to the head correctly and well.*

'I will solve this trouble with Rowan Scrivener,' he said after a while, confidently, but so quietly that he could have been talking to himself. 'I will treat him again with the electricity—again and again until he is remembering who he truly is.'

'Good,' said the director, hearty now with relief. 'Better make a start right away then, hadn't you, old chap, before he tries throwing his bed at someone, or goes leaping off the roof with one of my nurses in his arms.'

THE CAKE WITH NO SULTANAS IN IT

Summer took a long time to fade. The clear skies lasted through most of September, empty of clouds, and of enemy aircraft too. People relaxed a bit. Theatres and dance halls reopened and everyone moaned about the blackout.

In London, Rowan's nana and her friend Rosa planted purple and yellow crocus bulbs on top of their Anderson shelter. 'Let's hope we'll be around to see them in flower,' said Rosa, but she'd been saying that for years now, because they were both so ancient.

Daphne went dancing four nights a week with Eddie Dobbs. She wore Ashes of Roses perfume and thought more about kisses than bombs. Rowan's father started a new painting, featuring a gas mask, trampled lilies, and the face of a broken clock. His mother wrote an article about the new autumn fashions—'*over-boots of waterproof velvet or gaberdine . . . handbags incorporating a handy gas-mask container . . . a luminous brooch that glows in the blackout and can be seen for fifteen feet . . . and, if you're handy with the needles, try knitting yourself a nice warm scarf in a bright and cheery colour.'*

Young Laurel was given the option of returning home, since the Current Situation did not seem to warrant her staying away. But she was having such a good time, as an evacuee, that she chose to remain in Weymouth.

With Rowan, things were not so cut and dried. A week after his committal, the director telephoned the Scriveners to advise against all visits until further notice. Treating the mind, the director said, was a delicate matter and visitors had been known to jeopardize the whole process, however carefully they spoke and behaved around the patient. He hoped they understood, he said. And they did.

Rowan's mother missed her son terribly. She wrote letters twice a week, telling him the family news, and fretted, privately, over whether he was keeping warm and getting enough to eat. His nana said that if he wasn't home for Christmas they would jolly well take Christmas to him, whatever that pompous twit with the flashy gold pen had to say about it.

Dear Rowan (*his mother wrote on the first day of October*)

It is hard to believe you have been away for almost a month. We do miss you. This house is very quiet without you and Laurel bickering all the time! Last night your father and I lit all the candles in the drawing room—there are thirty-four of them altogether, did you know?—and what with the silence, the old wood panelling, and the old-fashioned light it seemed as if we had gone right back to the eighteenth century when French silk weavers lived in this house and boiled water for tea over a spirit lamp. I half expected to see a man in knee breeches and a curly wig come through the door to say goodnight!

Just before 9 o'clock there really *was* a knock on the door—the front door—and I almost jumped out of my skin. It was only the air raid warden, though, come to say he could see the candle light flickering through a gap in our shutters and could we please observe the blackout restrictions or we would find ourselves in trouble. I thought your father was going to hit him. Luckily he didn't and I managed to stuff the gap, temporarily, with two socks and a ball of wool.

Daff sends her love and says she hopes . . .

'Is that your mum, writing to you again?'

Quickly, Rowan folded the single sheet of notepaper and slid it back into its envelope. He would finish reading it later, if he got the chance.

'Yes,' he said. 'But it's just family stuff, nothing exciting.'

Dorothea sniffed. 'I thought you came to earth in a rocket ship,' she said. 'I thought your real parents were blasted to smithereens when Planet Krypton got destroyed in an inter-galactic battle that rocked the whole universe and shook up the stars.'

Rowan wasn't sure if she was mocking him or not. Usually she was but sometimes, like now, it was hard to tell.

'I did,' he told her, warily. 'And they were. Lawrence and Hazel Scrivener adopted me. They're good people and I'm like a proper son to them.'

'Really.' Dorothea sniffed again. 'That's why they've had you shut away in a loony bin, is it? Because they care?'

Rowan didn't answer. With every day that passed he was regretting more and more that he had ever said anything, to anybody, about who he truly was.

Doctor Von, for instance—could he really trust that man? Those treatments . . . they were awful. Dreadful. Worse than anything he could possibly have imagined before coming here. And how did he know they weren't draining his powers? After all, Doctor Von was a German, and he remembered enough, between treatments, to know that the Germans and the English were at war with one another, back in the outside world.

But then . . . other doctors here, and nurses too, claimed that the shocks were doing him good; making him less aggressive. Those people were English, so on his side for sure, and what they said made sense for he clearly remembered hurting Laurel and that had been wrong—a mistake. If Doctor Von's treatments worked . . . and he wanted, more than anything, to believe that they were going to . . . he would never misuse his powers like that again. Never.

And yet . . .

The nurse now, Sarah Jane. She was lovely and he wouldn't have minded her knowing who he was if only she believed it. She didn't though. She hadn't said anything, but Rowan could tell from her manner that she thought he was making it all up. It was wrong, he knew, to actively wish for some kind of disaster to befall the hospital, so that he could shrug off his dull, everyday self and become the person he was underneath. But part of him was hoping for precisely that: for an opportunity to prove himself to Sarah Jane; to be her hero. At least she had never taunted him, though, about his superhuman powers. Not like Dorothea.

Dorothea was scary, with her shaved head and smart remarks. And she saw things—angels perched like parrots on people's shoulders, or hovering mistily above beds and chairs. Everyone had a guardian angel, according to Dorothea, everyone, from the King of England down to the most helpless feeble you ever saw. It was what she'd told him, that first night on Ward Five, after the doctor had gone and the nurse had dimmed the lights.

'Does Hitler have one?' Rowan had wondered.

'Who?'

'Never mind.' He hadn't cared enough to ask about his own guardian angel, nor had Dorothea bothered to enlighten him on that score.

'Welcome to Ward Five,' she had called to him instead, across the space between their beds. 'An exclusive little hideaway with all the very latest comforts—a private bathroom with a fine view of whoever's still in bed; three meals a day, for those who can swallow; excellent security and—most important of all—a free and abundant supply of electricity. My name's Dorothea. Don't call me Dot—dots are small and insignificant—and never, ever, call me Dotty or I might have to kill you. Goodnight.'

How long ago could that have been? In some ways it seemed to Rowan ages since they had moved him to Ward Five but it could just as easily have happened yesterday. That was the trouble—one of the troubles—with the treatments. Just when you got a date fixed in your mind they gave you another zap, jumbling minutes, hours, and days like the flecks in a kaleidoscope.

Today, though, was a rest day, for Dorothea and for him, so they were sitting out on the lawn, in almost-autumn sunshine, waiting for Doctor Von to come by for a little chat. They had been wheeled out in bath chairs and a male nurse had tucked tartan rugs over their knees. It made Rowan feel like an old man, sitting there like that—an old man waiting for someone to come and push him around, or take him to the lavatory. It was a good disguise though, he had decided, for someone like him; a superhero biding his time.

Sarah Jane was not on duty today. She was at home in the village at the bottom of the hill, doing whatever she did on her day off. Rowan wondered (not for the first time) if she had a sweetheart and, if so, what they got up to together.

'What are you thinking, Superboy?'

'Nothing.'

'Yes you are. You're thinking about Miss Clacton-on-Sea, aren't you?'

'No.'

'Yes you are. You're blushing. You're stuck on her, aren't you?'

'No—no I'm not.' Rowan could see Doctor von Metzer ambling towards them across the lawn. *Hurry up,* he willed him.

Dorothea began picking at one of her scabs. There were two of them, congealing on her temples, and it didn't take much to make them bleed.

'I don't know what you see in that stupid little tart,' she said. 'Are you mad or what? Are you *completely* out of your mind?'

Von Metzer had stopped to talk to a helpless feeble. He was smiling, Rowan could see, as if the man tied to a bath chair and being pushed towards the rhododendron path by a nurse with strong arms, was his greatest friend in all the world. And as he spoke he squatted down on his haunches so that the feeble could see his face without having to crane his wobbly neck.

'Here comes our saviour,' observed Dorothea, bitterly. 'His guardian angel was a Christian martyr, did I tell you? The Romans threw him into a pit full of dust and animal dung, and a lion tore half his head off. He's quite young, as guardian angels go, and doesn't show himself often. Perhaps he doesn't like what Doctor Von does for a living. Perhaps he's given up on him in disgust.'

Rowan continued to watch as von Metzer shook the feeble's hand and said goodbye. 'He's all right, Doctor Von is,' he said, thoughtfully. 'I think he just wants us to be able to pass for normal, when we go back to the outside world. He's doing his best, I'm pretty sure of it.'

'Hah!'

Dorothea dabbed at her head with the flat of her hand, dabbed and dabbed until her palm came away smeared red.

'I'm going home on a blue moon,' she said. 'When fishes fly and the seas run dry—that's when I'll get away from this hell-hole.'

Rowan looked round at her and winced. 'You should stop doing that,' he told her. 'They'll never heal, if you keep doing that. And it upsets Doctor Von.'

'That's precisely *why* I do it,' Dorothea snapped back. 'Idiot.'

Today von Metzer had some particularly searching questions for them.

'Dorothea,' he said, pulling up a wicker garden chair and sitting down with his face to the sun, 'when Rowan says he has superhuman powers—do you believe him?'

Dorothea hesitated, smelling a trick.

'Ah. You hesitate. It is because you are not sure, yes? You suspect he is making it up?'

'No I don't. I don't think anything. I don't care. Stop asking me stupid questions.'

Von Metzer turned to Rowan.

'My guardian spirit,' he said, solemnly. 'Do you see it, Rowan, the way Dorothea does? On my shoulder perhaps?'

'I . . . '

'He won't see anything, stupid,' Dorothea cut in. 'He hasn't got the gift. And it's "angel" not spirit. Get it right.' Irritated, she mopped at her head. Von Metzer hadn't mentioned the blood. He never did. He was sitting in an ordinary chair, smiling his most irritating trust-me smile and waiting for her to say something else. He was always doing that—throwing out infuriating questions and then sitting back to see what effect they would have. They were like stink bombs or fireworks, those questions. They were like flesh tossed to cranky animals.

Rowan was watching the sky. There were swallows up there, swooping and soaring; preparing to leave the country. Somewhere close by would be nests made from spat-out clay and the birds' own saliva; abandoned now and already beginning to crumble.

'Dorothea,' he said into the silence, 'have *I* got a guardian angel?'

'No,' she said at once. 'They only do earthlings.'

Doctor von Metzer smiled and shook his head. This girl, this Dorothea, she was as bright as a buckle—brighter, it seemed, from one treatment to the next as if the electricity was opening new pathways in her brain. Back in June, when he had first arrived here, she had been sullen and unwilling to speak at all, except to the angels, and then only in a mutter so that nobody else would hear.

All her life, von Metzer knew, Dorothea had been smacked and shouted at for seeing her angels. When, at the age of nine, she had begun shouting and smacking back, her family had locked her away in a wing of their house, with a nurse to keep her clean and sedated. Two years after that, when she cut both of her wrists with sewing scissors, the family had had her committed.

Von Metzer was of the opinion that Dorothea's brain had been jolted enough, by successive electric shocks, to be working along more normal lines. True, she was still talking to, and about, guardian angels but he suspected that this was nothing more, now, than an elaborate pretence. He understood this—the need to cling to a delusion at all costs for fear of being nothing without it—but if Dorothea was ever to be properly cured the pretending was going to have to stop. Time alone, he hoped, would do that trick, now that the treatments had tamed her.

With Rowan Scrivener, it was harder to tell just yet what was going on. All von Metzer knew, and could write in his reports with confidence, was that there had been no repetition of the aggression the boy had displayed prior to his committal and just before his very first treatment. The Superboy fantasy, however, was proving harder to dislodge. It was the first time von Metzer had treated a delusion that had set in *after* treatment and, despite the inevitable concerns, he found it fascinating. Whether more shocks would put paid to this fantasy, or time and careful counselling would be enough to see it off, was something he had yet to decide.

A great deal depended on trust.

'You are watching the birds, I notice,' he said to Rowan. 'Are you wishing, perhaps, to be able to fly like them?'

'I don't need to, do I,' Rowan replied matter-of-factly. 'If I wanted to, if there was an emergency of some kind, and I had to get somewhere fast, I could leap an eighth of a mile in half a second or run faster than a speeding train. That's just as good as flying, isn't it—better, I'd say.'

'I see.'

Von Metzer turned, then, and made a signal with his

hand to someone hovering just beyond the glass doors that opened out from the dining room onto the lawn.

A male nurse appeared, carrying a tray loaded with tea things. He placed the tray on a low wicker table, within easy reach of all three chairs, nodded conspiratorially to Doctor von Metzer, then went back indoors.

'What, no ugly brown mugs with spouts?' said Dorothea in mock surprise. 'I'm not sure I can hold a tea cup, Doctor Von. I'm out of practice.'

'I'm sure you will do very well, Dorothea,' von Metzer replied. 'In fact, would you be kind enough to pour?'

Dorothea raised an eyebrow. Rowan looked from the swallows to the tray. He noticed the cake first and thought *yum.* But there was steam coming from the teapot's spout which meant the liquid inside was scalding hot. And there was a knife—a very sharp knife—for cutting the cake, which meant—well . . . that this little tea party could take a sudden nasty turn.

A movement caught his eye: a flash of white beyond the big glass doors. The male nurse, the one who had brought the tray, was still hanging about. Meeting Rowan's eye, the nurse pretended to be adjusting a curtain but Rowan knew he was really there to raise the alarm, should anything bad happen.

Afternoon tea . . . so very civilized. So very *ordinary.*

For a long time nobody moved or spoke. They could have been posing for a photograph, Rowan thought, or for one of Lawrence Scrivener's paintings. Overhead the swallows flew daringly low. Across the lawn, on the rhododendron path, somebody laughed—a long loud laugh, full of spit and garble.

When Dorothea's hand shot out towards the teapot, Rowan flinched. *Do something! Stop her!* He could feel the sweat forming in a wet band around his hairline and two slicks under his arms. The feeling was horribly familiar. *Is this it?* he wondered. *Is this how I start to change?*

Dorothea lifted the pot. There was a silver tea strainer which she picked up with her left hand and set, correctly, over one of the cups. Holding the lid of the teapot in place with one finger she began, very slowly, to pour.

Rowan held his breath. His heart was thumping and that, too, felt like part of a process of change. *If she splashes tea onto the tray—even a tiny bit—Doctor Von will die. She'll scald him, she will, or stab him with that knife.* He breathed out, and then in again, out and then in. The blade of the knife winked, nastily, in the sun. If this was how it happened, the switch from normal to superhero, it wasn't at all pleasant.

'Milk, Doctor Von?' said Dorothea, setting the pot back down. 'Or a slice of lemon?'

'Neither, thank you,' the doctor said. 'I like my tea black. Sugar though I will take. One lump.'

The tongs in the sugar bowl could have poked someone's eye out.

'There,' Dorothea said, dropping one perfect white cube into the brimming cup. 'I'll let you stir.'

She passed the cup and saucer, managing not to spill, and Von Metzer took them from her. 'Thank you, Dorothea,' he said.

'Don't mention it.' Dorothea picked up the teapot, reached for another cup and began, once again, to pour. 'Luckily for you,' she added, pleasantly, 'the cake is a chocolate one, and we like chocolate, Joan and I. Had it been plain, or full of sultanas, we would have had to kill you. Have I told you, Superboy, about Joan? *Saint* Joan, that is, of Arc. She's my guardian angel and she's with us now.'

Rowan didn't answer. He was staring at the tea, at the little pool of hot tea that had dripped onto the tray when Dorothea lifted the pot. *If she splashes some onto the tray . . .* But the Voice was fading, like an echo in a cave. It had barely been there in the first place and now it was gone. And the bit of spilt tea was no more or less than that—a spill. Not a bad omen, after all. *I am Superboy,* Rowan told himself, weakly. *If necessary, I can still lift this girl up and whisk her away before she does any harm. I can do that. I know I can . . .*

When the tea was all poured, Von Metzer asked Rowan if he would leave his, for a moment, and kindly cut the cake. It was very good cake, and it cut beautifully, in dark, moist slabs. When he had finished dividing it up, Rowan laid the knife carefully down, being careful not to clatter, or drop crumbs.

'Well now,' von Metzer said. 'How very pleasant this is.' He was very nearly beaming as he sipped his dark, sweet tea. These two, the girl who saw angels and the boy who believed he had superhuman powers . . . it warmed his heart to observe them now; to note how surprised and pleased they were (although trying hard not to show it) to be taking tea like any sane English person on a sunny afternoon.

He had gained their trust, just as he had hoped. Later on he would record this happy fact in his written report.

And he would cure them both, he silently vowed. He would give them back their sanity, if it was the last thing he did.

Dorothea and Rowan said nothing at all as they drank their tea and demolished their cake in big, childish, bites. There were smudges on the handles of their cups, where Dorothea's fingers had left traces of her blood. Behind the glass doors, the male nurse remained poised, on red alert.

'That was a test, wasn't it?' said Dorothea after a while. 'You can't fool me, Doctor Von. You were testing us just then, weren't you?'

Von Metzer set his empty cup down upon its saucer with a small triumphant chink. 'You are nobody's fool, Dorothea,' he said. 'It was a test, yes. And you have both passed, I am pleased to say, with a flying of colours. There will be no more treatments for a while, for either of you. For a month or so, we will see how we get on. And if all goes well I am hopeful that, by Christmas time, you will both be considered low-risks.'

No more treatments! Rowan was glad about that. Sitting there in his bath chair, with the taste of chocolate in his mouth and the sun warming the back of his neck he felt a wave of something that was not quite contentment but almost. His head still hurt when he moved it, and thinking too hard was a strain—he got confused so easily—but life could, he realized, be treating him a whole lot worse than this.

And what a relief, he thought, that he had not had to save von Metzer's life after all. Not that he wouldn't have done it, of course, but he really didn't feel up to being a superhero today. Maybe he was too groggy, still, from the treatments. More likely, he was simply out of practice.

He wondered, as he finished his tea, if Sarah Jane would be back on Ward Five tomorrow. That really would make his week, he decided. That and another piece of Joan of Arc's favourite sort of cake.

'THE BRAIN MUST WALK BEFORE IT RUNS'

Night-times, during early October, were a trial and a nuisance to Rowan. As the effect of so many treatments began to wear off he took to waking up at midnight, alert, cranky, and unable to go back to sleep. In the bed next to him Dorothea slumbered deeply, ten hours at a stretch, and resented being roused in the mornings. Being asleep, she said, was like being dead: utter bliss.

Rowan didn't like her saying that. It worried him. But 'I'm not saying I want to die right *now*, stupid,' Dorothea sneered. 'I just like a lot of sleep. It's the only way of getting out of this hell-hole.'

'Do you dream?' Rowan wanted to know.

'I travel,' she replied. 'With Joan. We go all over the place.'

Waking in the small hours Rowan envied Dorothea her travels. Then one night he opened his eyes to find Sarah Jane on ward duty and insomnia took on a far happier meaning. Getting up during the night was forbidden, unless you needed the lavatory, and Rowan had become an expert at controlling his bladder when Sarah Jane was there, watching his every move. It was enough, though, to lie quietly in the semi-darkness, gazing happily across at his favourite nurse.

She sat at the desk beside the door, her face and the waves of her hair lit by the glow of a lamp. If angels existed, Rowan thought, then she could be one easily. For a while she read a magazine, flipping the pages quickly as if it was really just the pictures she liked. Then she bent down and took something from a bag—long, slim knitting needles and a ball of bright pink wool.

I love you, Rowan mouthed, as silent as a goldfish. And he drifted back to sleep to the lullaby clicking of needles, *clickety-tick, clickety-tick*, marking the seconds until morning.

As male nurses began leaving the hospital, to do their bit for King and country, Sarah Jane swapped her day shifts for night duty and Rowan's happiness was complete. In the mornings, Doctor Von took over and Rowan was glad about that, too, for although he was allowed to wash himself, here on Ward Five, the bath tub could still be seen by whoever was on duty and he had begun to hate, and yet to want, Sarah Jane's cool stare upon him as he jumped, as quick as a frog, in or out of the water.

Doctor Von never looked, though, while either Rowan or Dorothea were in the bath and in the third week of October he arranged for a screen to be set up around the lavatory. 'I trust you,' he said to his test-cases. 'To be quick, yes, about your business and not do anything foolish.'

'Like what?' Rowan had wondered.

'Like sticking our heads down the lavatory pan until we stifle and drown,' said Dorothea. 'Or hanging ourselves from the chain—although I notice it's been shortened. Clever, that.'

Although there were eight beds altogether, on Ward Five, no other patients came and Rowan wondered about that as well.

'You are special,' von Metzer told him. 'You and Dorothea, you are unique, yes?'

Their days fell into a pattern. Breakfast with Doctor Von—just the three of them, on the ward—followed by a morning of tasks and talk. The tasks were easy and confined to the room: sweeping the floor, changing the bed linen, polishing bits of silver and brass brought in to them in a box. Sometimes Rowan and Dorothea did the tasks together, sometimes Rowan had his chat with Doctor Von while Dorothea worked, and sometimes it was the other way round.

The talks, like the tasks, seemed simple enough but Rowan soon came to understand how important they were—how every word he said to Doctor Von was being carefully weighed up and might count towards how soon he would be considered a low-risk and, then, be allowed to go home. And he did want to go back, eventually, to the big old house in Spitalfields even though it wasn't his real home, and the Scriveners weren't really his people.

To begin with, if it was Rowan's turn for a chat, Dorothea interrupted all the time. 'Joan's here,' she would call across the room. 'Come and say hello.' Or, if asked to do the sweeping, she would bang the broom on the metal legs of all the beds before riding it, like a witch, up and down the ward.

'Have consideration, please, for a fellow patient,' was all Doctor Von ever said to her. To Rowan he said: 'Ignore Dorothea, if you can. She is seeking some attention only.'

'No I'm not,' Dorothea would call out. 'I get enough of your stupid attention. I'm just bored, that's all. Bored out of my skull. Bored, bored, bored . . . '

If it was Dorothea's turn to answer Doctor Von's questions (or not, as was mostly the case with her) Rowan was as considerate as possible, making just enough noise to show he wasn't listening but not enough to be thought a nuisance. He was always considerate with Dorothea, never saying hurtful things about her angels or her head, and never, ever, watching while she took her bath.

'Does it bother you, Superboy, when I interrupt your talk time?' Dorothea eventually asked him.

'It does a bit,' he replied, honestly.

'Fair enough,' she said and, after that, she was better behaved.

After lunch they had a walk, skirting the rhododendrons in the hospital grounds and nodding at the helpless feebles. 'We'll end up like that,' Dorothea said one morning. 'If Doctor Von here keeps shocking our heads.'

'No, we won't!' Rowan protested, before the doctor could reply. 'We won't, Dorothea. That's mean.'

After the walk they took a nap. Rowan, exhausted from his broken nights, slept soundly at nap-time, waking only as the light was fading beyond the tall barred window. He would lie very quietly then, until it was time for supper, trying to fill in the gaps that still peppered his memory like holes in a certain kind of cheese. 'Doctor Von,' he asked, at the end of the third week of October, 'where are my comics?'

'Your comics?' the doctor repeated, hopefully. 'Which comics are you meaning, Rowan?'

Rowan thought hard. 'I don't remember, exactly,' he admitted after a while. 'I just know that I had comics, once, and that I liked looking at them.'

'When you remember what they are about,' von Metzer replied, 'let me know, yes, and I will seek to find them for you.'

'Give him the comics,' the hospital's director said. *'Then he'll see there is no Superboy, only a cartoon character called Superman who has never existed outside some artist fellow's imagination.'*

Von Metzer disagreed. *'No,'* he said. *'Rowan must see through this delusion of his naturally, and in his own time. To look at the comics now could be a dangerous thing. It may convince him that he is not alone—that Superman is his real father, maybe.'*

'Heaven forbid,' grumbled the director. *'That would be all we needed.'*

Instead of the comics, Doctor Von brought Rowan story books. He chose carefully from the library—nothing too upsetting, nothing to do with superheroes or saving mankind—and although Rowan read these offerings dutifully he found little about Beatrix Potter's bunnies or Enid Blyton's elves to interest or inspire him. Every day, though, he read a few pages aloud, so that Doctor Von would be able to write in his reports that the part of his brain to do with recognizing the written word had not been damaged by the treatments.

'I did Latin at school,' Rowan remembered one day. 'Before I came here. I did all kinds of clever stuff.'

'All in good time,' von Metzer replied. 'Using your mind after the treatments must be taken slowly, yes? The brain must walk before it runs, if you understand.'

Several times a week the tray with the photographs glued to it appeared and Rowan was asked to look at each member of his family in turn and to say something about them that he hadn't said before—anything he could remember, it didn't matter what, so long as it was new and off the top of his head, so to speak.

The hotch-potch of Rowan's recollections went something like this:

Father: He was a soldier once . . . he works hard . . . his paintings are like strange dreams . . . he isn't my real father . . . he says he eats to live, not the other way round . . . he wouldn't give houseroom to a Bakelite cup or anything made this century . . . or the last century either . . . or possibly even the century before that . . .

Mother: She mends my socks . . . she has a faraway look . . . she isn't really my mother . . . she can type very fast . . . she likes chocolate but says it doesn't like her . . . she worries about me . . .

Nana: She is as old as the hills . . . she is amazing for her age . . . she knows what dogs are thinking . . . there is a painting in our house of her that was done when she was young. She had very long hair, then, and is sitting in a tree . . . she drives a van with a blue cross . . . she stole my penknife . . .

Daphne: She smells of roses . . . she sings all the time . . . she doesn't understand me . . . she is a happy soul . . . she isn't really my sister . . . she wants two children, one of each . . .

Laurel: Her plaits are always wet at the ends, because she chews them . . . she torments me . . . I am not her real brother, thank goodness . . . she cannot play the piano to save her life . . . she wants a kitten but is not allowed one in case it scratches the furniture . . . once she used red oil paint to give all her dolls measles, and cried when it wouldn't wash off . . . I hurt her and that was wrong . . .

'Do you love your relatives, Rowan?' asked Doctor von Metzer.

'They are not my relatives,' Rowan replied. 'How many times do I have to tell you?'

Towards the end of the month he wrote his first letter home. It took a long time, not just because his writing was shaky, from lack of practice, but because the Scriveners hardly seemed real by then and he didn't know what to say to them.

Dear father and mother and Daff,
I am glad to hear that you are all well. I am well also and doctor . . .

'How do you spell your name?' he asked.

'V, o, n,' said von Metzer, 'then a space and then M,e,t,z,e,r.' He waited a moment before adding, 'It is a German name, as you know.'

Rowan nodded. England and Germany were at war, he hadn't forgotten that. He remembered, albeit vaguely, Hitler and Anderson shelters and apple pickers with their gas masks on. But no bombs had been dropped on London, or anywhere else in England (he'd asked Sarah Jane and she'd told him so) so it was all starting to look like a big false alarm.

'Why aren't you in Germany, fighting for your country?' he asked von Metzer.

'Because I am here, looking after you,' the doctor replied, promptly. 'And because my mission in life is not to kill people, but to keep them alive and happy in their minds.'

'I see.'

He squeezed the word 'my' between the words 'and' and 'doctor', then carried on writing:

. . . my doctor thinks I will soon be able to have visitors. I have become very good, you will be pleased to learn, at tidying up and making my own bed. My friend Dorothea says that if there were prizes for tucking sheets in I would get one. She is being sarcastic when she says that, but not unkind.

'Careful what you say, Superboy,' Dorothea called to him from her bed. 'The director will read it, before posting it off, and he won't be checking your spellings.'

The weather continues fine, Rowan wrote, *and I am getting plenty of fresh air. Do not worry about me.*

'Bet you've gone drivelling on and on and on about Miss Clacton-on-Sea, haven't you.'

'No I haven't. I haven't even mentioned her.'

'Bet you have.'

'Well, you're wrong. I've mentioned you though. I said you were my friend but if you don't shut up I'm going to change that bit.'

'Your friend, eh? What about Joan? Did you give Joan of Arc a mention as well?'

'No.'

'Why not?'

'Because they'd think you were bonkers.'

'Fair enough.'

THE PUMPKIN WITH THE FIENDISH GRIN

On the thirty-first of October von Metzer brought a pumpkin on to Ward Five. It had already been carved (*'Not trusting us with a sharp knife any more, then, Doctor Von, now that we're thinking more clearly*?' sneered Dorothea) and it sat on the desk by the door, grinning like a fiend and smelling vaguely of rot.

'Do you celebrate Hallowe'en in Germany?' Rowan wanted to know.

Von Metzer was pleased. For a patient to start asking questions about another person's life was always a good sign. It showed that he was looking beyond The Self.

'Not so much,' he said. 'In Germany we have "*Hexennacht*"—the "witches' night" but that is in the springtime, on the thirtieth day of April.'

'Hex-enn-acht,' Rowan repeated. The word felt rough in his mouth.

'You sound like a helpless feeble,' Dorothea teased him. 'A helpless feeble coughing up his dinner.'

Rowan ignored her. 'What is Germany like?' he asked.

Von Metzer looked into the eyes of the pumpkin and sighed. Then he looked at his patients' faces—the girl's so indifferent; the boy's so pale and serious; both of their brains as faulty, still, as radios thrown at a wall.

'I cannot speak for my country as a whole,' he said, 'but my birthplace in the north is very beautiful. The mountains there have snow on their tops from September until May and the mist is like a veil around their shoulder's blades.'

'Boring,' muttered Dorothea.

'Go on,' said Rowan.

'When it snows,' continued von Metzer, 'it is said that the old woman of the sky is shaking her feather bed. Then in April, when the snows are commencing to melt, ghostly riders come in a troop to chase the young goddess, Walpurga, all around the peaks and through the wet, green forests.'

'Oh,' breathed Rowan. 'Did you ever see that? When you were a little boy?'

'No,' von Metzer replied. 'It is a story, only. A way of explaining the coming of the summer.'

'He wouldn't see any young goddess,' Dorothea scoffed. 'He hasn't got the gift. I bet I'd see her though, and those other riders, and the old woman with the feathers.'

'Well . . . ' von Metzer went on, 'it is said that Walpurga flees fast from the riders of winter, with her long hair flowing behind her in the mists and her spindle trailing its threads. She gets tired, with this fleeing, so for the last nine nights of April the villagers are leaving open their windows so that she may rest, in safety, among mortal beings. Once, it is said, a farmer hid Walpurga in his stock of grain and when he woke in the morning his rye crop was sprinkled with speckles of gold.'

'Hah!' Dorothea began scratching her head. Her hair was growing back and it itched. 'You wouldn't catch an English person leaving their windows open all night. That's asking for trouble, that is.'

Von Metzer chuckled. 'They are very tiny windows in the houses of this German region,' he said. 'Too small for robbers with their big sacks but just right for the goddess of summer who is as slim as a rasher of breeze.'

'Hah!' went Dorothea a second time. But her expression was soft—wistful, almost—and she said nothing further to challenge, or ridicule, the story of the goddess Walpurga. Rowan, too, seemed taken with the tale and it dawned on von Metzer that he had given both these young people something a lot like nourishment—a welcome taste of a time and a place beyond the hospital gates.

Later, as they walked in the grounds, their feet crunching on fallen leaves, Rowan remembered something. 'The witches night,' he said. 'Your German one, I mean; the one at the end of April.'

'*Hexennacht?*'

'Yes. Is that to do with the goddess then? The summer goddess who flees from the ghostly riders?'

'That is a very clever question, Rowan,' von Metzer said. 'And there is a connection, yes, for the story of Walpurga has changed much, over time. It is long ago that she was a goddess. In modern thinking, she is considered a saint and the winter riders are said to be evil witches who meet in the mountains every year, on the thirtieth of April—the eve of Saint Walpurga's day.'

'Joan was burnt as a witch,' Dorothea piped up. 'And then she became a saint . . . in France though, not Germany.'

'I'm confused,' said Rowan.

'Of course you are, Superboy,' Dorothea said, sweetly. 'So am I. Perhaps we both need our heads shocking some more, before we can understand such madness.'

That night Rowan dreamed vividly of flight, waking with a jolt that felt just like a sudden landing. On his tongue, he was sure, was the taste of snowflakes. Remembering where he was he turned over in his bed, the pupils of his eyes already growing big as he thought of Sarah Jane.

His first sight of the pumpkin scared him, for he had forgotten all about it, and now there it was, lit up from within, its serrated grin flickering in the dark.

There was no sign of Sarah Jane but her knitting was on the desk, next to the pumpkin, so Rowan guessed she could not be far away. He waited, with his eyes fixed on the ball of pink wool, for her to come back. He waited a long time.

Maybe he dozed, he wasn't sure, but a giggling out in the corridor made his heart leap and his eyes widen and then she was there, her shadow thrown crazily against a wall by the light of the pumpkin lantern and someone . . . some*thing* . . . hurrying in behind her.

The person-thing had a black face and horns like a goat and he-she-it was growling low in his throat and making little grabs at Sarah Jane's blouse.

'Shhh . . . *Shhhh* . . . don't wake the loonies . . . In here, quick!'

The person-thing smacked at Sarah Jane's buttocks as she scampered ahead towards the bathroom. Then in one quick movement, and using both of his hands, he peeled off his face and flung it down on the desk. Underneath he was handsome, and about eighteen years old.

'Oh . . .' Rowan breathed, relieved that this was, after all, only a person in a Hallowe'en mask, but shot through, all the same, with a terrible envy.

'In here . . . come on!'

The young man did not need telling twice. In a few long strides he was through the bathroom doorway and had disappeared behind the screen that had been put up to hide the lavatory.

The giggling began again, followed by a little shriek, quickly stifled.

'Does that tickle?'

'YES! But don't stop, I like it!'

'Do you like this as well?'

'Mmmm . . .'

Rowan couldn't bear it. He pulled his sheet and blanket high over himself but the giggling and the whispers and the little stifled shrieks were still audible. He put his head under the pillow but that wasn't much better and after a while it became hard to breathe so he came out for air, his heart racing.

Sarah Jane had stopped giggling. Now she was panting, like someone doing exercises, and the man with her was grunting as if he still had horns and the face of a beast.

Is he hurting her? Is she in danger? She said she liked it a minute ago, when he tickled her, but now she sounds really odd. Rowan's heart was beating so fast that the thud of it, in his ears, was almost-but-not-quite muffling the noises coming out of the bathroom.

Then Sarah Jane began to yelp and *Right,* Rowan decided. *That's enough. I'm going in there.* The penny had dropped—better late than never—and although he had never heard anyone doing sex before he was pretty certain that girls didn't cry out like that while it was happening—not if they were having a nice time they didn't. So this was *it,* he realized. His chance to prove to Sarah Jane that he really was a boy with extra-special powers, and that no one was going to hurt her, or take advantage of her while he was around.

He clenched his fists and took a deep, steadying breath. *Any second now the change will happen . . . it will happen automatically, any second . . .* In his mind's eye he saw, already, his fist crashing through the lavatory screen *Bam! Kerpow!* and the look of terror on that beast-boy's face as he got lifted off his feet and flung, hard, into the empty bathtub. *Bam! Kerpow! Splat!*

And Sarah Jane . . . He would gather Sarah Jane up in his strong blue arms (Blue? Yes . . . blue, he remembered that quite clearly . . . bright blue sleeves and a cape that flapped like a sail) and together they would . . .

'Don't stop! That's wonderful!'

. . . they would launch themselves . . .

'You're wonderful, Sairs. You're fantastic . . . the best . . . girl . . . in the . . . world . . . '

. . . out of the window . . . and then . . . and then . . .

It wounded him. Hearing those words—the soppy love

words—echoing down the ward pained him far more, he would swear to it, than anything done, so far, to his head. Still, as the love-talk continued, in between the grunts and the yelps, he was forced to accept the obvious: Sarah Jane did not need rescuing. She was enjoying herself behind the lavatory screen and would not thank anyone for charging in and throwing her handsome friend across the room.

Don't bother, Rowan told himself. His other self. His super-human self. *Stay where you are. You're not needed here tonight.*

Scarlet with misery and embarrassment he curled himself up like a foetus or a prawn; curled himself up and stuck his fingers in his ears. It was what he should have done earlier, he realized, put his fingers in his ears, because it worked. It blocked everything.

He closed his eyes too after a while because the pumpkin seemed to be mocking him. *Careful. Don't wake the loonies . . .* and after a while it crossed his mind that any halfway decent person would be relieved that Sarah Jane wasn't being attacked. He ought to be glad, he told himself, that he hadn't had to rescue her, just like he'd been glad when Dorothea had managed to pour the tea, without scalding Doctor Von or stabbing him through the heart with the cake knife.

But he wasn't glad. Not this time. He was sorry.

Somehow . . . he told himself. His ordinary self. His curled-up, red-faced, insignificant little self. *Somehow, someday, I'll prove to Sarah Jane that I'm not what I seem . . . I'll show her I'm amazing. A true hero.*

'BUSINESS AS USUAL, MARGARET'

'What's up, Superboy?' croaked Dorothea partway through November. 'You've been a right old misery-guts recently. What's the matter?' She sniffed, then wiped her nose on the sleeve of her nightdress. She was recovering from a cold and confined to bed.

'Nothing,' Rowan snapped. 'And I'm tired of you calling me Superboy. You're only mocking me when you say it, so don't.'

'Oooooh! Temper, temper. Fetch me my brush, will you, and my looking glass.'

Rowan set the brass plate he was polishing face down on a sheet of newspaper and went over to the desk. 'Can she have her things?' he asked Doctor von Metzer.

The looking glass had a silver-coloured handle and a picture on the back of swans on a lake. The comb looked like ivory but wasn't. They were inexpensive items, purchased from a catalogue, but they were pretty, nonetheless and Doctor Von had given them to Dorothea for her birthday.

'My birthday is in May,' Dorothea had told him. 'I think.'

'For Christmas then,' he had answered her.

'And that's ages away too, stupid.'

'Dorothea,' he had said, 'you are looking the gift horse in its mouth. Do you want these items or not?'

'All right,' Dorothea had said as if presents were things she got showered with most days; as if she had more presents knocking around than she knew what to do with. 'If you insist.'

There had been a condition though ('Oh surprise, surprise' Dorothea had scoffed) and that was that both the comb and the looking glass should only be used under supervision. Director's orders.

'Why?' Rowan had wanted to know.

'In case I decide to jam the comb into Miss Clacton-on-Sea's stupid head,' said Dorothea. 'Or on the off chance that I'll smash up the mirror and cut my own wrists with the biggest, sharpest bit.'

Rowan had looked genuinely shocked. *I believe Rowan Scrivener has no suicidal tendencies,* von Metzer had the confidence to write in his notes. *Despite suffering some moodiness recently he shows no leaning towards more severe depression and it is now over two months since his last schizophrenic episode. The delusion that he is a hero from another planet persists, however, and I remain concerned that he may one day cause serious injury, to himself or to others, while acting out this role.*

I am reluctant, at this stage, to recommend further applications of electroconvulsive therapy. It may, however, prove beneficial to set up a carefully controlled situation within which . . .

'Can Dorothea have her things?' Rowan repeated.

Von Metzer stopped writing.

'Of course,' he said, unlocking a drawer beneath the desk. 'Take them.'

Rowan took the comb first and then the mirror, being careful to turn the glass away so that he wouldn't see his own face, not even by accident.

'You look pale, Rowan,' von Metzer said. 'Paler even than usual. Are you sleeping badly? Because if so I can give you something—a small sedative in a drink—that will help . . . '

'I'm fine,' Rowan insisted. 'Really.'

'Then maybe it is fresh air you are needing, yes? At lunch time a nurse will be replacing me here. I have a meeting with the director, but after that you and I will walk together.'

'All right.' Rowan was looking at the page of writing.

'Is that in German?' he asked, peering harder at the upside-down words. 'Or in secret code?'

'It is indeed in German,' said von Metzer. 'For my own personal reading only.'

'What does it say?'

'It is supposed to be—what is the word—confidential, yes? But it says most basically that you, Rowan Scrivener, are doing well, here on Ward Five, and that I am pleased with you.'

'Oh. Right.'

Rowan shrugged, to show he didn't much care just then for an expert opinion on the state of his mind. Then he turned and went trudging back across the ward, the comb and the looking glass like dead weights in his hands.

That boy is most definitely troubled, von Metzer observed. *His delusion of the hero must be worrying him, on a very deep level. He does not wear it lightly, like Dorothea with her angels, and the longer it lasts the harder it will be to help rid him of it. Time and careful talking have not worked with Rowan Scrivener. Another plan is needed—and soon.*

Rowan handed Dorothea her things.

'*Merci,*' she said, and then: 'Joan's here. She says my mirror's pretty. Joan liked pretty things. Her mother sent her half a yard of blue silk ribbon, before the siege of Orleans, and she pinned it to her helmet—not for luck, but because it was such a beautiful colour, like the sky.'

Rowan lay down on his bed, his back deliberately turned. He didn't want fresh air, or a sedative, or anyone fussing over his health, or prattling in his ear about ribbons and saints. He was sick and tired of both Dorothea and Doctor Von—there was just no escaping them.

I'm going out, he wanted to say. *Don't wait up.* He wondered, grimly, how far he would actually get before someone grabbed his arm and escorted him back to Ward Five. Not far, he decided. Not far at all . . .

Closing his eyes, he concentrated, hard, on the task he had recently set himself: the surprisingly difficult task of remembering what it had been like to be Superboy. Before coming here. Before the shocks had scrambled his head and turned his past into a half-forgotten story.

From somewhere came the memory of elephants . . . big grey elephants floating in the sky on the ends of enormous chains. London. He had been in London, then. And the elephants (*Surely not? Alien spacecraft more like, shaped like animals to fool people*) had spelled danger all right.

I am Superboy from Planet Krypton and I am here to protect humankind.

Had he made the change that day? To Superboy? He must have done . . . but the memory wasn't there . . . just the feeling . . . the sensation . . . that he had.

And then later . . . in that house . . . the house where a Nazi had lived and a dog had been left and the very air had been tinged with menace . . . *I am ready to defend my people.*

It was no good. He was groping . . . straining . . . fishing for recollections that flickered but then vanished, in teasing, scattering shoals. What was it Doctor Von said? 'The brain must walk before it runs.'

My brain is CRAWLING, he thought, bitterly. *My stupid brain can't even STAND yet! And I'm so, so tired of it . . .*

'Let me run through this again.' The director tapped his golden pen on the report in front of him—a translation of Doctor von Metzer's review of the patient Rowan Scrivener, and a recommendation that seemed to the director bizarre, to say the least. 'You want us to set up a situation—a false situation, a piece of play-acting—that will send this patient into a full-blown schizophrenic episode?'

'That is correct.'

'Well, forgive me, doctor, but isn't that rather dangerous?'

'It need not be, not if the preparations are careful.'

'Hmmm . . . so you think that by forcing Rowan Scrivener to confront his "Superboy" delusion he will realize the utter falsity of it and abandon it altogether?'

'That is my hope for him, yes.'

'Hmmm . . . '

For a long time the two men sat quietly, each one thinking the matter through. Von Metzer stared into the fireplace where logs of apple wood were burning. The sweet smell of the smoke was pleasant and there were more logs piled up ready in a basket to the left of the hearth.

There was a fireplace, von Metzer remembered, in the small private bedroom he had been allotted, here at the hospital, but no one had brought him any fuel for it yet and he hadn't thought to ask.

Certainly the weather had turned icy. Before long, von Metzer predicted, the old woman of the sky would be shaking her mattress.

'Sherry?'

'No . . . thank you.'

'You don't mind if I do?'

'Not the smallest bit.'

The director lifted the stopper from a heavy crystal decanter. 'It's an old ladies tipple, sherry,' he said, pouring a small amount of the amber-coloured liquid into a glass the size of an egg-cup. 'But I like it.'

Von Metzer waited, politely.

'I'm stumped,' the director admitted after a while. 'We might have to get the whole team together over this one. Trouble is, I don't want to broadcast the problem too widely. Doesn't reflect well on the effectiveness of the treatment, does it, or on my hospital either for agreeing to the trials.'

Von Metzer inclined his head. 'I understand your concerns,' he said, quietly. 'They are my concerns also, to a certain degree. But my priority, doctor, is to help Rowan Scrivener come back to his proper senses as quickly as possible.'

'And mightn't a few more treatments do the trick?'

'There is no reason to assume so, since he has already had so many. It may even be that the shocks are making matters worse—destroying the voice that told Rowan to hurt other people but making louder the belief that he is, instead, their saviour.'

'Interesting . . . ' The director set his empty glass down upon the desk. 'It has exciting potential, don't you think, Doctor von Metzer, this possibility that electroconvulsive therapy replaces an impulse towards evil with an impulse towards doing good?'

'It is indeed a fascination,' von Metzer agreed. 'But it has not happened in the Italian trials, or elsewhere in Europe, so I suspect Rowan's experience is unique. Certainly my other patient, Dorothea de Vere, has not had the same response. She is calmer, just as Rowan Scrivener is—as all known cases are following these treatments—but with her there are no surprises.'

'Dorothea doesn't matter so much,' the director said, with a dismissive wave of his hand. 'She's with us for life. Rowan Scrivener, though, is expected home one day so we need to—yes, what is it?'

The office door opened and Nurse Bradley bustled in. She nodded, politely, to von Metzer but her eyes, as she did so, were as chilly as his bedroom and she made no apology for turning her back on him as she said to the director:

'Everyone's wondering, sir, what's happening about Christmas this year. Because of the war.'

It was amazing, von Metzer thought, just how much disdain an English woman's back view could communicate to a German as she said the word 'war'.

'Business as usual, Margaret,' the director answered, briskly. 'The dinner. The pantomime . . . The low-risks look forward to a traditional do, and it will be good for staff morale.'

'Pantomime. . . ' von Metzer repeated, thoughtfully. 'A Christmas theatrical, yes? You have a pantomime-show here at Christmas time?'

Nurse Bradley turned and looked at him, down her nose.

'The staff and the low-risks,' she said. 'We put one on together. The patients who aren't in it are brought in to watch—the ones able to leave the wards anyway—and folk from the village come—a few relatives too, if they live close enough, and can be bothered to make the effort.'

'Interesting . . . ' Von Metzer caught, and held, the director's eye.

Nurse Bradley sniffed. 'We were thinking of doing *Peter Pan* this year,' she said. 'So if you're a fan of amateur dramatics, Doctor von Metzer, perhaps you would care to audition? The role of Captain Hook—the villain of the piece—might be right up your street.'

The insult was lost on von Metzer and overlooked, for the moment, by the director who said: '*Peter Pan*, eh?'

'I know of this story,' von Metzer murmured. 'And I am following your channel of thought.'

'How are you doing the flying, Margaret?' the director asked. 'Can't have ropes dangling around, can we. Too dangerous.'

'Only for the suicide risks, sir,' Nurse Bradley answered. 'And we don't audition those. Nor the new admissions either, just in case. We thought, for the flying scenes, we'd just tippy-toe along a raised platform at the back of the stage—that ought to be safe, so long as it's wide enough, and effective too against a nice background of silver stars. It's cutlasses for the pirates I'm most concerned about, but cardboard will do for those, I'm sure.'

'And the auditions are when exactly?'

'This Friday afternoon, if we're definitely going ahead. Two o'clock in the main hall.' She shot von Metzer a look. 'I was joking, doctor, about you playing the villain,' she said. 'It wouldn't be appropriate really, would it, what with families coming.'

'Oh, I don't know . . . ' the director opened his diary and checked his schedule for Friday afternoon. 'A Captain Hook with a German accent would probably bring the house down—give the audience an added incentive to hiss and boo and throw their streamers. What do you say, doctor?'

'I think Nurse Bradley is right,' von Metzer said, quietly. 'It would not be appropriate.'

'Nonsense!' The director shut his diary with a snap that said the subject, as well as the book, was closed. 'Now then, Nurse Bradley . . . ' (He sounded excited now.) 'Rowan Scrivener, the male test case on Ward Five. You know the one I mean? He'll be auditioning on Friday for the role of Peter Pan.'

'But . . . '

'No buts. The stage will be all set up and ready will it, including this raised platform?'

'Yes, but . . . '

'Excellent. And don't worry, Margaret. I know exactly what you're thinking, but this audition could be a turning point for young Scrivener. We need to thrash out the finer details, Doctor von Metzer and I, but trust me, Margaret—there is method in our madness.'

For the best part of an hour the director and Doctor von Metzer sat in front of the apple-wood fire, hatching their plan. In outline, it seemed simple enough: Rowan Scrivener would be given a reason, and an opportunity, to play the role of superhero. He would realize he couldn't do it and hey presto—delusion shattered.

The director had a couple more sherries and grew extremely animated. 'This has to be the craziest "cure" ever attempted anywhere,' he declared. 'But you know what, doctor? I have a good feeling about it. I think it might actually work.'

Von Metzer was more cautious. 'There must be safety measures in place,' he insisted. 'A soft landing for Rowan Scrivener, should he attempt to leap and soar. A second plan, as waterproof as this one, in case he makes no attempt at all. And whatever happens, doctor, that boy must never know—never suspect or be told—that you and I went beyond our way to trick him. I have worked hard to gain his trust, yes? To lose it now would be a big catastrophe.'

'Yes, yes . . . I understand all that. We'll make sure he auditions last of all, shall we, and we'll clear the hall beforehand. We'll make out we're doing him a kindness, auditioning him separately—making it less stressful for him. We'll put mattresses down, for a soft landing, and give him what—thirty seconds? a minute?—before admitting defeat and making it look as if we've diffused the situation ourselves. Now, who do we know who can act? Really act, I mean. Someone—a chap—who will be utterly convincing when he comes charging into our hall, threatening to torch the place? Not a patient, obviously, and not one of the staff either.'

In the grate a log shifted in a burst of violet and orange sparks.

'The young nurse, Sarah Jane Springfield,' said von Metzer, 'speaks often of a male friend who makes everyone laugh with his impressions and his antics. If he can act the fool, perhaps he can act the villain also? He is a young farmer, I believe, not too far from here.'

'Ask her,' the director said. 'Say we'll pay him. It'll be worth it.'

'Very good.'

Von Metzer stood up from the visitor's chair. 'I will go now and talk to Rowan Scrivener,' he said. 'We will take our walk and I will persuade him to make the audition for *Peter Pan*. He will not wish to do it, but I am thinking I can talk him around.'

'Excellent,' the director replied, tossing another log onto his fire. 'And I was serious, doctor, about you taking on the part of Captain Hook. I'm quite set on it, in fact, so no arguments.'

'We will see,' von Metzer said, heading rapidly towards the door. 'For myself, I think it best to keep my profile very low.'

'WE'LL BE FINE'

When Dorothea heard about the auditions for *Peter Pan* she startled Doctor von Metzer by wanting to know more about them.

'I know that story,' she said. 'I remember it. I could be Wendy, couldn't I, now that I've got a bit of hair? Hey, Superboy! We can be in this thing together.'

Von Metzer did his best to curb her enthusiasm. 'I believe the main roles are for staff and low-risks only,' he said. 'Except the part of Peter which may, or may not . . . '

'Well, there are other parts, aren't there? Pirates! I could be a lady pirate with a patch over one eye. Or you could shave my head again so I looked like a Lost Boy. Mind you, if Superboy here gets to be Peter Pan, it's going to look pretty stupid, isn't it, if the Darling children are played by ancient old staff.'

'They are not all such crocks, the staff,' von Metzer said, solemnly. 'Nurse Springfield is only a year or so older than you and there are . . . '

'Don't tell me little Miss Clacton-on-Sea is trying out

for Wendy!' Dorothea made a sicking-up noise. 'She'd be useless. Get her to do everyone's make-up. She'd be good at *that.*'

Rowan, who had been quietly eating his lunch, unwilling to even discuss the pantomime, never mind the possibility of being in it himself, brightened, considerably, at the mention of Sarah Jane.

'I think Nurse Springfield would be really good as Wendy,' he said, carefully. 'Is she auditioning then?' He kept his eyes on his dish as he spoke and made a big thing out of separating a stringy strand of cheese from a clump of macaroni. Doctor von Metzer was not fooled. Surprised, yes, and pleased, too, that this patient was looking far enough beyond the Self to show interest in a pretty girl.

'She may be,' he replied, honestly, and then quickly changed the subject before Dorothea could jump in with another of her barbed remarks. Later, though, he made a point of taking Rowan aside: 'Are you agreeing, now, to do this audition?' he asked.

Rowan pretended to be in two minds although, secretly, wild horses wouldn't have kept him away from the hall on Friday afternoon, not if Sarah Jane was going to be there, auditioning for Wendy.

'All right,' he said, shrugging his shoulders and pulling a face, as if he didn't much care now, one way or the other. 'If you think I ought to, I'll do it.'

'Good boy.'

Later still, while Rowan was taking his afternoon nap, Dorothea got out of bed and went padding on bare feet across the ward to where von Metzer was sitting, writing the day's reports.

'You should be resting, Dorothea,' von Metzer said, without looking up. 'You are recovering, still, from your cold.'

'My cough's completely gone,' she answered, sweetly. 'And your angel's with you. I thought you'd like to know. He's bending over your shoulder, trying to read your handwriting, but he can't, of course, partly because it's in a stupid language, partly because he never learned to read, and partly because the lion mauled both of his eyes out, so . . . '

'Dorothea.' Von Metzer put down his pen and did his best to appear stern.

'Yes, Doctor Von?'

Her hair, he noticed, was catching the light—the rays of winter sunshine streaming in behind her, through the big, barred window. It was all spikes and fluff still, that slow-growing hair, but she had brushed it as best she could and flattened the little bits at each side in an effort to cover the two raw patches left by the electrodes.

'This talk of angels,' he said, gently. 'It is no way, Dorothea, to convince me, or any of the staff here, that you are well enough to take part in the pantomime of Christmas.'

'Oh.' She sounded disappointed but von Metzer could tell that she had known all along what his response would be and had an answer already prepared. 'That's a pity,' she added, as if that answer wasn't dancing, fully-formed, on the tip of her tongue. 'And yet . . . ' she paused a moment, for effect . . . 'my friend Superboy over there . . . the one who thinks he can run faster than a train and leap an eighth of a mile . . . he'll be all right, will he, to play the leading role?'

Von Metzer sighed and shook his head. So bright, this girl . . . as bright and as bitter as a lemon.

'All right, Dorothea,' he said to her. 'You may come to the audition. But please remember you might not get the role of Wendy. It is not up to me and I worry that you are not well enough, yet, to deal with a rejection.'

'Hah!' She turned, then, and stalked triumphantly away across the linoleum. 'Don't you worry, Doctor Von. We've suffered far worse, Joan and I, than getting turned down for a part in some stupid show. We'll be fine.'

On Friday, after lunch, Rowan asked to borrow Dorothea's looking glass. He asked quietly, so that Doctor Von wouldn't hear and make a big thing of it.

'Get your own,' Dorothea told him, bringing the glass so possessively close to her own face that she had to squint down her nose to see herself. 'Or, if you really, really, *really* want to know what you look like, I can tell you.'

'Forget it,' muttered Rowan. 'It doesn't matter. I'm going to the bathroom.'

'You look super,' she called after him down the ward. 'Super-duper, Superboy. Joan says you remind her of the young dauphin of France, only he had more of a fringe . . . and more wealth, of course . . . and more freedom, naturally . . . Couldn't save his kingdom though. He needed Joan's help for that.'

There was no plug for the bathroom basin so Rowan

cupped his hands beneath the running water and bent to splash his face. And under cover of the splashing he felt his cheeks, nose, and chin the way a blind person might, to check for bumps and defects. When was the last time he had looked—really looked—at himself in a mirror? Doctor Von had tried to make him look, after the first few treatments, but he had screwed his eyes tight shut and refused.

'What are you frightened of, Rowan?' the doctor had said. 'This is you. The real you. What is there to fear about looking?'

So violently, though, had Rowan screamed and fought against the very idea of his own reflection that the mirror had been taken away. When he was ready to see himself, von Metzer had said, he only had to say. No one was going to force him.

Well, he was ready now. Today. This very minute. He knew he was no ordinary person, and was no longer afraid of a mirror suggesting otherwise. He just wanted to quickly check his face for blemishes, and his hair for neatness, but the only looking glass on the ward at the moment belonged to Dorothea, and she was hanging on to it for dear life. Was she being her usual contrary self, Rowan wondered, or had it been an act of kindness, not letting him look?

Surreptitiously he splashed a bit of water on his head and smoothed it in. His hair, being short to start with, had never been shaved completely for treatments, only razored in two broad arcs above his ears. The razored bits had grown back all prickly and, last week, a male nurse had come and cut the rest so that it all matched up (at least, Rowan hoped it matched up—that the nurse had treated him like a person, who might actually care about how he looked, and not like a bush of some sort, to be hacked at any old how).

The sore spots on his temples no longer troubled him and he dared to hope that the marks had completely faded. They should have done, he told himself, since, unlike Dorothea, he had never been daft enough to scratch or pick.

It shouldn't matter, he knew, what he looked like in everyday ordinary life. He had a vague idea that he was actually meant to look all puny and dull, to protect his true identity. But today wasn't ordinary, exactly, because he was about to go on stage. People . . . Sarah Jane . . . were going to be watching him very closely; judging his performance, his appearance . . . judging everything.

And although being stared at by Sarah Jane was hardly a new experience, today was going to be different. Today he wouldn't be just another patient—a loony in a bed, a nutter in the bath—he would be a person in his own right, a person who might . . . just might . . . be good enough to act in a pantomime.

Peter Pan . . . he couldn't recall the story anywhere near as well as Dorothea had, but it didn't matter. He knew that Peter Pan and Wendy went together somehow, like fish and chips, or man and wife, and that was exciting enough—or would be if he and Sarah Jane both got the leading roles. Anyway, there would be a script, Doctor Von had said. Something to read from. And he liked to read. He was good at reading. Good at acting too, he was sure, for he had been acting every single day for at least three weeks. Acting for all he was worth so that no one, not Doctor Von, not Dorothea, and particularly not Sarah Jane herself, would ever know or suspect that on the nights Ward Five's bathroom echoed with giggles and sighs he lay awake, and he listened, and it was breaking his heart.

'Rowan, it is time that we were going.'

'Coming.'

Quickly, he dried his face on a sandpapery towel . . . ran his hands over his head, checking the evenness of his haircut one last time.

Doctor Von and Dorothea were right there in the doorway, waiting for him. *We're like a family,* he thought, as he went towards them. *Me and Dorothea and Doctor Von. We're like a little family going somewhere for the afternoon.*

'I THINK I WOULD BE SCARED TO FLY. OR NO GOOD AT IT, MORE LIKE'

'We have a problem, doctor—two problems in fact.'

'Wait here, please, I will be swift.' Von Metzer left Rowan and Dorothea standing in front of the stage, appraising and being appraised by a group of low risks, and stepped quickly across the hall to give Nurse Bradley his full attention. The nurse's own full attention was on the clipboard in her hands, and she was frowning and pursing her lips.

'Dorothea de Vere,' she whispered, loudly, 'is not a low-risk. She's a Ward Five test-case and a former suicidal. She can't be in the show.'

Von Metzer glanced over his shoulder but it was all right, Dorothea was too intent on out-staring other patients to be listening in. She was wearing a blue velvet dress with a white collar—her best dress, she had told him; the one she had been wearing when she first came to the hospital. Really, von Metzer could not have said what saddened him the most about that: the fact that no one, over the last four years, had thought to provide this girl with a new best dress or that, at the age of fifteen, she remained so under-developed that a garment meant for an eleven year old still fitted her.

'Dorothea is auditioning only,' he informed Nurse Bradley. 'She knows she may not get the part. It was difficult, you understand. Once she knew that Rowan Scrivener was to try for the role of Peter Pan she—'

'There you have my other problem,' Nurse Bradley interrupted. 'Traditionally, doctor, the role of Peter Pan is played by a female, not a male. So however good this patient of yours is, and however close to being a low risk, he won't be getting the part.'

Von Metzer looked over his shoulder again and then all around the hall. The director should have been here by now but there was no sign of the man. He checked the stage. There were mattresses set out, as agreed, beneath the raised platform. The soft landing, at least, had gone according to plan.

'For Rowan to win the role of Peter,' he said, patiently, to Nurse Bradley, 'was never our main intention. Please . . . speak to the director. I'm sorry. I thought he would have explained to you, by now, what is to happen this afternoon.'

'Nobody tells me anything,' Nurse Bradley grumbled. 'I'm just General Dogsbody around here.' And away she bustled, still grumbling.

She does indeed have the body of a large dog, von Metzer mused, *and the swagger of a general also.* His amusement lasted all of three seconds and then he began worrying in earnest:

Had something gone wrong? Had Nurse Springfield's friend failed to show up, as arranged? This plan . . . this crazy scheme . . . already it was having unforeseen consequences . . . spinning out of control. For what troubled von Metzer the most right now, should the whole thing fall apart, wasn't the prospect of Rowan Scrivener clinging, still, to his Superboy delusion. No . . . it was the thought of the boy's disappointment at not, after all, being chosen to appear in the pantomime.

Failing this audition would not have mattered, von Metzer knew, had Rowan not developed romantic feelings towards young Nurse Springfield. But he had, so of course it mattered. It meant everything.

And Dorothea? Dorothea had set her heart on being in this show. Rejection, however much she might scoff in its face, could easily destroy what little bit of confidence she had recently gained.

I did not think this through . . . von Metzer fretted silently. *I did not consider well enough the havoc it might cause for my patients. We should have conducted this experiment in the privacy of Ward Five; not in this manner, with dreams and false hopes all tied up in it. Where is the science in this plan? Nowhere . . . it has all the makings of a great big shambles.*

Staring anxiously at the door, willing the director to walk in, hoping Nurse Bradley had gone to fetch him, he didn't hear Dorothea calling to him until she raised her voice and shouted:

'Doctor Von . . . DOCTOR *VON*!'

'Yes . . . yes, yes. Hush. What is it?'

Quickly he swung round and hurried back across the hall. More people had come in, without him noticing, and were perched, in rows, on hard wooden benches, waiting for the auditions to start. Sarah Jane Springfield was sitting towards the back, with a group of male nurses. Von Metzer tried to catch her eye. He was hoping for a nod, or some other signal, to reassure him that her friend had turned up, as arranged, but she did not appear to notice him.

Dorothea and Rowan had sat—or been told to sit—on separate benches towards the front. Rowan was looking fixedly at the floor and the blush on his face had spread all the way round to the back of his neck. It was taking every ounce of his self-control, von Metzer could tell, not to turn round, not even accidentally-on-purpose, for just one glance at Nurse Springfield in her off-duty skirt and powder-blue blouse. Von Metzer remembered that feeling, from a long time ago, and his heart went out to the boy.

'Hey, Doctor Von, I've saved you a space. This is John, this is Donald, and this is King Sid.'

The men sitting closest to Dorothea all rose to their feet. For a couple of muddled moments as he shook each of their hands in turn, von Metzer wasn't sure if they were staff or low-risks but the name 'King Sid' gave him enough of a clue. That and the way they all shook hands—so tentatively that you knew, straightaway, that normal social contact was something they no longer took for granted, if, indeed, they ever had.

'Donald is hoping to play Captain Hook,' Dorothea said cheerfully, as her trio of new friends sat down again. 'He's worried about forgetting the words, but he's done some acting before so hopes he'll be all right. Tell Doctor Von what you did, Donald . . . and do sit down, Doctor Von. I told you, I've saved you a place.'

The man called Donald had straw-coloured hair and a face full of creases and wrinkles. He could have been any age, from twenty-five to fifty, and he flinched before he spoke, as if drawing attention to himself, on stage or off, was really the very last thing he wanted to do.

'I played Hamlet, once,' he said. 'At Cambridge. But I'm not so bright about doing things any more.'

'You'll be fine,' said Dorothea. 'It's all a question of attitude, isn't it, Doctor Von? Tell yourself you'll be a star turn, Donald, and you will be. Doctor Von, are you listening to me? And sit down, will you, you're blocking people's views.'

The director . . . . *where was the director*? There was still no sign of the man, yet von Metzer was growing more and more desperate to know, before the auditions got under way, that there had been no last minute hitches; nothing to give him grey hairs. 'Excuse me,' he said to Dorothea, 'I need to . . . '

Too late. Here came Nurse Bradley, clapping her hands and shouting for quiet. She had returned to the hall alone, her clipboard clamped firmly against her bosom and a look of such grim determination on her face that the silence was immediate.

'Doctor von Metzer,' she bellowed. 'Are you staying or going?'

'He's staying,' Dorothea called back.

'Then sit!'

Von Metzer sat.

Nobody expected great things from the hospital's annual

pantomime. It was enough that everyone who took part said roughly the right thing, in approximately the right place, and loud enough for most of the audience to hear what was being said at least two thirds of the time. And if they got through the whole performance without anyone getting upset, or the scenery falling down, it was considered a roaring success.

As usual Nurse Bradley's sister (a teacher in a neighbouring county) had written a simple script and it had already been decided, pretty much, that a sprig of a girl who worked in the kitchens would play Peter Pan, Nurse Springfield would be Wendy, and Tinker Bell would be a splash of torchlight beamed all around the stage.

The villain, Captain Hook, would be played by the director if Nurse Bradley had her way, or by von Metzer if the director had his. No low-risk had ever been cast as the villain—or in any other major role, come to that. Auditions, though, had always been held, same time, same place, year after year after year. Like the cheap crackers that got passed around on Christmas Day auditions had a certain novelty value, even though the patients got very little out of them. And if the staff always got the best parts? Well . . . so what. None of the patients had ever really cared.

Until now.

'Right!' Nurse Bradley bellowed. 'Hands up who wants to be in the chorus. That's mermaids, pirates, and Lost Boys and you'll get a chance to help with the scenery, and the make-up as well, if you want.'

A forest of hands went up.

'Right,' Nurse Bradley said again, resigning herself to

long nights spent stitching silver sequins onto at least two dozen tails and worrying whether cutlasses made from cardboard might still cause bodily harm. 'Next on the list: Wendy . . . Wendy Darling . . . Nurse Springfield? Do you have a copy of the script? Let's run through page four shall we . . . the bit where Peter is about to fly back to Neverland and Wendy can't decide whether to go with him or not. I'll be Peter for now. Up you come.'

Dorothea's hand shot up. Quickly, von Metzer caught the velvet of her sleeve and gently pulled that insistent hand back down. 'All in good time,' he whispered. 'Sit still. Be patient.'

'She'll be rubbish,' Dorothea muttered under her breath. 'And her angel's got no clothes on. It's disgusting.' But she kept her hand down and said no more as Sarah Jane Springfield stepped onto the stage to an accompaniment of whoops and wolf whistles.

She's brilliant, Rowan thought, as the young nurse recited her lines.

She's rubbish, thought Dorothea. *Isn't she, Joan?*

She is no Marlene Dietrich, von Metzer thought. *But then we are a very long way from Hollywood.*

'You can stop there, thank you,' said Nurse Bradley after a while and everyone except Dorothea applauded—Rowan loudest of all—as Nurse Springfield stepped, simpering, from the stage. *If she's Wendy and I get to be Peter Pan,* Rowan fantasized, *I won't want anything else for Christmas. Not a thing. Not this year, not next year, or for the rest of my entire life . . .*

'Now then . . . unless anybody . . . '

'ME!'

Dorothea was up, and pushing past, before von Metzer could think of the right words to say on her behalf.

Nurse Bradley looked defeated, and then exasperated. 'All right,' she said. 'But be quick. Here . . . ' She practically threw a copy of the script into Dorothea's hands.

'Don't need that,' Dorothea said, calmly. 'Or . . . well all right, I'll hang on to it, then. In case I get stuck.'

Towards the back of the room someone sniggered. Von Metzer held his breath. Dorothea was looking up and all around the stage. 'Where's the window going to be?' she asked. 'The one they all fly out of . . . no, don't worry . . . I'll pretend it's over here.' Stepping away from Nurse Bradley, she clambered onto one of the mattresses, in front of the raised platform, and positioned herself carefully.

'Peter! Don't go, Peter!'

Von Metzer's breath came out in a gasp.

'Please, Peter!' She was standing on tiptoe, stretching out a hand, as if her whole life's happiness depended on whatever was just out of reach. And although her face was in profile, you could see the desperation in every line and limb of her. *'I know lots of stories. Stay here and I'll tell them to you.'*

'Um . . . ' Nurse Bradley blinked at the script on her clipboard, found an appropriate line and said it: 'Come with me, Wendy. Fly away with me to Neverland.' Before, while reading for Sarah Jane, Nurse Bradley had sounded all right—professional, almost. Now, she sounded flat, a true amateur, even though the line, and her delivery of it, were exactly the same as before.

'Fly? You can fly?'

'Yes, Wendy, I can.'

'But that's impossible. Swallows fly. I've seen them. Sometimes I've longed to go with them, to wherever they go in winter. I've yearned to go so much it's made me cry. But you're just a boy, Peter. And boys can't fly. If you try, you'll land on our railings and then it won't matter whether you have a shadow or not because you'll be as dead as the meat in Nana's dish.'

Nurse Bradley looked flustered then, and more than a little cross, as she checked and double-checked her copy of the script.

Keep going, von Metzer willed her. *Never mind that the girl is making this up as she goes along. She is marvellous, so humour her, please.*

'I can fly,' Nurse Bradley read. 'And I can teach you, Wendy. It is easy.'

'Is it? Is it really? Oh, Peter . . . I don't know. I think I would be scared to fly. Or no good at it, more like . . . ' She had backed away from the imagined window, and stepped down from the mattress, but you could tell, from her voice, and from the way she stood, that she was longing to go; that however scared she was, every bit of her skin, beneath the faded blue dress, was tingling with the urge to fly up and away through that non-existent space above the stage—to escape to Neverland.

Von Metzer found he was holding his breath again. And oh . . . *fool, fool, sentimental fool* . . . there were tears, real tears, starting in his eyes. All around the hall, you could have heard a pin drop. On his left, the man called Donald was leaning forward, entranced.

'Attitude,' he whispered. 'That's the question. Or was it the answer? I forget . . . '

'Please be quiet,' the man calling himself King Sid asked him, politely. 'I want to hear what happens next.'

Nurse Bradley lowered her clipboard. 'That will do,' she said, coolly, to Dorothea. 'Thank you.'

The applause was generous and sincere, too, so far as von Metzer could tell. Only Rowan looked crestfallen as Dorothea left the stage and made her way, triumphantly, to her place on the bench.

'Well?' she whispered as she sat herself down.

'You were very good,' von Metzer whispered back. 'I was most proud.'

'Good?' she sneered. *'Good?* I was a star turn, stupid. I was brilliant.'

'Now . . . ' Nurse Bradley consulted her clipboard. 'Next on the list . . . Captain Hook. Well, that's easy enough, isn't it, everyone? We would be absolutely delighted, wouldn't we, if our director, Doctor Thomas, would take the time, as in previous years, to play the villain of the piece?'

There were cheers then and an enthusiastic stamping of feet. Von Metzer kept quiet. Let this woman have her way. He would sooner eat a sandwich of his own toes than make a buffoon of himself up there on that stage. He was not, he knew, anywhere near good enough, as an actor, to win over even the most forgiving of audiences. Those who came at Christmas wouldn't see a doctor up there, or even Captain Hook. They would see and hear a Jerry and wish him only the stickiest of ends.

'Go on, Donald,' he heard Dorothea say, beneath the cheers. 'Say you want to have a try.'

'No, no, I've changed my mind.'

'But you were so keen a while ago.'

'Not really, no. Please don't mention it again.'

Swiftly, now, Nurse Bradley rattled on through her list. A couple of low-risks auditioned for John and Michael Darling. They were passable—you could hear the words and they didn't get upset—but: 'Can't they find us some proper children from somewhere?' Dorothea muttered. 'Those two might be puny but they're *old*.'

'Next,' Nurse Bradley called out, 'Mister Smee. Hook's right-hand man. A character part; not too demanding . . . '

Rowan turned round then, not to gaze at Sarah Jane but to seek out Doctor Von. *Well?* his face said, clearly. *How much longer before I go up there?* He had been told, already, that he would be auditioning last of all but all this waiting was making him nervous.

Von Metzer did his best to look reassuring. Confident, even. But as soon as the boy turned back to face the stage he swivelled round himself and frantically scanned the back of the room. No sign of the director. No sign, either, of Nurse Springfield. Perhaps, von Metzer thought, she had gone to meet her friend, to wait with him outside the hall until the time came for him to burst in. Perhaps . . .

The door opened and in came the director. He caught von Metzer's eye, looked away and then, unwillingly, back. *Well?* von Metzer mouthed, urgently. *What's happening?*

The director shrugged and raised his eyes to the ceiling. *Don't blame me!* said the shrug and the look. *It's not my fault.* And von Metzer knew, then, that their plan had hit a snag.

'And last but not least,' Nurse Bradley called out,

'Peter Pan himself. Mavis Carter? Where is Mavis? Up you come, dear . . . '

Up went Rowan's hand.

'One at a time, ' Nurse Bradley snapped at him. 'You'll get your turn in a minute.'

A farce and a shambles, von Metzer lamented, silently. *One delusion left intact and two bitter disappointments to come—one for each of my patients. This has all been a shameful waste of time. Unless . . .*

THE FROGS AS BIG AS SAUCERS

'Am I hearing you correctly?' The director raked his hands, distractedly, through his hair. 'You want both the Ward Five test-cases—Rowan Scrivener and Dorothea de Vere—to star in the pantomime? As Peter Pan and Wendy?'

'That is correct, yes.'

'Even though neither of them are low-risks—far from it in the case of the de Vere girl—and the boy still thinks he's a superhero from another planet?'

'Yes.' Von Metzer's voice was calm, but firm. 'For the sake of their self-esteems, doctor, I believe both of these patients should be given this chance. They have, still, their problems, but nevertheless I am pleased with their progress. Also, they did well at the auditions. Dorothea, in particular was—'

'Yes, yes, I heard.'

Von Metzer inclined his head. 'And we did, you and I, allow Rowan Scrivener to believe he might actually win the role of Peter, so surely it is only fair . . . '

'Yes, yes.'

Irritably, the director sloshed himself a small glass of sherry.

'Nurse Springfield, perhaps, can be given some other role,' von Metzer added. 'A good role—the Tinker Bell perhaps, or the Tiger Lily—to make up for losing the leading part of Wendy.' *And to keep young Rowan happy,* he added silently to himself.

The director sipped his sherry. He was making no promises.

'That friend of Nurse Springfield's,' he said after a while, 'can come another time. That's what he said when he telephoned earlier—that there was an emergency on the farm this afternoon . . . something to do with a cow . . . but he could come another day, during rehearsals perhaps. What do you think?'

Von Metzer didn't need to think, any more, on that particular subject. 'I believe we should shelve that plan,' he said. 'I am having some second thoughts about it. Also I have a hunch that taking part in the pantomime might be enough, by itself, to bring Rowan Scrivener to his correct senses. The responsibility of playing an important role, and the sense of a good achievement, could do the trick without any need for drastic measures.'

'Hmm.'

The director shuffled through some papers on his desk, and picked out a typewritten letter. 'This arrived yesterday,' he said. 'It's from the Scriveners—from Mrs Scrivener anyway. They're coming for Christmas—the whole blessed lot of them, by the sound of it. It says here . . . wait a minute . . . '

He put on a pair of reading glasses and focused, irritably, on the words on the page: '"Rowan's father, his grandmother and her companion, his two sisters, and I plan to take a six-bedroomed cottage, just outside Canterbury, for the week beginning Saturday December twenty-third. That way we will be able to visit Rowan and perhaps have him to stay with us on Christmas Day."'

He flung the letter across the desk—flung it petulantly, the way Nurse Bradley had tossed the script for *Peter Pan* into Dorothea's hands. 'There. Read it for yourself.'

Von Metzer read. 'This is good for Rowan,' he said after he'd finished. 'That he has a caring family is very good. And they would be proud, yes, to see him as a star of the pantomime? They would think it a fine thing, surely—a sign that he is doing well, since the treatments.'

'Hmm.'

'As indeed he *is* doing well,' von Metzer persisted. 'No violence. No enemy voice in his head. Just this strange delusion which could be gone of its own accord, maybe, by Christmas . . . '

The director sighed and raked his hands, once more, through his hair. 'Well, let's hope so, Doctor von Metzer,' he said, wearily. 'Otherwise, you and I could have quite a lot of explaining to do.'

Von Metzer, sensing victory, pressed stubbornly on: 'And Rowan and Dorothea: they will play the roles they are wishing for, yes? They will be Peter Pan and Wendy in the pantomime of Christmas?'

'All right,' the director agreed. 'It will look good on the reports, I suppose, if they do a decent job. It's on one condition though.'

Von Metzer's heart sank. He could see what was coming.

'You play Hook,' the director said. 'Not me. You. Is that a deal?'

'If you insist,' von Metzer replied, unhappily.

'Excellent! That way you'll be able to keep an eye on your patients, the audience gets a villain they'll genuinely dislike, and I get a break, this year, from the whole rigmarole. Lets me off the hook, so to speak—har, har!'

Von Metzer stood up. 'I have my paperwork to do,' he said, politely. 'So I will wish you a good evening.'

'Fine . . . fine . . . oh, but talking of paperwork . . . ' The director opened a drawer and took out a buff-coloured file with the word CONFIDENTIAL stamped across the front. 'John Wallace,' he said, passing the file across the desk. 'Sorry to spring him on you, but he wants to be in on the trials. He's a voluntary patient—checks himself in every year, at around this time. He's a depressive but not dangerously so—at least not yet. Hears voices though and says they're getting harder to ignore. Can you start on him first thing Monday morning? I know it's short notice . . . '

Von Metzer took the file. 'Of course,' he said. 'It is time, certainly, to take on more cases.'

'Excellent.' The director shut the drawer, locked it, and slipped the key into his pocket. 'There are a couple more in the pipeline. Both low-risks, but with a long history of interesting psychiatric disorders. I'll dig out their files, double check a few things, and then they're all yours.'

'Very well.'

'Oh, and, doctor?'

Von Metzer turned, at the door.

'These new cases, John Wallace and the others, they'll be easier to work on than the Scrivener boy. No concerned parties interfering with the treatments, no relatives to ask awkward questions should one or all of them develop—well—new and unusual behaviour patterns. It means we can really push ahead with these trials. See some results—some publishable results, I hope—by the spring.'

'Very well,' von Metzer said again.

'It also means you'll have a lot more leeway, old chap. No limits to the number of treatments per day, and feel free to experiment—quite radically, if you like—with both the duration of the shocks, and the voltage.'

Von Metzer felt his face darken.

'Ah,' the director said. 'That worries you, I can tell. Well, it shouldn't do, doctor, but if you want one or two helpless feebles or chronic dements to—um—experiment on, before continuing with the trials, that can be arranged. Just say the word.'

'No.' Von Metzer opened the door. His head was beginning to ache. 'That will not be necessary.' John Wallace's file was as light as a wafer in his hand but for some reason he felt the need to hold on to it tighter, as if the man himself was in there, pressed flat amongst his notes, listening to this conversation in mounting alarm, and in need of reassurance.

'You don't mind, do you, Superboy, that it'll be me playing Wendy Darling and not Miss Clacton-on-Sea?'

'Of course not,' Rowan lied.

'Are you sure?'

'Yes. I've just said so, haven't I?'

They were cleaning the brass and outside the ward snow was falling—huge whirling flakes patting at the window like cat's paws and piling up fast on the sill.

If he angled it right, the tray Rowan was polishing sort of reflected his face. Dark hair. Pale skin. Eyes, nose, and mouth in all the right places; just no clear expression; no sense of how he truly came across to other people: he needed a proper mirror for that.

'This is hard work,' he sighed, rubbing furiously once again at the tray. 'How come we only get given cloths to do this? You need polish—the runny sort—to make silver and brass shine properly. Why don't they ever give us polish?'

Dorothea pulled a hideous face at herself in the trophy she was cleaning (a sports trophy, awarded annually to the patient who ran the fastest up and down the lawn). 'In case we poison ourselves with it, stupid,' she said. 'In case we get an uncontrollable urge to get out of this hell-hole by taking a great big slurp of Brasso.'

'Stop it,' Rowan muttered. 'That's horrible.'

For a while they polished in silence. Then: 'Why do you call Nurse Springfield Miss Clacton-on-Sea?' Rowan asked. 'Is that where she's from? The place where she was born?'

'I don't know where she was born,' Dorothea said. 'And I don't flipping care. All I know is she's as common as muck and my nurse—the one who looked after me before I came here—always said that Clacton-on-Sea was full of common folk. "Heaving" with them, was how she put it, especially on bank holidays.'

Rowan set aside his tray and regarded Dorothea with

interest. She had never really spoken to him about her past life—her life before this one, here at the hospital—and he found himself wondering aloud what it had been like for her, living at home with a private nurse.

'I've forgotten,' she said.

'Why—because of all the treatments?'

'No. Because I wanted to.'

Rowan nodded. He understood—or thought he did. 'So . . . will any of your family be coming to the pantomime?' he asked. 'To see you as Wendy.'

'Not likely,' she told him, with a hard little laugh. 'And I wouldn't want them to, either, so don't you go feeling all sorry for me.'

But Rowan did feel sorry. He couldn't help it. The pantomime was to happen on Boxing Day and his lot would be coming—he'd received a letter that morning, telling him about their plans to stay somewhere close by, for the whole of Christmas week. It would be good to see them, he supposed, but strange too after all this time. If the director agreed, he was going to spend Christmas Day in the house the Scriveners had rented. Dorothea could come too, perhaps, if she wanted to.

'If you like—' he began, but: 'Hello, here comes the new recruit!' Dorothea cut in. 'Here comes poor old John. He volunteered for this, you know. He told me so at the auditions. His guardian angel is a little old lady—nobody famous, just a little old biddy who died in her sleep, about two hundred years ago. She still has her hair up in curling pins, under a frilly cap, and she despairs of John, she really does. She thinks he's made a big mistake getting his brain fried when he could have stayed quietly on Ward

Two. She says that's the craziest thing he's ever done in the whole of his crazy life.'

Rowan watched, with mixed feelings, as von Metzer and two hefty male nurses pushed the bed with John Wallace on it across the room to its place against the wall—a place closest to the window, but furthest from the bathroom. He had grown used, he realized, to it just being the two of them—him and Dorothea—on this ward. Doctor Von had said they were unique so how come somebody else was muscling in?

And yet, the man had just had his first treatment which meant he was going to wake up frightened and confused, with the feeling like woodpeckers drilling into his skull. Rowan couldn't help feeling sympathetic—protective almost—towards this new test-case as he thought about that, and shuddered.

'Who's watching us tonight?' Dorothea called across.

'I am,' said the heftiest of the nurses. 'It'll be me most nights, now that this ward's getting busy, so you'd better be good.'

'I'm always good,' Dorothea called back, cheerfully. 'As good as gold.'

Von Metzer was bustling around, checking the leather straps binding John Wallace's unconscious form to the bed. Rowan couldn't tell if he was tightening or loosening those straps and for the first time he wondered: *what does Doctor Von think about while he's zapping somebody's head?*

'Cheer up, Superboy!' Dorothea said to him. 'We've got a rehearsal this afternoon and Miss Clacton's playing Tinker Bell so you'll still get to dribble and swoon over her. A torch would have done a much better job as Tink, I reckon, but there we are . . . '

Silently, Rowan went back to polishing his tray. The pantomime . . . the Scriveners coming for Christmas . . . someone new on Ward Five . . . a lot seemed to be happening around here all of a sudden.

And when I wake up tonight, Sarah Jane won't be here. That was probably a good thing, he told himself. A very good thing, considering how envious he was of her man-friend and of the things that went on behind the lavatory screen.

Rowan didn't see von Metzer leave the room, or notice his return until Dorothea looked up and started chuckling. 'What on *earth* have you got there, Doctor Von?' she called out. 'Are we having planks on the window now, as well as bars?'

'No. You'll . . . see. Just a . . . minute . . . please.'

Von Metzer had staggered onto the ward carrying a vast rectangular *thing* in front of him. You could see his hands, his feet, and his sticky-out hair, at the sides, below and above the thing, but that was all. Because he couldn't see where he was going he had to feel his way forward with his feet, before turning sharp left, and staggering, comically, into the bathroom.

'There!' he said, depositing the thing on the floor, with a loud clunk. Then he tugged, hard, until the thing opened out—opened so suddenly that he almost fell over. It was another screen, Rowan realized. One for the bath this time only, unlike the hospital's normal screens which were made out of coarse cloth on metal frames, this one had been fashioned out of what appeared to be four cupboard doors, haphazardly joined with hinges. Most bizarrely of all, someone had painted the whole contraption with a pattern of bright yellow ducks, and frogs as big as saucers.

'That,' said Dorothea, 'is truly hideous.'

Von Metzer was still catching his breath. 'It is for . . . privacy,' he gasped. 'For you . . . Dorothea . . . especially . . . now that you are to be . . . outnumbered . . . by the male . . . patients.'

'Thanks,' she sneered. 'Who did you get to paint it? One of the paralytics, or a three-year-old child?'

Rowan gave her the smallest of shoves. 'I think it looks all right,' he said, so that von Metzer would hear. 'Nice and cheerful.'

'Cheerful. *Cheerful?* Superboy—please!'

In the bathroom von Metzer smiled, ruefully, and tested the cobbled-together doors for stability. 'The hospital's screens are all in use,' he said. 'I could not beg or borrow or thieve one. These doors were waiting to be chopped up for firewood, so I thought . . . why waste? The frogs, I agree, are maybe not so perfect.'

'Perfect?' Dorothea chuckled some more. 'They look like pea-green cowpats.'

Rowan gave her another shove. 'Stop it,' he whispered across the glitter of the brass. 'I think he made that screen himself. He was being thoughtful, Dorothea, so don't be so mean.'

Dorothea shoved him back. Hard. But she looked chastened and, after pretending to polish a dish for a while she flung down the cloth and turned back to face the bathroom. 'I suppose the ducks are OK,' she called, grudgingly, across to Doctor Von. 'I can live with the stupid ducks.'

'THIS IS YOUR DAD, I TAKE IT?'

The taunting of Dorothea began at the first rehearsal. But it was so subtle—a snigger here, a look there, a carefully-timed cough or two—that nobody, apart from Dorothea herself, picked up on it.

Afterwards, over supper, she broached the subject to Rowan and Doctor Von, but in a way that, typically, earned her no sympathy. 'That Miss Clacton,' she said, 'is *furious* about me playing Wendy. She's as green as those stupid frogs with envy. She was trying to unnerve me on stage this afternoon but I knew what she was up to so I called her bluff. I didn't let her get to me and I didn't mess up my lines.'

Von Metzer frowned across the table. 'You are being dramatic, Dorothea,' he said. 'It is best saved for the rehearsals, I think.'

Dorothea chewed, thoughtfully, on a mouthful of food, swallowed and grimaced.

'Oh no, she's jealous all right,' she said. 'Joan can see it even if you two can't. Joan says I need to be on my guard and she should know. The French generals were all *seethingly* jealous of Joan. They pretended to look up to her but, really, they were as jealous as cats and the first to think "good riddance" when Joan got burnt at the stake.'

Von Metzer had nothing to say to that and neither had Rowan.

'Oh well . . . ' Dorothea set down her fork and pushed her plate away. 'I suppose I can live with it—being distracted and made to feel bad, when I'm trying to act. But she's definitely not watching us at night any more, is that right, Doctor Von? Nurse Springfield, I mean. Because I hate to think what she might do to me while I'm fast asleep and no one's looking. Honestly, she really, *really* hates me. Worse than poison. Worse than Tinker Bell hates Wendy. It's written all over her stupid little face when she thinks nobody's looking.'

There was a hint—a real hint—of worry in her voice now, but neither Rowan nor the doctor picked up on it.

'Dorothea . . . ' von Metzer began, but then John Wallace woke up.

John Wallace . . . He was no trouble, no trouble at all, and after a couple of days Rowan was glad to have him around. He had grown used to Dorothea but, crikey, could she be tiresome, and although John was old—around the same age as Lawrence Scrivener, by the look of him—he was male, and a fellow test-case, and as such a potential ally.

At first all John wanted to do was sleep. This was natural, after the treatments, Rowan remembered that. The headaches, too, were only to be expected, and the sickness, and the strange feeling, upon waking, that you weren't quite human.

The first time John Wallace left his bed, to sit by the window in a bath chair, Rowan was tempted to go straight over and say hello. He was wary, though, of intruding upon whatever thoughts the man might be silently and carefully untangling, now that he was fully awake.

It was early evening. The hefty new nurse had come on duty a few hours earlier than usual, and Dorothea was already in bed, going over and over her script for *Peter Pan*.

There was nothing to see through the un-curtained window, except the winter's dark and reflections sliced up by the bars. John Wallace's eyes were as black as the night and he looked so . . . *sad* . . . sitting there strapped in his chair with a blanket slipping gradually from his knees, that after a while Rowan took a pillow from his bed and went across to sit with him. To keep him company.

'Tell me to shove off if you want,' he said, setting the pillow down on the linoleum. 'Or make a "go away" sign if it hurts to talk.'

John Wallace smiled weakly. 'Sit down, do,' he croaked. 'It's fine. Only, I'm afraid I've forgotten who you are.'

Rowan hesitated. *Me too,* he almost said. *I've forgotten who I am as well. At least . . . I know who I believe I am, but it's getting harder to be sure.*

'Doctor Von calls me Rowan,' he said, sitting down on the pillow and shuffling forward a bit, so that John could see him better. 'Rowan Scrivener.'

'I see,' John Wallace croaked. 'So . . . should I call you Rowan, or not?'

Behind them Dorothea's voice—a low mumble up until now—grew louder, suddenly. *'Look at me, Peter! I can fly! I can fly!'*

'No yelling!' the male nurse yelled, from his chair beside the door.

John Wallace winced and his blanket slid all the way to the floor.

'Ignore Dorothea,' Rowan said, moving to pick the blanket up. 'She only does it for attention.' He replaced the blanket clumsily, being careful not to touch the man's skinny legs in their faded pyjama trousers.

'Thank you.'

'Don't mention it.'

For a while they both sat quietly—John Wallace in his bath chair, Rowan on his pillow. The question of names had been set aside, it seemed, and Rowan, for one, was happy to leave it there.

'Aren't you cold?' John asked.

'No. I'm all right, thank you.'

The silence, after that, could have grown uncomfortable but for some reason it didn't. It felt peaceful, to Rowan—companionable even. And after a while, John Wallace nodded towards the window and said: 'If you look very carefully, right through your own reflection, you can see that it's snowing outside. You have to concentrate, mind, and ignore everything else.'

At first all Rowan could see, as he leaned forward, concentrating hard, was the jigsaw of his own self between the bars—a vague imperfect reflection, much like the one he caught from time to time in well-polished silver and brass.

'Can't see anything,' he said.

'Try again.'

'I can't. It's making me go cross-eyed.'

John Wallace smiled. 'Close both eyes for a bit and then open them again,' he said. 'Come to it fresh, as if it's the first time you've looked.'

Rowan closed his eyes, kept them shut for about ten seconds and then opened them wide. Straight through the bars he peered, focusing so resolutely through and beyond the black glass and the pools of his own eyes that his face went tight, from concentrating, and his jaw began to ache.

Then: 'Oh . . . yes . . . ' he murmured, happily. 'I can see it now. I can see the snow falling. It's really *whirling* down out there.'

'It certainly is,' John Wallace replied in his sore and husky voice. 'We'll be snowed in by morning, I reckon. Cut off from the rest of the world.'

Good, Rowan thought. *The rest of the world can keep its distance. I'm not ready, yet, for the rest of the world.*

The following evening, and the one after that, Rowan sat at the window with John Wallace. Two more patients had arrived on Ward Five: Donald—the man who had changed his mind about auditioning for Captain Hook—and King Sid (who clearly had about as much royal blood in his veins as the hospital's Christmas turkey). Both men were in bed. Unconscious. Zapped. And von Metzer had stayed on duty, to be there when they woke up.

Von Metzer looked worn out. His face had a greyness about it, like an old vest, and his hair was sticking up even more than usual, as if he, not his test-cases, had just had a massive electric shock. He was sitting by the door, writing frantically, but looking up from time to time to check that everyone was still where they ought to be: Dorothea in bed, lost in her script; Donald and Sid strapped tightly to their beds, lost to the world, temporarily; Rowan and John watching the window and finding—yes, von Metzer felt quite confident about this—an affinity of the spirit that would be a blessing under any circumstances but was something of a miracle here on Ward Five.

'You three already know one another, don't you?' Rowan was saying to John Wallace. 'You and Donald and Sid—King Sid, I mean. Dorothea says you were all on Ward Two together.'

'That's right,' John answered. His voice was a lot better now, just naturally quiet which, compared to Dorothea's parrotty screech, was soft music to Rowan's ears. 'I'm not a resident though. I just book myself in when my nerves get really bad.'

Rowan was surprised. 'Booking yourself in' . . . it made this hospital—this lunatic asylum—sound like a posh hotel. 'Do you have family?' he asked.

'No,' John replied. 'Do you?'

It had been almost a fortnight since Rowan had looked at the tray with the snaps on it and longer, still, since he had found anything new to say about Nana, or Daff, or the rest of them. What with rehearsals for the pantomime, and the new test-cases arriving, there hadn't been time for long talks with Doctor Von, only for short chats during which Rowan had talked, mostly, about how excited he was to be playing Peter Pan.

'Just a minute,' he said to John Wallace. 'I'll be back in a minute.'

The tray was in the desk drawer, along with Dorothea's mirror and comb. Doctor Von unlocked the drawer, slid out the tray and handed it over.

Don't ask, Rowan willed him.

'You are introducing John to your relatives?'

'Uh-huh. To the Scriveners, yes.'

'Excellent. Good. He will be pleased about that, I am sure.'

Back over by the window, John Wallace took the tray respectfully in both hands.

'Oh yes,' he said after a while. 'I can see the likenesses. You're the spit of your dad, aren't you, but with your mother's nose. This is your dad, I take it? The man here, in uniform?'

For what seemed like a very long time Rowan did not reply. He simply stared at the tray, over John Wallace's shoulder—stared and stared at the face that was the spit of his.

I am Superboy, from Planet Krypton.

He opened his mouth to speak, but then closed it again, and John Wallace did not press him further. 'So, he survived the last war then, your dad?' he said, instead. 'Was he at the Front?'

Rowan wasn't quite sure what that meant, or perhaps he'd known once but had forgotten. *At the front of what?* A military parade, he supposed, or some kind of a queue, for medals or food.

'Silly question,' John Wallace continued. 'Of course he was. I can tell by the look on his face. He was there all right, slap bang in the thick of it all.'

'But . . . that picture was taken before he left for France,' Rowan told him, as the penny dropped about 'the Front' and he remembered his mother—Hazel Scrivener—leaning over his shoulder while he glued the image to the tray. 'I know it was. I remember, now, being told. He hadn't done anything—seen anything—to do with the war when that picture was taken.'

'It's there though,' John insisted. 'If you look through and beyond. The knowledge of it . . . of what was to come . . . it's there in his eyes, poor soul.'

Poor soul?

'John,' Rowan asked then, 'did you book yourself in this time because of the current situation? This new war, I mean. Does what's happening now, between us and the Germans . . . does it trouble you, more than most people, because the last war was so awful and you were in it?'

John Wallace looked at him then, really looked at him, through and beyond. 'Why are you here?' he wondered aloud. 'You clever child. Why ever did they think this was a suitable place for someone like you?'

Rowan grinned, enjoying the compliment. If there was ever a right moment to tell this man who he truly was, this was surely it.

'Doctor Von is a Jerry,' he said instead. 'Does that bother you?'

John Wallace looked back at the tray. At the little girl with the chestnut-coloured plaits. At the elderly woman with a pack of dogs seething around her ankles. At the young soldier with a premonition of Hell blurring his eyes like sleet.

'On the contrary,' he replied. 'It reminds me that the

enemy has a face, and that it is not always an ugly one. Those Bosch boys, they were just like us really. Scared witless. Bored, a lot of the time. Missing their families. Cursing the mud. All of that . . . '

He fell silent then. Rowan waited, respectfully, for a while and then said: 'You're remembering a lot more than I could, after my first treatment. I'm impressed.'

John Wallace handed him back the tray. 'To be honest,' he said, in such a low voice that Rowan had to lean closer to hear it. 'To be totally honest, I don't think mine worked very well. I'm going to need a few more, I reckon. A bigger jolt, maybe, next time around.'

Von Metzer looked up, hopefully, as Rowan approached him with the tray. 'You are finished with it?' he said. 'You are sure?'

'Yes, thank you,' Rowan replied. 'I'm going to bed now. Goodnight.'

He had been sleeping a lot better recently, waking later and often managing to doze straight off again until morning. He put it down to all the hard work involved in rehearsing for the pantomime—all the thinking, and memorizing, and running up and down that raised platform like a boy in flight. Or maybe it was because Sarah Jane wasn't on night duty any more, distracting him.

'You are looking well, Rowan,' von Metzer said. 'There is colour in your face lately. Do you wish to see?' His left hand was poised over Dorothea's looking glass . . . over the picture of swans gliding on water.

'No,' Rowan told him, sharply, and hurried away across the linoleum, before anything else got said . . . before he gave in, and looked.

'Night night, Superboy,' Dorothea called to him as his shadow crossed her script. She said that name naturally and easily nowadays—as naturally and easily as she said 'Joan' or 'Donald' or 'Miss Clacton-on-Sea'. Rowan couldn't fault her for the way she said his name. *And yet . . .*

'Night . . . ' he mumbled, climbing into his bed.

And as he slept he dreamed of home; of lying on a couch in his father's studio, looking up through the cupola at a sky full of stars and falling snow. In the dream his father was hunkered down beside the couch, his face lit by the starlight, one hand pointing.

'You see, son?' his father said, in the dream. 'You see up there?'

'What?' Rowan replied. 'Where?'

His father shook his head, disappointed. 'Until you see it,' he said, 'until you recognize the obvious, there's really no point in me being here.'

'Wait!' Rowan cried. 'I just need a bit more time, that's all.' But his father's face was dissolving . . . melting and tipping the way candles did in their drawing room if they were set too close to the fire.

'Don't go! Don't go!'

'Rowan—Rowan, wake up. It is a dream you are having. Just a dream. Wake up now.'

And there was Doctor Von, tufty-haired funny old Doctor Von, bending over the bed, looking worried.

'Did I wake . . . anyone . . . up?' Rowan gasped, struggling up from the dream like a diver towards the light. 'I didn't wake the new people . . . did I? I didn't . . . frighten them?'

'No. It's all right. No one is disturbed. It was a bad dream, yes?'

'Yes . . . no . . . I don't know.'

Von Metzer hunkered down, next to the bed. 'This dream,' he said, in his tell-me-all-about-it voice. 'What was it all about? Tell me.'

'My father,' Rowan said. 'I was with my father.'

Von Metzer nodded. *Don't let him see how important this is,* he reminded himself. *Don't lose him now. And don't allow him to drop the thread of this dream. Keep him focused.*

'Your father,' he repeated.

'Yes.'

Von Metzer waited, keeping very still. His heart, though, had taken a sudden leap and it was hard to keep the excitement from showing, on his face or in his voice. In a minute—two minutes at the most—Rowan Scrivener, he was certain, would agree to look in a mirror. He would see himself, and know himself, and this Superboy delusion would take wings and disappear.

'WHERE AM I?'

It was a cry louder than anything Rowan Scrivener had uttered while dreaming about his father. It was a roar. A terrified bellow. And it woke everyone else on Ward Five as effectively as a pail of cold water or a slap around the head.

'I CAN'T MOVE. IS ANYONE THERE?'

'For crying out loud!' Dorothea yelled, blearily. *'Will somebody please shut that person up? Where's his angel? Don't tell me you fried his guardian angel, Doctor Von, along with his brains.'*

'PLEASE—I'M SCARED. IS ANYONE THERE?'

'That's King Sid,' Rowan whispered. 'He's just woken up.'

John Wallace was already out of his bed, stumbling down the ward on shaky legs and going, 'Shush, shush' as if to a crying baby.

'Doctor Von!' Rowan whispered, louder this time. 'What are you waiting for? Go and see to King Sid—go on.'

'SOMEONE—PLEASE!'

Rowan threw aside his blanket . . . began swinging his feet over the edge of his bed. 'No,' von Metzer said then, pressing him back. 'It's all right. I'm going. But we will talk later, yes, about the dream?'

'All right,' Rowan agreed. But, already, the moment had passed. And by the time King Sid had been soothed and unbuckled and had remembered, to von Metzer's relief, that he was plain old Sidney Victor Eccles from Kingston-upon-Thames, Rowan no longer wished to discuss his dream. Not with his doctor, not with his new friend John Wallace, not with anyone.

What will it take? von Metzer fretted silently, as his patients—all peaceful at last—slept heavily through the dawn. *What will it take to finally end this delusion of Rowan Scrivener's? He is so close . . . so very close to parting with it. It is like a tooth coming loose, hanging by a thread. One tug and it will be gone. One quick, sharp tug . . .*

THE HAIR LIKE AN OLD YELLOW MOP

Three weeks before Christmas, with rehearsals in full swing, Nurse Springfield suggested—loudly and with calculated sweetness—that Dorothea de Vere might look a lot better in a wig. 'It's just that Wendy Darling would have had normal-looking hair, and no marks, wouldn't she?' she shouted, from halfway down the hall. 'And anyone looking at Dorothea, even from this distance, can tell that something's been done to her head. I can see you're doing your best, Dorothea, by brushing those straggly bits forward, but with the lights on you—as they will be, on the night—well, those red blotches are still going to show, aren't they?'

Dorothea's hands flew protectively to her temples.

Don't, Rowan willed her. *Don't get angry. Sarah Jane's right. And it's your fault for picking and scratching.*

The stage and the hall were crowded. Everyone—the mermaids, the Lost Boys, the people painting scenery, the nurses sitting around on benches bemoaning the prospect of sugar being rationed . . . everyone turned to stare at Dorothea. And Nurse Bradley, as director, went bustling onto the stage to stare the closest and hardest of all.

'Perhaps this can be considered later,' von Metzer suggested unhappily, from his place among the pirates.

Nurse Bradley ignored him.

'Hmm,' she said, standing almost on Dorothea's toes and breathing, meatily, into her face. Then she pivoted away and yelled out across the hall: 'You knit, don't you, Nurse Springfield? Got any yellow wool at home?'

'I'm sure I have,' Sarah Jane called cheerfully back. 'I'll dig it out and see what I can throw together for her.'

'Excellent! Now then, people, back to Act five, line . . . where were we now? Yes, your cue, Doctor von Metzer. *"Enough of this shilly-shallying. They're going to walk the plank!"*—and put a bit more venom into it this time, man. You sound more like a mother ordering groceries than a villain sentencing children to an untimely and terrible death.'

'Are you all right?' Rowan asked Dorothea, back on the ward.

'What do you care,' she snapped at him. 'Go talk to Johnny boy and his fussy old angel. Leave me alone.'

The following day, Doctor von Metzer brought brightly-coloured paper chains onto Ward Five and a small fir tree, in a pot. He also brought Rowan permission from the director to spend Christmas Day with his family. Not at the cottage near Canterbury, however, but right there in the hospital.

'With any luck,' the director had said privately to von Metzer, *'we'll be snowed in by then so nobody will be getting past the village, never mind up the hill. Either that or your lot will have started bombing the Hell out of the capital, and the Scriveners, along with everyone else, will have put Christmas on hold.'*

'Your family can use the visitor's lounge for the day,' was what von Metzer said to Rowan. 'And the hospital will cater the lunch. You are doing well, Rowan, but you are not ready, yet, to be away from the hospital. You need nurses on hand, still, in case of any . . . problems.'

Rowan looked sideways at him and then away.

'It's been ages,' he said, 'since I tried to hurt anyone. I can't imagine wanting to do that ever again. Not good people—ordinary citizens—anyway. Only villains, and only when it's really necessary.'

'All the same,' von Metzer told him, 'it remains early days. You are not out of the forest quite yet.' He looked like a joke convict, with paper chains draped over his shoulders and hanging all down his body. Then he pulled his chair away from the desk, stood up on its seat and began looping the chains all along one wall.

'What will everyone else be doing?' Rowan wondered. 'On Christmas Day?'

'I believe it is traditional,' von Metzer said, stretching to stick a pin through a segment of scarlet paper, 'for everyone who is not . . . confined, yes? . . . to the wards, to share Christmas dinner in the hall. They have long tables for the purpose and everybody has a paper hat to wear. There are no knives provided, of course, and the pudding is not set on fire. Otherwise, according to the director, it is a most jolly and festive occasion.'

'I see.' Rowan eyed the paper chains, critically. Back in Spitalfields, they would not have been given house room. Holly and ivy, yes; mistletoe and pine cones, yes; but not anything artificial. He remembered that.

'So where will you have your Christmas dinner?' he asked Doctor Von. 'In the hall with all the others? Or in the visitor's lounge, so you can keep an eye on me?'

Von Metzer got down from the chair, moved it along the linoleum, then clambered back on to pin up another loop. 'I do not expect to be in either place,' he said. 'It is irrelevant. More important for you, surely, is the seeing, once more, of your family. The director tells me they are looking forward, very much, to being with you. But if you are anxious about spending time with them—if you do not feel ready—you have only to say so.'

'It's fine,' Rowan said. 'If the Scriveners want to have Christmas Day in a lunatic asylum instead of their own home, that's up to them.'

Von Metzer pinned the last chain, sighed and got down from the chair. Donald and Sid were sitting up in their beds, recovering from treatments and looking, dizzily, at the decorations. Dorothea was reading her script, mumbling words and paying no attention to anything else.

'John won't like those things,' Donald called across. 'I forget what they're called, my brain is still so slow, but I know they're for Christmas and I do remember that John hates Christmas. It disturbs him.'

'That's true.' Sid rubbed and rubbed at his whiskery

old chin—one of several nervous habits that the treatments had yet to cure him of. 'John gets very upset at this time of year. That's why he's here.'

John Wallace was deeply asleep. He'd had two treatments, in rapid succession, and von Metzer was hoping they had been enough to finally conquer the voice that had been haunting John for twenty-five years—a voice that always grew louder, and more reproachful, as Christmas Day drew near.

'I asked John,' von Metzer said. 'And he said it would not be causing a problem. He said he was not the only person here on Ward Five and that it would be good for the young ones—for Dorothea and Rowan—to have the decorations of Christmas to look at.'

Rowan waited for Dorothea to say something snide then, about the decorations being stupid or a complete waste of time, but she kept her head bent over the pages of her script and said nothing at all.

'He's a good chap, John,' observed Donald. 'He says he has no heart and cannot love but, really, he's a very sincere person—one of the best. There's a lot I don't know any more, but I never forget that, about John being kind. He's the salt of the earth, John is. Why, I remember—'

Dorothea slammed her script flat down on her bed.

'I can't hear myself *think*,' she cried out. 'What with all of you . . . and your stupid angels . . . gabbling on all the time . . . how can I learn my *words*.'

'But you don't stick to the script,' Rowan reminded her, needled by her rudeness, and her intolerance of a man whose wits, despite the treatments, were nowhere near as sharp as they used to be, and certainly no match for hers. 'You're always adding stuff of your own, confusing everyone.'

'When *exactly* have you been confused?' she challenged him. 'Go on . . . you can't think of a single time, can you? It's because I "add stuff" brilliantly, stupid, and always, *always* finish on the line I'm supposed to say before you, or anyone else, starts droning on.'

Rowan couldn't really argue with that, although he did his best. 'It's still confusing,' he said. 'Confusing and really annoying. Nurse Bradley must have asked you about fifty times to stick to the script, so why don't you?'

Dorothea looked wildly down at the pages on her bed, snatched one up at random and ripped it, swiftly, in half. 'There!' she shouted, ripping again and again before hurling the strips and bits onto the floor. 'Make more paper chains! Make a pretend angel for the top of that stupid tree! This script's rubbish. And if it wasn't for me, the whole show would be rubbish, so shut up, Superboy—just *shut up*.'

Von Metzer moved quickly, and quietly, to talk and to soothe. 'She makes me anxious, that girl,' said Sid, beginning to scratch and scratch at the sides of his arms, with the nails of both hands. 'She's a noisy one. A disruptive. She should be on Ward Four. Someone should tell the director to move her to Ward Four. I'll tell him. I'll tell the director. If I can find the courage I'll go straight out and tell him tomorrow.'

'Ward Four,' Donald mused. 'Where is that, exactly? Have I ever been on it? I forget . . . '

Turning his back on all of them, Rowan walked to the end of the ward. *Wake up, John,* he thought. *Wake up.* He thought of how he had almost-but-not-quite invited Dorothea to spend Christmas Day with him and the Scriveners. Well, he wouldn't be asking her now. She could take a running jump. And he didn't care what she did instead. It was . . . what was the word Doctor Von had used? . . . that's right . . . it was irrelevant.

'Rowan—Peter Pan—you need to face the audience. You need to appeal directly to the audience, after Tinker Bell drinks the poison, otherwise they won't hear a word you're saying, and might not realize that they're supposed to have started clapping.'

Blushing, Rowan turned away from the lovely form of Nurse Springfield, lying motionless on the dusty floor of the stage, to address himself to Nurse Bradley, a few other members of staff, and the low-risks sitting out in the hall. And as he begged them to clap their hands, to show that they believed in fairies, he suddenly felt a lot more confident about this acting thing.

He wasn't anywhere near as good as Dorothea, but then nobody was. She outshone the lot of them, despite the infuriating way she kept adding to the script. But now, as he begged for help for Tink, he began to feel that, actually . . . maybe . . . he was doing all right. His voice was soaring, almost the way Dorothea's did, and there was a genuine note of pleading in it.

'Do you believe in fairies? Please say you do! Please clap as loudly as you can for me . . . for Tink!!'

It was because it was Sarah Jane, lying at his feet, that he was acting so well, he knew that. If it had been a circle of torchlight down there, growing fainter by the second, he would not, he knew, have felt so moved, or so eager to impress.

And as the clapping grew louder, and his voice grew with it, he experienced such a lifting of his spirits . . . such a powerful surge of energy . . . that had his body risen up from the stage, to hover easily above the rest of the cast, he would not have been at all surprised.

'You were really good just then,' said Sarah Jane, smiling sweetly up at him as she flapped her arms and came alive.

'Well done, both of you,' shouted Nurse Bradley, from halfway down the hall. 'If you do as well as that on the night I'll be very pleased.'

At the side of the stage, Dorothea's hands tightened on the hateful wig that she had been given earlier but refused to put on.

'Right,' said Nurse Bradley. 'Who else is here this afternoon? No Captain Hook, I see.'

'He's in a meeting,' Rowan informed her. 'He's going over his reports, with the director, but he said he'd try and be here by three o'clock at the latest.'

Nurse Bradley flipped some pages over on her clipboard.

'How annoying of him,' she grumbled. 'Particularly as our crocodile has arrived.'

All eyes turned to the crocodile—just a head, as it turned out, but what a head! Four feet high, and about as much again wide, it rested on the plinth of its neck, towards the back of the stage, with its enormous jaws wide open at an acute and greedy angle. Inside it was hollow, with just enough room for an average-sized man to scrunch himself up and pretend to have been swallowed.

'Amazing what the professionals can do with a bit of chicken wire and papier mâché,' Nurse Bradley declared. 'It's on loan from the Theatre Royal in Margate and is to be returned intact—in*tact*, did everyone hear that? I'm so *cross* with Captain Hook . . . he really needs to practise, if he's to land inside that crocodile without damage or mishap.'

To enter the jaws of this extraordinary amphibian, von Metzer was going to have to jump from the ship's plank. The plank wasn't set terribly high but it was wobbly, and anyone leaping from it would need to judge the distance very carefully indeed, to avoid a painful crash-landing. When Nurse Bradley talked about damage and mishap, though, she meant to the crocodile, not the doctor. No one was in any doubt about that.

'So . . . ' Nurse Bradley continued, grumpily, 'since we have no Captain Hook, I suggest we go right back to the beginning of the play and brush up on the first act. Page six, everyone. Peter Pan has got his shadow back and Tinker Bell is so jealous of Wendy that she is about to pull her hair . . . John and Michael—are you there? To your mattresses, please. Peter Pan—up on the platform. Hurry up—*mind* the crocodile . . . thank you. And Wendy? Where's Wendy? Out you come, Wendy—and put that wig on, will you? It really is a vast improvement and will give Tinker Bell something to actually pull.'

The platform was properly fixed, now, against the back of the stage and you got on and off it using steps at either end. It was pretty high up—higher than the plank—but safe enough since it was nice and wide and Peter Pan and the Darling children had been told to fly in slow motion, more like dancers than birds. Rowan liked being up there, looking down. The low-risks playing Michael and John grinned up at him from the mattresses below. 'Don't fall on us, Rowan,' one of them called up. 'Don't land on us and squash us flat.'

'I won't,' he whispered down. 'Shush now.'

Dorothea stepped onto the stage. The wig was still in her hands, scrunched as small as she could make it. From his own position, directly above her, Rowan could see where her own hair was matted and flat, where she couldn't see to comb it.

'I said "on",' Nurse Bradley scolded. 'Put that wig on, please. We don't have all day.'

'It's too tight,' Dorothea replied. 'I can't hear anything, with it on. And it looks like a mop.'

'Oh dear,' said Nurse Springfield, sweetly. 'That took me *hours* to make last night. I used all my yellow wool, and the bathing cap it's attached to is my sister's. It's a brand new bathing cap, but my sister didn't mind us having it because we thought it would be *perfect*. It's no good for swimming any more, of course, because the wool is threaded right through . . . what a shame it's no use.'

'It's just right,' Nurse Bradley insisted. 'Dorothea—put it on! I won't tell you again.'

Quickly, as if she herself had just decided to, Dorothea crammed the yellow wig onto her head. Out in the audience, one or two people sniggered.

'Properly!'

Dorothea shrugged. 'There is no properly,' she answered, dangerously, through dangling strands of yellow wool. 'This is as good as I can get the stupid thing.'

'For *Heaven's* sake . . . '

'Stay there, Nurse Bradley. It's all right. I'll see to her.'

In growing alarm, Rowan watched Sarah Jane go skipping across the stage. He thought that maybe he should say something, but wasn't sure who to . . . couldn't decide, quickly enough, whether to tell Sarah Jane to be careful or ask Dorothea to please, please, just do as she'd been told.

Dorothea stayed exactly where she was, her expression mutinous. Perhaps she didn't see Nurse Springfield coming. Perhaps there was too much wool over her eyes. But when a pair of hands began tugging, hard, at the cap on her head her own hands jerked upwards, instinctively, to knock them away.

'Careful, Dottie. You've just slapped your precious Joan of Arc in the face. Oh look—she's crying. Poor Saint Joan. She's gone right off you, Dottie. In fact she's leaving you. She's leaving you for good.'

Later, Rowan would go over and over those words, trying his hardest to excuse them. He would repeat them to John Wallace who would sigh and shake his head and say: 'That's fighting dirty, that is; that's using words just like a bayonet, to run a person through.' He would tell Doctor Von precisely what Nurse Springfield had said, and Doctor Von would look angrier than he'd ever seen him look, in all the weeks he'd known him.

But up there on stage, alone on the raised platform, there was no one Rowan could turn to for a second or third opinion. *Excuse me,* he wanted to ask. *Was that a wicked thing she just said, or did I hear it wrong? Please tell me I heard it wrong* . . . Briefly, hopefully, he peered down at the space just above Dorothea's shoulders although he knew, even as he strained his eyes to see, that there would be nothing visible there—no misty, weeping, figure; no smacked guardian angel, fading away.

He turned his gaze to the audience, seeking some kind of a response from Nurse Bradley . . . from anyone . . . but getting none. They hadn't heard—weren't meant to have heard—what Sarah Jane Springfield had just said to the test-case with the frazzled head.

Dorothea was standing very still, so still that Rowan dared to hope that she hadn't heard anything either, that the yellow wig really was clogging her ears.

But Dorothea had heard all right. She had heard, and absorbed, every barbed and poisonous word. Too shocked to move or to speak straightaway, she could only stare soundlessly at her tormenter, through the hateful strands of wool, while she, like Rowan, replayed what had been said to her, over and over again.

It was the smile that did it. The little smirk that lifted the corners of Nurse Springfield's mouth.

'Nyaaargh . . . '

Ripping the wig from her scalp, Dorothea rammed it, hard, into the young nurse's face, blotting the smirk with bathing cap and wool, filling the mouth with yellow, to stop more words coming out. Sarah Jane staggered backwards—from the force of the attack, initially, and then, as she regained her balance, in a desperate, backwards-scramble to get away. With another warrior-cry, Dorothea sprang forward, grabbed Sarah Jane by her upper arm, shook her like a bag of rags, raised her up, and then pushed her, hard, to make her walk.

'*Someone stop her!*' Nurse Bradley bellowed.

Rowan froze. Should he jump? Of course he should! It was the obvious thing to do only . . . he was too high up to do it safely and, anyway, John and Michael were lying right where he would land, curled up on the mattresses, with their eyes closed and their fingers in their ears, too scared to move even if he asked them to. Further along might have been easier . . . but no, the wretched croc was in the way . . .

Think, think . . . you could run back down the steps, then round the side of the stage and up . . . no, no, there isn't time . . . there isn't time for any of that.

There were two male nurses on duty in the hall—at least there had been until five minutes ago, when they'd both nipped out for a smoke. Nurse Bradley was lolloping towards the stage but nowhere near fast enough, and the low-risks were getting upset, and the female nurses were having to calm them down, and there was no one else . . . no one at all . . . who could step in immediately, right that second, to rescue Sarah Jane . . . no one strong enough or close enough . . . unless . . .

He tried. In the few moments that it took for Dorothea to push and drag Nurse Springfield across the stage, and then to slam her, hard, into the waiting jaws of the crocodile, Rowan willed with all his might that the change . . . the longed-for change . . . would happen.

And with his eyes scrunched tight shut and every fibre of his being tensed and waiting, he saw once again, in his mind's eye, the blue and red outfit, like the garb of an acrobat . . . felt the rush of air past his ears . . . heard the gasps of amazement as he swooped down, in the nick of time, to rescue Sarah Jane.

He saw it all, felt it all, even as it dawned on him that it wasn't going to happen. Not now. Not ever.

'Right, de Vere. Let her go. Let her go this instant. Don't make this worse for yourself. Nurse Cartwright? About time too—pin her down—mind she doesn't bite. And you, Nurse Atwood, go and fetch the director—and tell him to bring a straitjacket. Now. Immediately. I'll see to Sarah Jane . . . '

Nurse Bradley was there. Nurse Bradley had taken charge—practically, sensibly, without either the need, or the wish, to hurl a bench, or change into a tight-fitting outfit with a big yellow 'S' on her chest.

With his eyes still shut Rowan pressed his spine and the palms of his hands flat against the back of the stage and then slowly, very slowly, slid down onto his haunches. Defeated.

And as he squatted there, listening to Sarah Jane cry, and Nurse Bradley give more orders, he felt a sense of loss every bit as overwhelming as the elation he had known, such a short time ago, as he'd called upon his audience to show that they believed, that they really, truly believed, in fairies.

I am Superboy, from Planet Krypton . . .

No you're not, said a new voice in his head—a voice he recognized, immediately, as his own, to be trusted absolutely, for the rest of his life, however weedy and pathetic it sounded. *You're Rowan Scrivener. Ro-the-Strange. Get used to it.*

THE HOUSE WITH NO WINDOWS

They took Dorothea straight to Ward Four. It went without saying that she had lost the part of Wendy. It was less clear, that first night, how long they would need to keep her sedated.

'But it wasn't her fault,' Rowan wept to Doctor Von. 'Not really. Can't you do something?'

Tight-lipped, von Metzer got up from his desk and went straight to the director.

'You're supposed to be on duty, aren't you?' was the first thing the director said to him. 'Who have you left in charge of Ward Five?'

'My patients are fine,' von Metzer told him, abruptly. 'I trust them, for a while.'

'Shame you couldn't trust Dorothea de Vere not to attack one of my nurses,' the director snapped back. 'Shame that particular test-case gave in to an overwhelming urge to smash my nurse's head between the jaws of a pantomime crocodile!'

'I can explain how that . . . ' von Metzer began.

The director made a sound between 'pah!' and '*Please*!'

' . . . My patient was goaded,' von Metzer pressed on. 'Taunted beyond her endurance. Nurse Springfield made remarks about the state of her mind. Unacceptable remarks, which sent her into a fury.'

'How do you know this?' the director wanted to know. 'Who says so? According to Margaret—Nurse Bradley—de Vere simply flipped. Something to do with not wanting to wear a wig.'

Von Metzer took a deep breath. He was not, and never had been, a drinking man, but tonight he could have done with a very large sherry.

'Rowan Scrivener was close,' he said. 'Rowan Scrivener heard everything.'

'Ah yes . . . ' The director began drumming his fingers on the desk. 'Peter Pan. The schizophrenic who tells everyone he's from planet Krypton. Well, it's his word against Nurse Bradley's, and half a dozen other witnesses—all of them staff and most of them sane—so no prizes for guessing who I'm siding with. Anyway, the fact of the matter remains: Dorothea de Vere launched a violent attack on a member of my staff, so what do you intend to do about it?'

Von Metzer knew exactly what he intended to do, if only to get Dorothea out of Ward Four and back among friends.

'She will have more treatments,' he said. 'Starting straightaway—tomorrow.'

The director readily agreed. 'Increase the voltage,' he said. 'Anything to calm her down. Oh, and, doctor . . . '

Von Metzer turned, at the door.

'This came for you this morning. It's been halfway around Europe by the look of it but got here in the end. The censors have opened it, and I took the liberty of checking it again myself. Can't be too careful nowadays, as I'm sure you'll understand.'

Von Metzer raised his eyebrows.

'Nice card,' the director added, handing over a well-fingered and clumsily re-sealed envelope. 'Hand-painted by the look of it. Artistic.'

Von Metzer said goodnight. Back on Ward Five he slipped the envelope into the drawer of his desk, his heart sinking, in pity, as he caught sight of Dorothea's mirror and comb. John Wallace, Sid, Donald, and Rowan were all sitting on their pillows, looking out of the window like disconsolate cats about to howl at the moon.

It is ridiculous, von Metzer thought, *that the only chairs on this ward, apart from my own, and the bath chair with the straps, are bolted to the floor, so cannot be moved from place to place. My test-cases are not the types to hurl chairs at one another. I will get them more chairs, for looking out at the snow.*

Rowan, hearing the desk drawer being closed, turned round from the window, his face bleak as he called across: 'Well? What did he say? What did the director say to you, about Dorothea?'

Von Metzer shook his head to show that the director had said little of any use or consequence.

At that, Rowan got up from the floor and almost ran across the linoleum to the desk.

'He didn't believe it, did he? He thinks I imagined it, or made it up.'

Von Metzer sat down, exhausted. 'The director was not convinced,' he admitted. 'I'm sorry, Rowan.'

'Nurse Springfield should lose her job,' Rowan said, through gritted teeth. 'She shouldn't be allowed to look after patients any more. I thought she was lovely but she isn't.' He rubbed his eyes and sniffed before asking: 'Can I go and see Dorothea? I want to tell her that I'm on her side; that I don't blame her for going crazy after what Nurse Springfield said to her.'

Von Metzer said no, that wouldn't be possible. Tomorrow, perhaps, or the following day, maybe, but not now. 'Dorothea will be sleeping,' he said. 'But when I see her in the morning I will send her your regards, yes?'

'Give her my love,' Rowan corrected him. '"Regards" sounds too stuffy. It's what an old person, like my nana, would say. Tell her: "Rowan Scrivener knows what really happened, and he sends you his love." You can say "love" when someone's ill, or having a bad time, without it being soppy, or like you want to marry the person.'

Von Metzer had been staring dejectedly into space and not really listening but the words 'my nana' and 'Rowan Scrivener' struck him, immediately, as significant and brought his head up so suddenly that he felt dizzy for a second.

'Your nana, Rowan?' he said, quickly. 'Do you really mean *your* nana? And "Rowan Scrivener" is what you wish me to say to Dorothea? Definitely "Rowan Scrivener", and not . . . ?'

'All right,' Rowan interrupted, with a rueful smile. 'Don't start. And don't get the tray out either. There's no need. I know who I am now—that I'm not Superboy and never was—but I don't want you, or anyone else, going on about it. It's embarrassing.'

Von Metzer waited, weak with relief.

'But if you know where my Superman comics are,' Rowan continued. 'I'd like them back. It's a long time since I read them and, after I've looked at them again, I thought I'd pass them on to John.'

'Of . . . of course. And what else . . . anything else? The mirror perhaps. Would you like to . . . ?'

'Not tonight,' Rowan said. 'I've waited this long, haven't I, to see how plain and boring and stupid I really am. I can wait a bit longer—until tomorrow anyhow.'

'You are not plain or boring or stupid, Rowan,' von Metzer told him.

But Rowan shrugged, turned away, and walked back across the ward, leaving von Metzer to give silent thanks that some good, at least, had come out of the day's terrible shambles. He considered going straight back to the director's office, to share the good news, but decided that no . . . like Rowan Scrivener's first honest glimpse of himself for months, that too could wait until morning.

By the time the night nurse came on duty von Metzer had clean forgotten about the envelope in his desk. He remembered it halfway up the stairs that led to his private room, and hurried back to Ward Five to retrieve it.

'Rowan Scrivener has turned a corner today,' he couldn't resist telling the nurse, while unlocking the desk drawer. 'He no longer believes he is Superboy, from planet Krypton.'

'Righto,' said the nurse, through a mouthful of sandwich.

'Who does he think he is now then? Jesus of Nazareth or Mickey Mouse?'

Back up the stairs von Metzer went. Once inside his room he locked the door before sitting down on his narrow bed and placing the envelope on his knees. It was so cold in that room that his breath came out in dragon's puffs. There was a small bucket of coal up here now, and a few sticks of apple wood, but he hadn't the energy to light a fire in the grate. Not yet.

On his knees the envelope lifted slightly, in draughts criss-crossing the room like radar. Von Metzer could feel those draughts himself, but all the same, it was eerie to see the envelope move as if urging him to, remove the card and look. No excuses. No more putting it off.

Slowly, von Metzer turned the envelope over and just as slowly opened it and slid out a Christmas card.

There was no need to check the signature. He knew who this was from. He knew, also, that Professor E. would not have signed his real name but used an alias—'Fritz' was what they had decided on, together, before von Metzer left Germany.

'If you stay,' Professor E. had said to him, *'we could try to stop this . . . this barbarism before it takes a hold.'*

'It won't come to anything,' Von Metzer had replied, eager to be away. *'Last summer, in Berlin . . . all those lecturers of psychiatry . . . all those hospital directors . . . some of them are known to me and, I tell you, they would not be supporting a programme of calculated euthanasia in the asylums. Not when it came to the crunch of it. Like me, they were simply not prepared to say so in front of the head of the SS and you, my friend, should not be blaming anyone for that. I just hope you*

will not come to regret expressing your own misgivings so publicly.'

'"*Life unworthy of life,*"' Professor E. had murmured, sadly. '*That, so I'm told, is the Führer's personal view of the mentally ill. We should have seen this coming, Hans. Two years ago, when you and I agreed to the sterilization of children with hereditary defects . . . we should have known it was just the beginning; that the writing was there on the wall . . .*'

'*Stay,*' Professor E. had urged him. But von Metzer had not stayed. He had left for Italy the following week, promising to keep in touch and agreeing, for the sake of peace and quiet, with the professor's farcical-sounding plan to communicate, in a Christmas card, whatever came of Herr Hitler's abhorrence of the mentally and physically impaired.

'*Remember,*' Professor E. had said. '*White candles on the card will signify all is well, red candles will tell you quite the opposite. And if I have drawn children, check the trimmings on their clothes for clues as to . . .*'

'*Please,*' von Metzer had appealed to his friend. '*We have only just celebrated Christmas. It is eleven months before it comes around again. Believe me, this scheme of the Führer's will be nothing more, by then, than a list of statistics turning yellow in a drawer.*'

'*And there will be a tree. Look at the tree,*' the professor had urged, as if von Metzer hadn't spoken. '*If it is simply a tree, with no ornaments on it, all will be well, but any decorations will tell you of the method, or methods, being used to dispose of the little children.*'

'*Please,*' von Metzer had repeated, after listening patiently, and for long enough, to the professor's proposed use of symbols on a card he wouldn't even be posting for another fifty weeks. *'From Italy, I plan to go to England. There is a hospital there that, depending on the results of the Italian trials, is keen to run its own assessment of electroconvulsive therapy. I will give you the name of the hospital, and look forward to receiving your Christmas card. But all will be well, I am certain of it. Adolf Hitler's views on the mentally ill are too extreme. His proposed "solution" will never be taken up by those who are running the hospitals. Trust me.'*

And now here was the card. And what was it the English said? *'A great deal of water has passed under the bridge.'* A torrent, he thought, a torrent has rushed under the bridge and threatened to sweep it away. And with Germany at war, Hitler and his ministers would surely have had more urgent matters to attend to recently than the numbers of retarded children in the country's institutions.

There will be white candles, I am sure of it. White candles, an evergreen tree, and no messages on any clothes—just the good wishes of a friend, for a happy and peaceful Christmas during this testing time of war.

He turned the card over, braced to study the picture. Painting had been Professor E.'s hobby for a great many years. He could not do hands, and his perspective was sometimes odd, but his watercolours had always had a certain charm and this one was as sweet to look upon as the lid of a chocolate box.

The children looked so innocent, clutching their red candles and hurrying towards, and through, the entrance of a *Lebkuchenhaus,* a gingerbread house as the English would say. Beside the house stood a fir tree decorated with baubles as round and clear as soap bubbles.

Von Metzer, his gut already tightening because of the red candles, sat up straighter on the bed and trawled his memory for the correct interpretation of plain, glass baubles. Holly on the tree, he recalled, would have meant lethal injection; candy canes: starvation; bunches of feathers: suffocation . . . how sinister, yet impossible, that list had sounded to him then, and still sounded now. But what had the professor said about baubles? What horrors did baubles signify?

Setting the card down, von Metzer lit the lamp on the table beside his bed and rummaged in a drawer for his spectacles. Then he remembered the magnifying glass he used for checking electrical wires or to read the very small print on medicine bottles. It was in his doctor's bag and, as he fetched it, he remembered the way Rowan Scrivener had taken Dorothea her looking glass; reluctantly, with the mirror pointing away, for fear of catching even a fleeting glimpse of the person he truly was.

The magnifying lens was like a third eye that von Metzer did not want to use. And then it was like a single eye—the terrible eye of a Cyclops—as he positioned it over the Christmas card and looked.

The baubles on the tree had identical markings on them, barely discernible if you weren't examining them minutely. And even if you were, they could easily have passed as a pattern, for the tiny letters, 'C' and 'O' had been carefully intertwined. CO. Carbon Monoxide. Clear, odourless, and deadly.

No . . . surely not. It cannot be. Even Professor E., in all his morbidity and pessimism, had not foreseen this . . .

Setting the magnifying glass aside, von Metzer closed

his eyes. He did not want to see—to know—any more. He had to force himself to look again, and when he did the clues that did not need enlarging jumped straight out at him. The gingerbread house was lavishly decorated in sugary loops and swags but it had no windows—just that wide open door. And the smoke coming out of its chimney was not white, in keeping with the cuteness of the scene, but thick and black where it blended with a background of deliberately-dark firs.

'And check the trim on any items of clothing.' The professor's words rang urgently down the weeks and months as von Metzer lifted the magnifying glass. Again, the interlinked letters—two, three letters at the most—repeating insistently, in the pattern of a coat, in the detail of a little boy's lederhosen, around the crown of a jaunty hat and the hem of a little girl's skirt.

'Ep', 'Unt', 'Kr', 'Bl', 'Tau', 'Sch'. . . the epileptic, the retarded boy, the cripple, the blind girl, the deaf and dumb girl, and the schizophrenic . . .

Appalled, von Metzer opened the card:

Die Kinder gehen in Scharen zu einem besonderem Haus im Wald.

Alles Gute zu Weihnachten, Fritz.

'They go in droves, the children, to a special house in the woods. From Fritz, at Christmas.'

Too sickened to move, von Metzer simply sat. He sat a long time until his fingers and toes turned so numb, from the cold, that he could no longer feel them. Freezing, though, was what he felt he deserved. Freezing to death, in the guest room of an English asylum, would have seemed to him, just then, like a perfect form of justice.

I should have stayed, he berated himself, over and over again as the sky began to lighten, ice-cold and unforgiving beyond his small, barred window. *I am a failure to myself and to all German children deemed 'unworthy of life'. And what, now, can I do? I am too far away. I have signed papers, here, pledging to finish the trials. And the time for resistance has clearly passed. The children are going in droves . . .*

It is too late, now, to stop it.

'THOSE DOCTORS, THEY CAN WORK MIRACLES NOWADAYS'

The following morning Rowan was summoned to an emergency pantomime rehearsal. He did not go willingly, for he no longer cared about being Peter Pan and would have walked off the show, in support of Dorothea, had Nurse Bradley not been such a scary woman and he himself such a pathetic weedy little boy (for that, now, was his opinion of himself—an opinion strengthened, earlier, by his first proper look in a mirror).

Nurse Springfield was nowhere to be seen. She was on sick leave according to Nurse Bradley; recovering from shock and severe bruising. 'Sarah Jane is a very lucky young woman,' she told the assembled cast. 'Very lucky indeed. For if we hadn't placed a cushion inside the crocodile's mouth, to ensure a soft landing for Captain Hook, Dorothea de Vere would have cracked Sarah Jane's skull like an egg.'

She might not have done, Rowan thought, angrily. *You can't know that for sure.*

Mavis Carter, the girl from the kitchens who had lost

the role of Peter Pan to Rowan, had reluctantly agreed to take on the part of Wendy. She had been up all night, learning her lines, and was wilting over her script. Tinker Bell was to be a pool of torchlight after all, and there was a bit of a clamour going on among the low-risks over who would get to switch the torch on and off and wave the beam around.

'Either we all pull together,' Nurse Bradley bellowed, 'and make the best of a bad job, or the whole show gets cancelled! Is that what you want? Is it?'

One or two of the low-risks began to rock backwards and forwards on their benches, distressed by the very idea of this unprecedented change to the pattern and ritual of Christmas.

'No, it isn't, is it,' Nurse Bradley answered for them. 'In the thirty-odd years I've worked here, we've had a pantomime at Christmas come hell or high water, and this year's to be no exception. So . . . let's make a start. And yes, Mister Smee . . . the crocodile, as you've noticed, has remained mercifully intact. Actually, it lost a couple of teeth but we've glued them back in and let's just hope to goodness they stay put. '

They rehearsed for hours, going over and over each scene for the benefit of the new Wendy. Von Metzer appeared just in time to do his bit and got told by Nurse Bradley, in no uncertain terms, that out of the whole sorry cast he was the sorriest of the lot and if he didn't start acting the villain instead of drooping around the stage like a Lost Man she would personally give him a very great deal to be villainous about.

Von Metzer listened to her courteously for a while, and

then left the stage. 'Forgive me,' he said, holding up a hand as if that gesture alone might halt the flood of angry words following him out of the hall. 'You are correct in your judgement. I am a very poor Captain Hook. Tomorrow I will try harder but for now I must see to my patient.'

Dorothea was back on Ward Five; still unconscious after her treatment, still strapped to her bed. Donald was bending over her, like a shambolic prince wondering whether or not to kiss the Sleeping Beauty.

'Any sign that she is waking?' von Metzer asked the nurse on duty.

'Nope,' the nurse replied, and went back to reading his newspaper. 'LEAVE THEM WHERE THEY ARE!' shrieked the front-page headline. The nurse saw von Metzer looking and said: 'The kiddies. The evacuees. The government's telling parents not to have them home for Christmas even though there's been no bombing. "Safety before sentiment," it says here. The authorities have got the wind up themselves, if you ask me. They reckon the kiddies'll go home and stay home and the whole evacuation scheme'll go to pot.'

Von Metzer tried, and failed, to appear interested in the choices of these English parents whose sane and perfect children could surely expect to have parties, and presents, and the turkey with its gravy and sprouts, wherever they spent Christmas Day.

The nurse, seeing the sour look on his face, but not knowing the reason for it, flicked over the page. 'Sorry,' he said, sarcastically, 'I forgot. It'd probably suit your lot, wouldn't it, if the little 'uns all went home.'

'Pardon?' Von Metzer was already moving away, anxious to check on Dorothea.

'Your lot,' the nurse repeated. 'It would suit the Jerries a treat, I expect, if all our evacuees went back to the towns and cities, to be blown to kingdom come in a surprise attack. '

Von Metzer didn't hear him. He was already across the room, taking Dorothea's pulse and staring anxiously into her face.

'All right, don't listen to me then,' muttered the nurse. *'Flaming Jerry. Ignorant Kraut.'*

In Spitalfields, Rowan's grandmother pushed a copy of the day's newspaper across the kitchen table. 'Read that, pet,' she said to his mother. 'It's saying exactly the same as I've been telling you for weeks. Laurel's best off staying in Weymouth. She's happy there, after all, and you can't blame the child for not wanting to spend Christmas Day in a hospital.'

Rowan's mother was writing a list. *Things to take Rowan.* So far, apart from his vests, and a cake, she couldn't think of anything. No more comics had come from America—because of the war, she supposed, and the way it had messed up the post—and she hadn't a clue what to get him for Christmas.

'Let me see that,' she said, putting down her pen and sliding the newspaper closer. 'LEAVE THEM WHERE THEY ARE!' . . . 'Oh, I can't be bothered to read it,' she exclaimed. 'Honestly. I get so tired of being told what to do all the time, by the powers-that-be. Laurel's had her hair cut, did I tell you? She's had it bobbed, she told me so in her last letter. A hairdresser-friend of the Weymouth family did it. Don't you think she's too young, still, for a bob? I keep trying to picture her without her plaits . . . '

Rowan's grandmother picked up the newspaper, folded it in half and tucked it into her bag. Before the day was out, an abandoned puppy at the rescue centre would have piddled all over the government's views on evacuees and Christmas.

'It's Rowan we should be thinking about,' she said, briskly. 'Not Laurel. Laurel's fine. What did that ghastly director-chappie have to say, the last time you spoke to him? About the fits?'

Rowan's mother forced a smile. 'They've stopped,' she said. 'For the time being anyway.'

'Time being my foot,' said Rowan's nana. 'Think positive, Hazel. They've cured him! I knew they would. Didn't I say . . . those doctors, they can work miracles nowadays.'

'Hmm.' Rowan's mother picked up her pen and went back to her list. *A Meccano set? A Dandy annual? A scale model kit of a Wellington bomber with a 38-inch wingspan?* Only last week one of the women's magazines had published her article on 'economy toys for all ages' and now here she was unable to decide on a single Christmas present, economy or otherwise, for her only son.

She smiled, wistfully, remembering some of the cheap homemade playthings featured in her article. What would Rowan and Laurel make, she wondered, of a rubber bath toy cut from an old hot water bottle, stuffed with chopped up corks and stuck together with rubber solution? *('Patterns available include Polly the Plaice, Charles the*

Crocodile, and Monty the Mackerel, price 1d each') They were lucky, both of them, that their father's paintings, and her bits of writing, were selling well enough for the family to be able to afford nice things, despite the Current Situation and all the cut-backs it involved.

At least, thank heavens, the predicted raids hadn't happened. No bombs. No poisoned gas. And, for all she knew, Rowan might quite like a Polly the Plaice. The truth was, she didn't know what he wanted and nor could she guess. It was so long since she had seen him . . . and although it was a huge relief, of course it was, to know that his fits had stopped, she couldn't help but wonder: at what cost? Twice, recently, she had dreamed that her son had regressed right back to babyhood. That everything he'd been able to do for years . . . walking, talking, using the lavatory, eating with a knife and fork . . . was having to be re-learned, even though he remained, physically, a boy of thirteen.

'Eddie Dobbs wants to come with us, to Canterbury,' she said, to distract herself from the worry and the dream. 'He'd have his own bedroom, of course—the one that was to have been Laurel's. He has some leave due, and wants to be with Daff over Christmas. What do you think?'

'Not up to me is it,' Rowan's nana replied. 'What does Lawrence say?'

Rowan's mother smiled. 'Only that it might be useful having a policeman around,' she said, 'if only to handcuff you and march you straight back to the house if you start prowling the streets of Canterbury, looking for strays to feed.'

'Hah!' Rowan's nana reached for the teapot, to pour

herself another cup of tea. 'I won't be doing that. And we'd better start praying for a thaw—or no more snow at least—otherwise we'll need all the dogs we can lay our hands on, to pull us to Kent in a sleigh.'

'Is she going to be all right?'

Rowan had been standing, all morning, next to Dorothea's bed, talking to her, and willing her to answer. To call him stupid, to tell him to shut up, to say anything at all so long as she spoke. The strap across her forehead had been unbuckled, because it was chafing, but the other two, across her chest and over her legs, were still firmly in place.

'She will be all right, won't she?'

Von Metzer said, of course. Dorothea was going to be fine. It was just taking her a bit longer than usual to come to full consciousness.

'But she was awake just now,' Rowan insisted. 'She woke up, saw where she was, looked at me and then closed her eyes again. It was like she recognized everything but couldn't be bothered. That's not like her, is it? She used to wake up furious after a treatment. She used to wake up cursing everyone, especially you.'

Von Metzer tested the pulse at Dorothea's throat. It was normal. All her vital signs were normal. It could be, he thought, that despite her closed eyes and perfect stillness she was actually wide awake and listening to every word he and Rowan Scrivener were saying. It could be that she was bluffing—creating a brand new drama in which to star.

And although the Christmas card from Professor E. was

upstairs in a drawer, the image of those children trooping so trustingly into the house with no windows was etched so painfully on von Metzer's mind's eye that wherever he was, and whatever he was doing, it was all that he could see.

Dorothea de Vere, von Metzer concluded, was in buttercups—no, clover—compared to any insane and troubled girl in Germany. Yes. Dorothea was in clover, here in this English hospital, receiving the very best medical treatment and the kindest of care.

'She will be fine,' he repeated, gruffly, before striding back to his desk. John Wallace, walking past towards the bathroom, paused as if he might say something, but then carried on without a word. Donald and Sid were still in their pyjamas, staring dreamily out of the window.

He should be looking after them, von Metzer knew. Making sure they got dressed before counselling each one individually and then writing his reports. John Wallace, especially, was relying on him to get him through and beyond Christmas. And Rowan—Rowan's confidence was low, since the shattering of his delusion. Rowan would need a lot of support before he met once again with his family . . .

'Where are my comics?'

Von Metzer jumped. He hadn't seen Rowan approach the desk; hadn't been paying attention.

'Your . . . ?'

'My Superman comics. You said you'd bring them to me. The day before yesterday you said you'd do it.'

'Ah, yes.' Von Metzer scratched his chin. He hadn't shaved. The bristles felt like splinters. 'I'm sorry, Rowan,

I forgot. As soon as I can, I will go to the director and get your comics back for you.' *And I have yet to inform the director,* he realized, *of this boy's good progress. Indeed, I have yet to write a proper report about it. My mind is far away from here and too troubled to care.*

'And the paper chains have fallen down,' Rowan added, coldly. 'I'm surprised you haven't noticed.'

It was the oddest thing, Rowan discovered, having his comics back. Odd and . . . well . . . disappointing. His first thought, when he saw them, was that the comics themselves had got smaller, like items shrunk in a wash.

They hadn't, of course; it was only that the frames of each story had loomed so large in Rowan's mind, as he'd looked forward to reading them again, that the real ones seemed titchy by comparison.

Superman, too, was proving a bit of a let down—instantly recognizable as the man of steel, but no longer with quite the same power to dazzle and inspire. After poring over several stories, Rowan set the comics down on the floor. He wasn't in the mood for reading, he decided. He was too worried about Dorothea.

Lying back down (it was afternoon nap-time, supposedly) Rowan glanced across at the next bed and '*Oh!*' he gasped, for Dorothea was staring straight back at him. Staring blankly, with no sign of recognition.

Too shocked to call out immediately for Doctor Von, Rowan found he was holding his breath. *Was she . . . ? Surely she couldn't be . . . ?* Then Dorothea blinked and he breathed out a huge sigh. She was fine.

'Shall I shout for Doctor Von?' he mouthed, just loud enough for her, but no one else, to hear him. 'Do you need to be sick?'

She didn't answer; just blinked again and licked her lips which were cracked and dry and peeling.

'I'll fetch you some water in one of those spout-cups, shall I?' Rowan pushed aside his covers.

'No.' Such a small word, that 'no', and so quietly spoken, yet the distress in her voice was obvious, and troubling to hear.

'All right.'

Checking quickly to see if Doctor Von had been watching or listening (he hadn't) Rowan lay back down. He expected Dorothea to turn her head away then and close her eyes, blocking him—blocking everything—but she didn't. How much did she remember, he wondered, about her fight with Sarah Jane? And did she know she was out of the pantomime? It probably wouldn't be wise, he decided, for him to mention any of that. Not until Doctor Von had spoken to her first.

So, wanting only to keep Dorothea awake, and to maybe entertain her a little, he said: 'There'll be no point in you calling me Superboy from now on. You can still call me stupid, though, since that's exactly what I am for ever believing I had superhuman powers. Stupid, dull, and boring. That's me—the real me.'

For a moment or two it seemed as if Dorothea hadn't heard him properly, or had maybe not understood. Then, she swallowed and cleared her throat, preparing, obviously, to say more this time than one tiny word. Rowan found himself hoping, more than anything, for a nice ripe insult; for something truly scathing to show that Dorothea had come back from her treatment with all the old fight still in her.

When he saw the tears pooling in her eyes, then trickling sideways down her face he realized that he had never seen her cry—never seen it, and never expected to. Like silence, and courtesy, and putting other people first, without a song and a dance, it simply wasn't her.

He didn't know what to do. Perhaps she was in pain—more pain than usual. He was definitely going to shout, this time, for Doctor Von; had taken a deep breath, ready to do so, when Dorothea spoke:

'She's gone,' she croaked, the tears rolling faster and faster. 'I can't see her any more. I can't hear her. Joan's gone. She's really, really gone.'

'SILENT NIGHT, HOLY NIGHT'

Christmas week was bitingly cold, but no more snow fell, and the Scriveners got safely to Canterbury on December the twenty-third before the sun set and the roads into Kent froze solid for the night. They took two cars; Rowan's parents and Daphne travelling in the family's old Vauxhall, and his nana, Eddie Dobbs, Rosa, and the four dogs in the van with the blue cross.

'You sit up front, dear boy,' Rosa said to Eddie Dobbs. 'I'm perfectly happy in the back with the animals—unless, of course, you actually *want* to be slobbered to death and covered all over in hairs.'

Neither Eddie Dobbs or Rowan's grandmother said one word about the journey Eddie had been forced to make, back in September, locked in the back of the van. They had let that drop, and never mentioned it to a soul—Eddie out of sheer embarrassment, Rowan's grandmother because the whole incident was done and dusted and, anyway, she had grown rather fond of this earnest young constable. He wasn't the brightest star in the firmament but he was steady and well-meaning and dear Daphne thought he was wonderful, which was all that really mattered.

'Tell you what, ladies,' said Eddie, now. 'Why not let me drive? Then you, Mrs Mull-Dare, can just sit back and enjoy the ride.' (*And we'll be more certain of getting there in one piece,* he added silently.)

Eddie Dobbs was feeling a lot better about himself nowadays. He was in love, for one thing and, for another, he no longer felt bad about shirking active service.

Active service? The very words made Eddie Dobbs chortle. Here in England, the war seemed to have ground to a halt. Trained soldiers were kicking their heels in camps. Members of the Auxiliary Fire Service, on stand-by for enemy raids, were spending most of their time pumping flood water from disused Anderson shelters.

No bombs had been dropped. No homes destroyed. In fact, the way Eddie saw it, with hundreds of civilians being killed on the roads, due to blackout regulations, being on traffic duty in the heart of London was probably the most active and useful service a chap could be engaged in right now.

Indeed, so cheerful was Eddie Dobbs, as the van with the blue cross chuntered and chugged across the capital, that had the hairiest, whiffiest dog in the whole of Europe been panting in his ear, or draped across his knees, he would still have kept a smile on his face.

Rowan's father was driving the Vauxhall. His overcoat smelled of turpentine and he was trying not to mind about the house—his house—being left empty over

Christmas. Not because of The Current Situation but because he didn't like to think of it in an abandoned state. No sound of wrapping paper being torn away from presents. No smell of the goose roasting. They hadn't even arranged holly on the mantelpieces this year, since there hadn't seemed much point. *Dust and ghosts,* he thought to himself. *Dust and ghosts and the ticking of a clock. Those are the things we've left behind, to inhabit the place in our absence.* There could be a painting in that, he thought.

'Have they said, yet, when Ro will be coming home?' asked Daphne, from her seat in the back.

'Not yet.' Rowan's mother opened a paper bag bulging with boiled sweets, turned round and offered it to her daughter. 'He's doing very well but no . . . they've not said when he'll be home.'

Daphne took a sweet and looked out of the window. She had not missed her brother at all, but she did feel sorry for the poor little chap, and had no objections, really, to spending Christmas Day at the hospital—not now that her Eddie was going to be there too.

Dear Eddie. *'They can't black out the moon,'* he had whispered to her just a few weeks back, while kissing her goodnight beneath a moon as full and round as a dish. And she had tingled from head to toe, even though *'They can't black out the moon'* was the title of a popular song, not something Eddie had made up on the spur of a romantic moment.

'Got the painting safe, Daff?' her father asked over his shoulder. 'It's not under anything heavy, is it?'

'Hmm?'

'Wakey-wakey, dreamboat.'

'Oh—yes.' Pink-faced, her head still swimming with moonlight and kisses, Daphne placed a protective hand on the rectangular canvas, wrapped in jolly paper and tied up with string. Rowan's Christmas present. 'It's fine, Daddy. I'll keep hold of it, so it doesn't slip.'

Rowan's mother dug a pear drop out of the paper bag and popped it sideways into her husband's mouth. As a child, it had been a ritual—hers and her father's—always to have sweets on a car journey. Mints, mostly. No crunching allowed, she remembered, and no talking either while she ate them. Not because her father had been particularly strict, but because he had loved her so much that just the thought of her choking, or breaking a tooth, had been more than he could bear.

'Shthankshyou,' said Rowan's father, through the pear drop on his tongue before starting, very loudly, to crunch.

The dress rehearsal for *Peter Pan* was scheduled for Christmas Eve. 'But my parents might visit me,' Rowan said to Nurse Bradley. 'My nana too, and my sister.'

'They won't,' Nurse Bradley replied. 'They know the drill. You're to spend Christmas Day with them in the visitors' lounge, then they'll be back up again on Boxing Day to watch the pantomime. And that's a sight longer than any other patients get to spend with their families, young man, so be grateful. Now, stand still and hold your arms out, will you? No, not out to the front, dafty, to the sides . . . I need to get this right.'

They were in Ward Five's bathroom, and Rowan was being measured for Peter Pan's shadow.

'Does it have to be exact?' he whispered, aware that Dorothea was awake and watching, listlessly, from her bed. 'It's not like I have to put it on or anything, only dance with it, for about five seconds, during the first scene.'

'I'm a perfectionist, Rowan,' Nurse Bradley answered, running a tape measure from his left wrist to his right one. 'A rare thing in this place, I know, but . . . will you stand *still*, for goodness' sake.'

'Dorothea is a perfectionist,' Rowan insisted, quietly. 'She was perfect as Wendy. You know she was. We all know it.'

'Yes . . . well . . . ' Nurse Bradley slung the tape measure over the bath screen while she noted the measurement for Rowan's arm span in her '*Panto 1939*' notebook. 'She's only got herself to blame for the way things turned out. Herself. No one else.'

'Shhh . . . She'll hear you.'

'Don't talk back to me, you little whipper-snapper!' Nurse Bradley's scolding was loud enough for the whole ward to hear. 'I don't care if she does. And if she thinks she'll be allowed out of here on Boxing Day, to watch the performance with everyone else, she's very sadly mistaken. Now—stay exactly where you are. Head to heel and we're done.'

Rowan winced as the flat of Nurse Bradley's hand came down, hard, on the top of his head, to hold the end of the tape measure in place. *Go on,* he silently willed Dorothea. *Yell out that you wouldn't want to watch her stupid pantomime for all the tea in China. Tell her you and Joan will have better things to do on Boxing Day than sit through such a load of old rubbish.*

But Dorothea said nothing at all.

From his desk, von Metzer looked across at the bathroom and then away, his expression as mopey and disinterested as Dorothea's had been. In a minute it would be his turn for the tape measure—Nurse Bradley would be fitting him with a cardboard hook and warning him not to bend or break it. He would let her get on with it, not caring, any more, what anyone was going to think about his performance as pantomime villain.

Let the English hate me, he reflected, bitterly. *Let them throw their rotten apples, and eggs with bad smells, should they feel so inclined. I should not have come to this country seeking glory for myself while plots were being hatched in my homeland to kill innocent children with gas. I deserve only scorn . . .*

John Wallace had requested another treatment. The voice was still there in his head, singing carols, more urgently than ever. *'Stille Nacht, heilige Nacht . . .'* Such a sweet voice, John Wallace had said, and the Bosch lad no more than eighteen, walking across no-man's land, all those years ago, with his arms raised and his pockets full of photographs and ready-rolled smokes.

Christmas 1914. The great truce, they called it afterwards. Tommy and Fritz laying down arms on the Western Front to meet and shake hands. To swap tunic buttons and addresses . . . to light each other's smokes . . . to play football, so it was reported, with bully-beef cans for kicking and steel helmets as the posts.

Less than fifty yards there had been, between John Wallace's trench and the Bosch. Fifty yards of mud and slime, with corpses from both sides splayed out there, rotting.

'Stille Nacht, heilige Nacht . . .'

John Wallace and his men had heard the guns fall silent, further down the line. They'd heard the rumours, also, of a Christmas truce, but were uncertain . . . disoriented . . . in no mood, if the truth be told, for any kind of a party.

The young German had been just feet away, and still singing like a nightingale, when John Wallace shot him through the heart. How many more John had gone on to kill, before being invalided out of the war, he could not have guessed. But it was just the one who haunted him, and sang to him at night.

'Doctor von Metzer? I'm ready for you now. Left or right?'

Von Metzer blinked. 'I . . . I beg your pardon?'

Nurse Bradley rolled her eyes. 'The hook, doctor. Left hand or right? It's all the same to me . . . '

Lacklustre.

That was the only word Nurse Bradley could think of to describe the way the dress rehearsal had gone.

Lacklustre: devoid of force, brilliance, and/or vitality.

'Cheer up, Margaret,' the director said. 'It'll be all right on the night.'

'It had better be,' Nurse Bradley answered, grimly.

The director leaned back in his chair and put his feet up on his desk. 'Have a sherry, Margaret,' he said. 'Go on—just a small one. It's Christmas Eve. Be a devil.'

The director, like Eddie Dobbs, was feeling merry—pleased with life in general and with himself in particular.

The Scrivener boy, thank heavens, had finally accepted that he was not from another planet. The de Vere girl, by all accounts, had stopped seeing angels. Sidney Eccles, although still a bag of nerves, no longer believed he was the rightful King of England. Donald Granger, a brilliant scientist before mental illness addled his brain, had suddenly remembered how to calculate volume and was working out how many cubic feet of air they were all breathing in Ward Five. And John Wallace, although still hearing Christmas bells, or whatever, was at least taking a friendly interest in his fellow patients and talking, openly, to old von Metzer about his troubles. Mellowing, in other words. Coming out of his shell.

The trials were going well. Very well. Before long, the director hoped, he would be able to cobble together an article for *The Lancet* or *The British Medical Journal* extolling the benefits of electroconvulsive therapy for schizophrenics, manic depressives, and all manner of other defectives. Such an article, as well as earning him a bit more respect among his peers, would be excellent for business. More patients. More fees. More money in his own account.

'It's been a good year, Margaret,' he said, raising his sherry glass in a toast. 'A very good year.'

'It's not over yet, sir,' said Nurse Bradley, downing her own drink in one syrupy gulp. 'And there's a war on, don't forget.'

'Ah yes.' The director refilled both of their glasses. 'It's easy to forget about all that up here, don't you find?'

Nurse Bradley swirled her second tipple thoughtfully round her molars, swallowed, and then shook her head. 'Not when I've a Jerry in my pantomime,' she said. 'Not when I've a Captain Hook who's going to be lucky to get off stage in one piece. There have been mutterings, doctor. Some of the staff, they reckon von Metzer's a spy.'

'Poppycock!'

'It's what they reckon, sir, and with all due respect how can you be sure he isn't? There's something not quite right about the man. Did you know he's put screens around the bath, and the lav, over on Ward Five? He's even gone and painted one. Ducks and frogs all over it. I've never seen the like! I said to him: "Doctor von Metzer, it's strictly against hospital policy to screen the bath and the lav. Patients have to be watched at all times." And do you know what he said to me?'

The director stifled a yawn.

'Go on.'

'He said: "Nurse Bradley, this is my ward and these are my test-cases. Should I wish to install a flying trapeze, or paint a rainbow on the wall, it would be my business, not yours."'

'Hmm.' The director got up, to put another log on the fire. 'An unusual approach, certainly, to the rehabilitation of the mentally ill. Don't quite see how it makes him a spy though.'

Nurse Bradley sniffed. 'It makes him an odd fish,' she declared. 'An odd fish *and* a Jerry. And folk round here . . . some of the staff, people down in the village . . . well, they don't think he should be working for us, doctor. Not now. Not with the way things are. And he's been getting parcels, Nurse Atwood says.'

'Christmas presents,' the director reassured her. 'For the test-cases. He ordered them from a catalogue—it's all above board, Margaret. No explosives wrapped in tinsel. Nothing sinister.'

'Hah . . . well . . . let's . . . *hic* . . . hope not, doctor, for . . . *hic* . . . everyone's sake.'

The director checked his watch. Alone, he would happily have stayed another hour or so with his nice blazing fire and the remains of the bottle of sherry. But: 'Come along, Margaret,' he said, briskly. 'I'll give you a lift down the hill. Busy day tomorrow. Is the visitor's lounge ready? Fire laid? Table set?'

Nurse Bradley rose, unsteadily, to her feet. It tasted like nectar, her annual tipple, but it got to her every time.

'I expect . . . *hic* . . . so,' she said. 'Not my . . . *hic* . . . department, doctor. I've got a pantomime to put on the day after . . . *hic* . . . tomorrow. A pantomime with rotten . . . *hic* . . . actors . . . a Jerry spy . . . *hic* . . . and a crocodile . . . *hic* . . . with broken teeth . . . and . . . '

'Come along, Margaret,' the director repeated, offering her a steadying arm. 'Let's get you home.'

John Wallace and Dorothea both had treatments that evening. Because the dress rehearsal went on longer than expected, Doctor von Metzer went to work in full make-up and with the fingers of his right hand badly cramped from being stuck inside a flower pot, clutching the end of a cardboard hook.

What was the point, he wondered, *in having my hand measured by that general dogsbody, Nurse Bradley, when all they were going to do was stick a pretend hook through the drainage hole of a pot? It is too cumbersome and uncomfortable an arrangement. No thought has been put into the creation of that hook.*

John Wallace went like a lamb to the treatment room and solemnly wished von Metzer a very happy Christmas. 'Any chance, doc,' he said, before the rubber bung went into his mouth, 'of knocking me out until the New Year?'

'No,' von Metzer replied, sharply. He could, he knew, have been kinder, for John always joked at the last moment, to ease the fear they all inevitably felt, however much faith they had in the treatment, but he wasn't in the mood to be kind.

Dorothea went sullenly, with none of the quips and insults von Metzer had grown accustomed to. He was gentle with her, but distracted, as he buckled the restraints.

Christmas Eve . . .

In Germany, so small children were told, rivers would turn to wine tonight, mountains open up to reveal precious gems, and church bells be heard chiming from the bottom of the sea.

In Germany . . .

'Dorothea,' he said, as he dabbed conductive gel on her temples, 'I would like your thoughts, in these next few seconds, to be happy ones. Can you do that for me, please?' The sides of her head were red raw and he flinched as he positioned the electrodes. But: *Be stern,* he chastised himself. *Be professional. This girl does not know how lucky she is, compared to others in this world.*

'Tomorrow is Christmas Day,' he added, after getting no reply. 'I am hoping, Dorothea, that you will wake up from this treatment in a friendlier state of mind, and be joining other patients, in the hall, for the dinner with all the trimmings.'

The apparatus seemed heavier than usual as he pulled it closer to the bed. 'I want Joan back,' Dorothea whispered, closing her eyes against him. 'Get Joan back for me.'

Exasperated, von Metzer filled her mouth with the rubber bung and turned the dial that determined the voltage. And whether his cramped fingers were making him clumsier than usual, or he simply wasn't concentrating, the figure he arrived at was higher than any he had ever dared to set on purpose.

Realizing the error he hesitated, his fingers still touching the dial. The higher the voltage, he already knew, the more effective the treatment in stabilizing a patient's mood and suppressing abnormally active brain circuits. But this . . . this was unknown territory. Was it worth the risk? Could this slip of a girl absorb such a shock?

This and more, he told himself, grimly. *This and more . . .* Recent treatments, after all, had made little difference to the state of Dorothea's mind. Losing the role of Wendy was, he was certain, solely to blame for her continuing silence and heavy sulks. For cruel though Nurse Springfield's comments had been, Dorothea's angels, he remained convinced, had been banished long ago.

Carefully timed—no more than 0.5 of a second—a more powerful shock might just tip the balance, dispelling both this Joan of Arc nonsense and the girl's self-indulgent peevishness at no longer having a part in the pantomime.

Quickly, allowing no time for second thoughts, von Metzer flicked the switch; flicked it hard—brutally, almost.

Dorothea's body arched in agony against the leather straps, thudded back, and arched again. And in that minuscule flash of time, as he both thrilled to, and shrank from, what he had just done, von Metzer could have sworn . . . sworn . . . that a voice, a woman's voice, high and wild and unmistakably foreign, rang in swift, burning judgement through his head: *Shame on you, monsieur . . . Shame, shame . . .*

'ENJOY YOURSELF, KID'

The Scriveners had the best part of a morning to kill, before going up to the hospital for lunch. There were presents to open and breakfasts to cook but no one could pretend that this was going to be a straightforward, run-of-the-mill Christmas Day. Rowan's mother, in particular, was so anxious about seeing her son again that she was like a cat on hot tiles and couldn't eat her toast.

The house they had rented for the week was a large stone property surrounded by a tumbledown wall and the frozen shapes of apple trees. On a scale of one to ten, with one being squalor and ten unashamed luxury, the facilities scored around three and a half. But, as Rowan's father said, a holiday let in rural Kent was never going to give the Ritz a run for its money. And if the washing water didn't freeze, and you weren't being bitten to death by bed bugs, you were doing all right. He had, he concluded, spent Christmas in far worse places, and they all knew, without another word needing to be said, that he meant a trench.

The dogs were in their element, bounding around in the frosty garden and licking at the edges of an iced-over pond. Daphne, too, was as happy as any girl could be because Eddie Dobbs had given her a necklace set with real emeralds, to match her eyes.

'*Eddie*,' she had squealed, lifting the glittering thing from its silk-lined box. 'You shouldn't have!'

'Yes I should,' he had beamed. 'I saw it, like, and I thought, hang wartime economy and making do, I want something perfect for my girl.'

They were all pleased for Daphne. So pleased that when Eddie put his uniform on, before leaving for the hospital, no one had the heart to suggest that ordinary civvies might be more appropriate for a man who was not on duty that day or even on home ground.

'I'll leave off the helmet,' he said, catching the exchange of glances. 'I just thought it might be a good idea if one of us went up there looking official, like. In case—you know—in case of any trouble. From the inmates . . . ' He trailed off, embarrassed. Daphne took his hand and stroked it, forgivingly. Rowan's father smiled, sadly, and shook his head.

'There won't be any "trouble",' Rowan's mother said, gently. 'We've been given a private room, and the hospital has plenty of its own staff to look out for the patients—not as many men as there used to be, of course, because quite a few of them have joined up. But . . . well, you look very smart, Eddie, doesn't he, mother?'

Rowan's grandmother was brushing dog hairs off her good skirt; brushing so hard and fast that the hairs were floating everywhere and would land, in a moment or two, on everybody else.

'Very dapper,' she agreed, without looking up. 'Very dapper indeed.'

Old Rosa went to the back door to call the dogs in: 'GRETA!' she hollered. ' GRETA GARBO! ERROL FLYNN!' The dogs would be staying in the house, with a pig's ear each as a Christmas treat.

'MARLENE! CLARK GABLE!'

'It's a good job the nearest neighbours are more than three fields away,' chuckled Rowan's father. 'Or they'd be queuing down the path any minute, with their autograph books . . . '

It didn't feel very Christmassy on Ward Five. In spite of the paper chains, and the tree in the pot; in spite of the gifts Doctor Von had left at the end of each bed, it felt to Rowan like a day to be endured.

Bathing quickly, behind the frog-and-duck screen, he started rehearsing little bits of speech in his head; going over stuff he could say to his family that would sound normal and pleasant—words to reassure everyone that he was as sane as sixpence now and a pleasure to be around.

A pleasure to be around? Who was he trying to fool?

'Hurry up, Rowan,' Doctor Von called out. 'Your family will be here in less than half an hour.'

'I am hurrying,' Rowan called back, beginning to splash.

Peter Pan. He could talk to them about that for a bit. But then what? His mother, he knew, would want to know all about the friends he had made—about Dorothea and anyone else he might have chummed up with.

Everyone on Ward Five gets along famously, he imagined

himself saying over the turkey and the sprouts. *Me. Doctor Von—who's a Jerry by the way. King Sid, who's not really a king, John Wallace who is afraid of Christmas, Dorothea who . . .*

'Rowan. Half a minute more and I will be coming in to pull you from the bath.'

'Right. I'm done. I'm getting out.'

Dorothea had not opened her present. It was still at the end of her bed, round like a croquet ball, or a Spanish orange, and wrapped in pink tissue paper. Dorothea was still unconscious and she looked ghastly. 'Her ears have been bleeding,' Rowan had informed Doctor Von on his way to the bathroom. 'Not a lot, but enough to muck up her pillow. Is she all right? Is that normal?'

Doctor Von had told him not to worry.

'Will she be awake in time for her Christmas dinner?'

Doctor Von had said it was highly unlikely that Dorothea would be in any mood for a Christmas dinner even if she did wake up in time.

'That's true,' Rowan had said. 'It's probably best for everyone that she misses it.'

'Rowan? You have five seconds only!'

Quickly, Rowan stepped out of the bathroom. He had put on a clean shirt and his best trousers, and his shoes had been cleaned the night before. He would probably do, he thought, and yet had Doctor Von, or anyone else, told him to change back into his pyjamas and return to bed he would have obeyed, like a shot.

I don't want to do this, he thought. *I want to stay right here on Ward Five. I want to polish the brass, or talk to Dorothea, or watch through the window in case it starts to snow. I don't want to see my family. It's too soon. It's too difficult.*

'I'm a bit worried,' he said to Doctor Von. 'They've come all this way and what if . . . what if they don't like me?'

'Nonsense.' Von Metzer's tone was so dismissive that Rowan wished he had kept his fears to himself. It hurt, too, that Doctor Von hadn't been kinder. It seemed to him that the man had changed—grown sterner—recently. Or could it be that the fault was all his own? Maybe he was just downright irritating, and unworthy of anyone's attention. Perhaps these facts about himself had simply not registered while he believed he had superhuman powers.

'OK,' he said, stiffly. 'I'm ready then.'

'Have a good day, young man,' Donald called from the far end of the ward.

'Yes,' added Sid. 'Enjoy yourself, kid.'

John Wallace was sitting up in his bed. He was holding the socks von Metzer had given him as if he wasn't quite sure what to do with them, and the paper they had been wrapped in had fallen to the floor. This was the worst day for John's voice, Rowan knew that. And although he hadn't been told all the details he was aware that it had something to do with the last war—with being over in France, killing people, while families back in England went about the usual business of an ordinary year.

'I'll maybe see you later then, John,' he called, tentatively. 'After lunch, in the visitors' lounge—remember?' He had invited John Wallace to meet his family, if he wanted to; if he felt up to it. He'd thought it would distract him and make the day pass more quickly. He'd also thought that John Wallace might get on rather well with his father.

'You have the same cigarette cases,' he'd told John. 'My father's is exactly like that—brass with a lady's head on it.'

'Princess Mary,' John Wallace had replied. 'It's the profile of the young Princess Mary. We all got sent one—all of us who were out there, that first Christmas. There was a card with it. A cream card, I remember, although mine got dropped, and tramped into the mud. Nineteen fourteen it said on the front, and then a greeting inside: "With best wishes for a happy Christmas and a victorious New Year from the Princess Mary and friends at home." I've often wondered what she'd have made of things, if she'd made a point of coming over, to deliver those greetings personally. Most likely she'd've fainted. Or thrown up.'

'Come and meet my family,' Rowan had said to him then. 'On Christmas Day. I'd really like you to.'

'John?' he called now, a little louder than before, and was glad when John Wallace looked up and nodded. *Yes,* the nod said. *After lunch, Rowan. I'll see you after lunch.*

Rowan hadn't been to the visitors' lounge before and his first impression on walking in, was *It's normal! It's a normal room!* What he meant was there were pictures on the walls, and a fire in the grate and comfortable chairs to sit on. Chairs with cushions. A table had been set for lunch, with napkins and silver cutlery. Rowan wondered who had polished the knives and forks. It certainly hadn't been him. (*'Too dangerous, stupid,'* Dorothea would have said.)

'Well, it's all looking nice and jolly in here, isn't it?' the director said, rubbing his hands together in a satisfied way as if he, personally, had lit the fire and plumped up the cushions. 'Very festive, don't you think?'

'Yes,' Rowan agreed. 'But where is everyone?' He had expected his whole family to be there, waiting for him.

'They'll be here soon,' the director said, checking his pocket watch. 'Any minute now, I expect.'

The director had come to Ward Five to collect Rowan and escort him to the lounge. And he had asked Rowan not to discuss with his family the exact nature of his treatments. A report about them was in the offing, he'd said. In an important medical journal. All a bit hush for now (can't have some other hospital stealing our thunder, can we?) so . . . 'If they ask,' he'd said, 'just tell them the doctors here know their stuff and that you've had plenty of rest and so on. Will you do that?'

Rowan had said that he would.

'Just one more thing,' the director had added. 'Best keep mum about your little Superboy episode too. All right?'

'All right.'

'Good chap.'

The director was due in the hall where staff and patients were already wearing daft paper hats and sniffing, hungrily, but he wasn't about to leave a test-case all alone. Later on, the Scriveners' Christmas dinner would be served, and discreetly monitored, by a male nurse who would behave like any attentive waiter but would also know exactly what to do should Rowan Scrivener suddenly go berserk. Not that anyone seriously expected the boy to turn violent, after all this time, but better safe than sorry.

'I suppose . . . ' the director began, but then the door flew open and in they all came—the difficult mother first, followed by a man who looked so much like Rowan Scrivener that he was surely the father, followed by the grandmother helping a second, even more eccentric-looking, old biddy along, then by an extremely bonny young girl and then—*Oh, for heaven's sake,* the director thought—a policeman.

The women descended upon Rowan with little cries of welcome and delight. Rowan breathed in their combined scents of dog, and roses, and the outside world and felt a rush of something . . . nostalgia? . . . longing? . . . he couldn't tell what, exactly, as his mother hugged him tight.

'I've brought your vests, pet, but no comics, I'm afraid.'

'Who's been cutting your hair, my darling? It looks like Errol Flynn's hindquarters doesn't it, Rosa?'

'You've got taller, Ro. Another year or so and you won't be my "little" brother any more. You'll be towering over me, just like Eddie here!'

Rowan couldn't speak, could only smile and nod and stand there while they clucked and fussed. His mother, his sister, his nana, old Rosa . . . as familiar as his own feet, all of them, and so happy and pleased to see him . . . He ought, he knew, to be just as happy and pleased to see them, so why did he feel so . . . tired?

'We've got crackers to pull,' he said, politely, 'with paper hats in, I believe.' And he took a step or two away, so that they couldn't hug him any more. He wasn't used to hugs, he realized. They overwhelmed him.

'Paper hats, eh?' His father stepped forward to clap

him on the shoulders. 'Hear that, young Dobbs? Anyone gets a blue paper helmet, pass it down to Dobbs.'

Eddie Dobbs grinned, while everybody else laughed, then he nodded across at Rowan. 'All right, mate?' he said, gruffly. Rowan nodded back, far more at ease with gruffness than with tears or hugs. Even his father's pat on the back had unnerved him, it had been so hearty and so loaded with expectations. *Chin up, son,* it had said. *A stiff upper lip, and no funny behaviour over dinner. I'm relying on you.*

The director left them to it but not before making meaningful eye contact with the male nurse who was hovering just inside the door, a cloth over one arm and a tureen of hot soup held awkwardly in both hands, like a very full bedpan that he was anxious to empty out.

And so the family sat down around the table—Rowan's father at the head of it, Rowan between his mother and his nana, Daphne opposite, next to Eddie Dobbs, and old Rosa at the far end with a doggy bag at the ready, for bits of sausage and turkey. And they all pulled their crackers, and put on their daft paper hats; and Eddie Dobbs read out a motto which they all roared with laughter over even though it wasn't particularly funny; and the nurse poured water from a cut-glass jug into cut-glass tumblers; and Rowan sat very, very still, looking down at his plate.

'How is the girl you mentioned in your letters?' his mother asked. 'Your friend—Dorothy, is it?'

'Dorothea,' Rowan replied, still looking at his plate. 'She's . . . she's all right.'

'Is she in the pantomime as well?'

'As well as what?'

'As well as *you*.'

'No,' he answered. 'She isn't.'

His mother took a sip of her water. 'Ah, well,' she said. 'Acting isn't everybody's cup of tea, is it? I'm sure she has other talents.'

The soup was pea and barley and very, very thin.

Rowan's nana said to him that he was looking extremely well. A bit pale, she said, but then he'd never been a child with rosehips in his cheeks.'You're not sleeping *all* the time are you, pet?' she asked, trying not to sound too anxious. 'They haven't woken you especially, have they, just for today?'

Rowan's mother tutted and set down her spoon. 'Didn't we agree?' she exclaimed. 'Didn't we say—no interrogations.'

'It's all right,' Rowan said. 'And don't worry, Nana. I only sleep at night now, like . . . like normal people. I used to have a nap in the afternoons sometimes, like you and Rosa do, but I don't any more.' He paused. 'The doctors here know their stuff,' he added. 'I've had plenty of rest and . . . and so on.'

Reassured, his nana took another mouthful of soup and his mother, too, picked up her spoon, saying: 'Laurel sends her love. We went down to see her last weekend. She sits her piano exam next month, and she's had her hair bobbed—can you imagine? It's so short. I'm not at all sure I like it.'

'Oh, I thought she looked sweet,' said Daphne, gaily.

Rowan was glad to hear about the piano exam, for it meant that his sister's fingers must have healed. But talk of her new hairstyle left him cold. *My friend Dorothea has been trying to grow her hair,* he imagined himself saying. *She tried for weeks—but it's all been shaved off again now. If you think Laurel's hair is short you should take a walk along the corridor, step into Ward Five, and take a look at Dorothea . . .*

The nurse carved the turkey, over on the sideboard, and Rowan felt a flicker of sympathy for his father who, he sensed, had expected to do that job himself, as head of both the table and the household.

And then: 'What are you going to eat, Nana?' he asked, in a rush of anxiety, for his grandmother was a vegetarian—hadn't eaten meat since she was forced to, as a child.

His nana placed a settling hand on his arm. 'Don't you worry about me, pet,' she said. 'I'm having a nice macaroni cheese. It's all sorted.'

Rowan swung round in his chair—swung and almost toppled over, he was so used to the chairs on Ward Five being bolted to the floor.

'Don't put any gravy on my grandmother's macaroni cheese,' he called out to the nurse. 'It'll be turkey gravy, made with the turkey's guts. I know, because I used to help make it at home. And my grandmother doesn't eat . . . '

'Hush . . . ' His mother was holding tight to both the chair and his left arm. 'Hush, it's all right . . . ' Rowan swivelled back round to face the table. The others had stopped eating—Daphne's soup spoon was actually poised in mid air—and Eddie . . . Eddie Dobbs . . . looked suddenly just like a police officer getting ready to make an arrest, despite the yellow paper crown slipping foolishly over his ears.

'I *know* it's all right,' Rowan told them all, calmly. 'I was only saying . . . only letting him know.'

'Of course you were, my darling,' his nana said, heartily. 'Thank you. Most considerate.'

They thought I was going into a panic, Rowan realized. *They've been told I'm all right but they don't really believe it. I was just talking normally though—wasn't I? Normal for this place anyway . . .*

Dinner was served. Rowan ate it obediently although each mouthful went down his throat like a pebble. This family of his . . . it exhausted him. Just trying to fit in—to belong again—was wearing him out.

'That was delicious,' Rowan's mother said to the nurse, when they had all finished. 'But I think we'll wait a while for pudding, so that my son can open his presents.'

'Of course, madam,' the nurse said. 'Whatever you wish.' He was doing a fine job, Rowan thought. It was a shame he hadn't auditioned for *Peter Pan,* he was that good.

The presents had been placed in a pile beside one of the chairs. New pyjamas from Rowan's nana, a sponge bag with his initials on it from Daphne and Eddie Dobbs, a tin of sweets and a box of writing paper from Rosa.

'Thank you,' he said to each of them in turn. 'Thank you . . . thank you . . . thank you . . . ' He was sitting in the chair, with them all clustered round, making him feel important, yet inadequate, both at the same time.

Then, just as his 'thank yous' were beginning to sound desperate, the nurse came over and coughed, politely. 'Excuse me, sir,' he said to Rowan's father. 'The King will be addressing the Empire in just a few minutes, so if you and the other gentleman would care to follow me, there'll be a wireless on in the director's office.'

Rowan held his breath. His father, if he remembered correctly, had stopped listening to the wireless the day war was declared. And on top of that he wasn't a man to care tuppence what the King had to say, to the Empire . . . to him personally . . . to a cloud in the sky or a dog in the street . . . not today or at any other time.

Rowan, though, was not the only member of the Scrivener family who could say a polite 'thank you', through gritted teeth, and sound as if he really meant it. 'Much as I hate to miss such an important broadcast,' his father told the nurse, 'I'm here to see my son. So far as I'm concerned, Rowan is king for the day. And he still has his main present to open—here you go, old chap. From your mother and me.'

Taking the gift in his hands, Rowan knew at once that it was one of his father's paintings.

'Thank you,' he said and this time he wasn't pretending. Carefully, in case he should accidentally touch and mark the canvas, he prised open a section of wrapping paper and folded it away from the top of the frame. It was a good frame, the colour of polished steel, and Rowan began to hurry, eager to see what his father had painted for him . . . for *him* . . . not for a client, or a gallery, or some smart exhibition in Paris or New York, but for his own son.

The painting wasn't enormous, but it was an awkward shape and Rowan almost dropped it as he tugged and pulled at the paper.

'Here,' his mother said, 'I'll hold the top, while you finish unwrapping.'

After that it was quick and easy. The wrapping paper came down in one big piece, like a drape being whisked away and: 'Isn't it marvellous?' his mother said, proudly. 'We know how much you love the comics Tommy John sends over from America. And we knew you'd be disappointed that no more have come in time for Christmas. So . . . well, what do you think, pet? Do you like it?'

'It's . . . ' Rowan groped for a word. The right word. A word that would please his father without sounding lame. A word he could hide behind while he dealt with the surprise—the shock—of seeing this . . . this . . .

'He's lost for words, bless him,' old Rosa said.

'First family portrait I've known you do, Lawrence,' said Rowan's grandmother. 'I must talk to you, later, about doing the dogs.'

'I think it's *marvellous,*' sighed Daphne. 'What do you think, Eddie?'

Eddie Dobbs said it was pretty marvellous all right—as good as a photograph, in his opinion.

'Stand back from it, son,' Rowan's father said. 'You'll be able to see it better.'

Obediently, Rowan stumbled backwards, almost treading on his father's toes. And everyone fell silent as he looked, again, at the canvas. It was his turn to speak, and they were waiting.

He felt his father's hand, gentle on his shoulder. 'You can keep it here, if you want, or I'll take it back to Spitalfields and hang it in your bedroom.'

Rowan nodded. *Now. Speak now. Say something—anything!*

'It's . . . ' he repeated, forcing the word up his throat and out of his mouth as he stared, and stared, at the perfect likeness of himself: Rowan Scrivener, Ro-the-Strange, pale-faced, dark-haired, leaping through the air above a London street—his own street in Spitalfields by the look of it—in the blue and red outfit . . . the scarlet boots and yellow belt . . . the flapping cape . . . of Superman.

'It's . . . it's astonishing, father. Thank you.'

'So you're not keeping it here? They're taking it home?'

'Yes. Was that wrong? Do you think they guessed I don't like it, because I said to hang it in my bedroom? Do you think I should have asked Doctor Von to hang it up here? People would have laughed, John. Dorothea would have . . . '

'I think you made the right choice.'

'Do you? Well . . . I'm going to bed now. I'm really tired. Goodnight, John.'

'Goodnight, lad. Oh—and, Rowan?'

'Yes, John?'

'Sorry I never made it to the lounge. Slept like a baby all afternoon I did. Missed dinner. Supper too. That last treatment must have really hit the spot, eh?'

He's fibbing, thought Rowan, wearily. He didn't sleep, I know he didn't. He just lay there in bed with his eyes closed, waiting for the day to be over. Dorothea did the same. She's still doing it. She hasn't even opened her present from Doctor Von and soon it won't be Christmas any more.

'Those treatments,' John Wallace added, trying to sound hearty, 'they could knock out the poorest sleeper in the world, they could. I swear, I would have slept until New Year if von Metzer hadn't woken me up with that turkey sandwich.'

'It's all right, John,' Rowan said to him. 'I understand.'

THE RAINBOW WITH NO ORANGE OR BLUE

Dorothea was stubbornly refusing to open her present. 'Come on, Dorothea,' Rowan said to her, on Boxing Day morning. 'Doctor Von went to a lot of trouble. I got a kaleidoscope—look.' But she turned her head away and blocked him out. It had taken two nurses to wash her earlier, and coax some food into her mouth, even though she had been fully conscious and Doctor von Metzer had declared her perfectly capable of getting to the bathroom by herself and of lifting a spoon. Now she was back in her bed and showing no signs of getting up again.

'If you need the lavatory you'd better say,' Rowan warned her. 'Now that you're awake, you'd better say so, Dorothea.'

Von Metzer beckoned him over to the desk.

'Leave her be,' he said. 'She is sulking, only, and you and I, we do not have time for such dramas. Not today. Pay her no attention and do not mention the pantomime. By tomorrow, once the show is over, Dorothea will be very much better and we can all get back to normal. Trust me.'

It suited Rowan not to mention the pantomime. He was already nervous and the last thing he needed was Dorothea saying something catty, to make him feel worse. He needed to go over his lines, though, so asked to be excused from the afternoon walk.

Von Metzer wasn't sure about that. 'There will be no nurse on duty,' he said. 'Because of Christmas, and the pantomime, there is no one, today, who can take my place, here on Ward Five. Dorothea can be strapped down while we walk, and again, later on, while the show is being performed. In her present mood she will not care. She might even thank me. But you . . . '

'I'll be fine,' Rowan said. 'Honestly. I was fine, yesterday, with my family even though I didn't think I would be, and I'll be fine here while the rest of you have your walk.' He paused and grinned. 'Trust me,' he said.

'Very well,' von Metzer agreed.

'You can strap me down too, if you like,' Rowan added. 'I can still look at my script if you leave my arms free. Of course, it might upset Dorothea if she sees what I'm reading . . . but I could hide the pages inside one of my comics and . . . '

'Rowan,' von Metzer said, 'I see no need to strap you down. I trust you. It is all OK.'

With the men gone, and no one at the desk, Rowan felt strangely important—in charge of himself, for the first time in months, and of Dorothea too. Through the bars of the window he could see snow clouds piling up like grubby washing. Inside, close to where he stood, the paper chains moved gently, in a draught. He wandered into the bathroom, smiled at the screen with the ducks and the frogs on it, and then wandered out again.

'Are you awake?' he whispered, leaning over Dorothea's bed. 'They've gone for a walk, Doctor Von and the others. You could look at your present now.'

Dorothea's eyes opened quickly, like the eyes of a doll being lifted from its box. 'Gone?' she croaked. 'Are you sure?'

'Yes.' Rowan beamed at her. 'Your voice still works then? We were starting to think, John and I, that we might never hear it again. We were sort of pleased about that, if you must know.'

He was teasing her, in the hope that she would tease him back, but she was looking up at his face as if his presence in the ward—in the world, even—was neither here nor there.

Then: 'I need the lav,' she croaked. 'Urgently.'

'Oh . . . ' Rowan took a step away, frowning. 'I'm not sure . . . '

'Unbuckle me, stupid, or I'll mess the bed.' And because there was a hint of the old Dorothea in the way she said that, and because he really did not want her to mess the bed, Rowan did as she'd asked.

'I'm coming with you, though,' he said, as she eased herself, shakily, to the floor.

'What? No you're not. You're not watching me on the lav. Only dirty boys watch girls on the lav—dirty boys and stupid nurses.'

She staggered, almost falling. He reached for her arm but she motioned him away, almost falling, again, from the effort. Her hospital nightdress was too long for her and, as she set off across the linoleum, her bare feet got tangled in the material, stopping her in her tracks. For a moment she stood still, a puzzled look on her face as if she didn't understand what was happening. Then she lifted the hem of the nightgown, like a girl walking through dew, and carried on towards the bathroom.

'Go. Away,' she hissed, as Rowan skittered anxiously along behind her. 'Have you turned into a pervert or something?'

'I'll wait for you here, then,' he said to her, 'by Doctor Von's desk. I'm just worried you might faint, that's all. Your ears were bleeding yesterday and that's not right. I don't care what Doctor Von said, your ears shouldn't bleed after a treatment. Mine never have and neither have John's. I asked him.'

Dorothea disappeared behind the lavatory screen.

'Don't be long,' Rowan called, anxiously. 'Don't dawdle just to worry me, and if you need any help you'd better shout. In fact, talk to me, will you, so I know you're all right? Go on—or I'm coming in to check.'

'For goodness' . . . *sake.*'

He heard, with relief, the chain being pulled. Then she was out, and visibly washing her hands.

'I'm sorry,' he said, as she returned, dizzily, to her bed. 'It's just that without Doctor Von here . . . '

'Forget it,' she said. 'And pass me that present.'

Delighted that she was finally showing some interest Rowan picked up the ball-shaped parcel and placed it in her hands. 'Oh . . . ' he said, as she tore the paper away. 'It's a snowstorm.'

'So it is. I'm tired now. Go and look out of the window or something.'

She bent from the bed, meaning to put the fake-glass globe down on the floor, but Rowan took it from her. 'Look,' he insisted, giving it a good shake. 'There's a rainbow in it, with something at the end—a pot of gold, I expect, since that's what you usually find at the foot of a rainbow. And the snow has bits of glitter mixed in. Look!'

With a sigh, Dorothea took back the snowstorm and pretended to care. Inside the globe, flecks of fake snow were settling on and around a gaudy plastic rainbow with a gold-painted blob at one end like an ugly mistake.

'There are two colours missing,' she said.

'What? What are you talking about.'

'The rainbow. It should go: red, orange, yellow, green, blue, indigo, and violet. *"Richard of York gave battle in vain."* That's the rhyme. That's how you remember. But this one's got no orange, and no blue either.'

Rowan shrugged. 'It's still pretty though, isn't it?' he said, persuasively. 'And you can't really tell.'

'I can tell,' Dorothea said. 'I can tell it's not right—not the way it's supposed to be.' And she thrust the snowstorm back at Rowan as if she never wanted to see it again, lay down and closed her eyes.

Defeated, Rowan placed the snowstorm on the floor. He'd done his best with Dorothea for today. Now all he wanted to do was go over his lines, while there was still time.

'I'd better do your straps up,' he said. 'Doctor Von will undo them for you, when he gets back from the walk.

You'll have to have them done up again later though, just for an hour or so while we're . . . busy.'

A flicker—realization? understanding?—crossed Dorothea's face, making her closed eyelids tremble, like a dreamer's, and Rowan winced to think he might have accidentally reminded her about the pantomime and made her sad. There was a pillowcase on the floor, between his bed and hers, with his Peter Pan outfit stuffed inside it (they had all been told to look after their own costumes, so that nothing got muddled up) and it worried him, now, that she might have seen a bit of his tunic sticking out and guessed what it was.

'Show me your costume then.'

'What?'

'Your Peter Pan stuff, stupid. It's in that pillow case, isn't it? Go on. I won't laugh, I promise.'

'Dorothea,' he said, slowly, 'that's so *odd*. I was just thinking about that. It's like you read my mind.'

'Hah!' she said. 'Not difficult, Superboy. Your head's like that stupid snowstorm; completely transparent and not much in it.' Her eyes were open again, with a hint of a sparkle in them, and she was hauling herself up in the bed.

'All right,' Rowan agreed. 'But I'm not putting it on. There isn't time. I need to go over my lines.' *And I won't have you laughing at me in my leggings,* he added, silently, *or saying something rude about the tunic not quite covering my man-bits.* He was worried about that tunic, now that he came to think of it. Hopefully, on stage, the shortness wouldn't notice, or he'd be able to tug it down.

'What's Wendy wearing?' Dorothea wanted to know,

as she fingered the green tunic, stuck all over with fake autumn leaves and cobwebs made from wool.

'I can't really remember,' Rowan said. 'A nightie-thing, I think; a bit like the one you're wearing now. She's not as good as you though, Dorothea. Nowhere near.'

Dorothea had picked up Peter Pan's shadow and was holding it, thoughtfully, in both hands. 'Of course she isn't,' she said. 'She'll be rubbish. Useless. A complete failure.' Carefully, she spread the shadow out on top of her blanket—the stocking legs, the stocking arms, and the stockinet body and head, all painstakingly stitched together by Nurse Bradley and dyed to a shadowy-black. Rolled out it was exactly the same height as Rowan and covered most of the bed.

'My shadow,' said Rowan, in case she hadn't guessed. 'I have to dance with it, only the head flops all the way back so it looks like I have a headless shadow. Silly, really . . . '

Dorothea didn't answer. She had twisted the shadow into a long dark scrunch and was pulling and stretching it, this way and that.

'Stop it,' Rowan snapped. 'What are you doing? Give it here. You'll ruin it.'

He stuffed everything back in the pillowcase, annoyed now.

'My straps,' Dorothea reminded him.

'Oh—right. Hang on.'

He put the pillowcase down and turned to do up the restraints. Only: 'What if I need the lav again?' Dorothea said, her voice small and worried. 'Later on, while the rest of you are "busy"?'

Rowan wasn't sure what to say to that. 'It wouldn't be for long,' he ventured. 'An hour . . . an hour and a half at the most. You'd be able to hang on wouldn't you?'

'Not necessarily.'

'Well then . . . I don't know. Ask Doctor Von when he gets back. Maybe he'll leave you undone.'

'He won't. He doesn't trust me. Tell you what, do them up just tight enough so I won't fall out of bed but not so tight that I can't wriggle out if I need to. Oh, and leave my arms free. Then, when old Von gets back, tell him I've been to the lav . . . opened my *beautiful* present . . . talked myself hoarse . . . and now I'm sound asleep. Tell him you've done the straps up and put an extra blanket over me because I was cold. Then say that if anyone goes near me—or even touches my blanket—I'll wake up and want to go to the pantomime. Tell him I threatened to scream the place down if I woke up before the thing started, and wasn't allowed to go.'

'And would you?'

'No, stupid.'

'So . . . you're not going to turn up in the hall, are you, if I don't do you up tight enough? You're not planning on making a big scene in front of everyone, to spoil the show because you're not in it any more?'

'Are you mad?'

'Promise me, Dorothea. Promise me, on your life, that if you do get out of bed later you won't go anywhere near the hall. Promise.'

'I promise.'

'On your life.'

She looked at him then—really looked at him—and her eyes were sad and kind and very, very tired.

'On my life,' she said, softly. 'I promise you, on my life, that I will not go anywhere near the hall tonight.'

Reassured, Rowan buckled the restraints over her legs and her chest, leaving her arms free, and just enough slack for her to ease herself out if she needed the lavatory. Then he shook out the extra blanket from the end of her bed and covered her with it, up to her chin.

She was still looking at him in that sad, kind way, and he couldn't help but ask: 'Your angel. Is she . . . ?'

Dorothea's expression hardened immediately. She was blocking him, Rowan could tell. And Joan had gone—gone for good—he could tell that as well. He wanted to say to Dorothea that everything would be all right; that she would get used to being without her guardian angel just as he was having to get used to being just a dull and ordinary boy, not a superhero after all. But he didn't think Dorothea would welcome any reassurances just then and, anyway, he still had his lines to go over, one last time; so he picked up his script, along with his pillow, and walked away.

'Thank you, Superboy,' Dorothea called after him, unexpectedly.

'I'm not Superboy,' he called back, without turning round. 'I never was.'

'You are to me,' she answered, as he sat himself down by the window, with his back to her.

'We are all rather lonely in Neverland, Wendy, for we have no female companionship . . . '

Would Sarah Jane be coming, to watch the show, he

wondered? No one had said whether she would be there or not and, in all honesty, he hoped she would stay away—not because her presence would turn him into a tongue-tied, blushing idiot (he was beyond all that, he was certain) but because if he saw her, to speak to, he would feel compelled to say something on Dorothea's behalf.

'You hurt my friend. You were cunning and cruel and I don't like you any more.'

No.

'Why did you do what you did? How could someone like you—someone pretty, and popular—be so mean to a girl like Dorothea?'

No.

'I loved you. I really, really, loved you. Now I'm just sad and confused.'

No, no, definitely no!

He lay down on the linoleum, with his head on the pillow, and closed his eyes while he silently mouthed more pantomime lines. He must have dozed, for the light was fading from the window when Doctor Von and the others came in, waking him with a jump that cricked his neck.

'What time is it?' he asked.

'Time to go,' said Doctor Von. 'I have just seen Nurse Bradley and she is wanting the whole cast, right now, in the hall. She plans a big talk, I suspect. John and Sid and Donald will come with us. But first I must see if Dorothea is needing anything.'

'Don't,' said Rowan, quickly. 'Don't disturb her.' And he repeated, word for word, all that Dorothea had told him to say. Von Metzer shrugged. 'More dramas—how typical. But she was talking, you say? Making sense? And she was able to get to the bathroom unaided?'

'Yes,' Rowan answered, honestly.

'Good. Then no, we will not disturb her.' He sounded relieved; extremely relieved, Rowan thought. Perhaps the bleeding ears had worried him, after all, a lot more than he'd cared to admit.

'Fetch your costume, Rowan,' von Metzer added. 'And let us go and break a leg.'

'WHERE IS MY SHADOW? WHERE IS IT?'

The Scriveners were sitting in the front row, clearly visible to Rowan as the curtain went up and he tiptoed out onto the raised platform. Below him, on the mattresses, Wendy, John, and Michael were feigning sleep, sucking their thumbs and cuddling bears.

Rowan's heart was thumping. He was a bag of nerves. Old Rosa raised a hand and waved to him. She might have been as deaf as a post, that woman, but there was nothing wrong with her sight and Rowan felt a flash of panic in case she should suddenly shout out 'Yoo-hoo, pet!'

One of the cobwebs on his tunic was tickling his neck, and his conker-brown leggings felt tight and hot. *Get into character,* he told himself. *Forget that you're really only a useless boring boy. Be Peter Pan—really be him. That's your family out there, watching this show. Impress them, go on!*

Slowly, taking his time, he stretched like a cat and took a few steps along the platform. Light steps.

Dancer's steps. Then he went up on tiptoe, raised a hand to shield his eyes and peered down, out, all around . . . searching, searching . . . *Where is my shadow? Where is it?*

In the wings, the low-risk entrusted with the torch held his breath and began, with great care and precision, to shine Tinker Bell's light all around the stage: flickering over the mattresses . . . darting to a coat stand . . . lingering on the pocket of a coat . . . away to a small chest of drawers . . .

The appearance of the light was Rowan's cue to move. Down from the platform he hurried, to burst onto the stage calling 'Tink! Tink! Have you found it?'

The audience cheered, or maybe it was just his family, making enough noise to sound like the whole audience. It was nice though—particularly as he'd barely said anything yet to deserve such a warm response. Down on his knees he went, in front of the chest of drawers. There were three drawers, and the shadow, he knew, would be in the bottom one.

From the top drawer he took a jack-in-the box, raised the lid and then fell back in exaggerated amazement as the jack popped out. That got a laugh and, inspired, he opened the middle drawer and got another laugh for trying on a child's seaside bucket as a hat.

This is fun, he thought, sliding open the bottom drawer. *I'm enjoying this.* The bottom drawer was empty. Nothing there at all. Frowning, he felt all around, his fingers touching only wood. It had been the stage-people's responsibility to take the shadow out of the pillowcase and put it in the drawer, while he was having his face painted, but they hadn't done it. They must have forgotten, he thought, or maybe they'd put it in one of the other drawers by mistake and he'd missed it.

Quickly, he checked the middle drawer, and then the top one—both empty. Well then . . . he would have to pretend—make the best of a bad job.

'HERE it is, Tink!' he cried out. *'But how am I to fix it back on?'* And he held up an imaginary shadow . . . danced around the stage with an imaginary shadow . . . thrust an imaginary shadow at a perplexed and tongue-tied Wendy . . . did a pretty good job, overall, he thought, in covering up for the stage-people's blunder.

When the first act was over, he stood in the wings, feeling extremely pleased with himself.

'What happened to the shadow?' Nurse Bradley hissed in his ear.

'I don't know,' he whispered back. *'It wasn't in the drawer. It's not my fault . . . '* And then he forgot about the shadow as Doctor Von edged past him, looking utterly miserable, and went out to break a leg.

Captain Hook. Dastardly villain. Would-be child killer. All-round bad egg. Von Metzer didn't even try to win favour by giving the role his all, and by the time he left the stage he was clearly, already, a failure. *The audience is against him,* Rowan realized. *Nobody's supposed to LIKE the baddie, exactly, but it's more than that . . .*

And Rowan was right. Nobody booed, and nobody hissed, but discomfort spread, palpably, across the hall as von Metzer recited his lines. Discomfort tinged with dislike. Had Rowan been able to pick out the faces of hospital staff, out there in the dark, he would have seen a sourness in their expressions that had nothing to do with the character von Metzer was struggling to portray, and everything to do with the man himself.

People who had never actually met von Metzer—including Rowan's own family—were thrown, more than anything, by the accent. Was it real, or phoney? Was this man a Jerry or not?

As he waited for his cue, Rowan noticed Daphne whisper something to Eddie Dobbs, and saw how the policeman patted his sister's arm, reassuringly. His mother and his nana were staring coldly at von Metzer as if trying to work him out and his father had a look on his face that said if Hook's accent was somebody's smart idea of a joke it was in pretty poor taste, given The Current Situation.

Only Rosa—deaf old Rosa—still had a smile on her face.

Doctor Von is a good man, Rowan wanted to yell from the wings. *Give him a chance will you?*

Then he was back on stage himself, and the audience cheered to see him—a slim, gawky lad, self-conscious yet endearing in his leaf-and-cobweb tunic; a nice English boy doing his best to act well.

Away from the spotlight von Metzer eased his hand from the flower pot and took a deep, steadying breath. He had felt the audience's hostility and although it was no less than he'd expected it was unsettling.

It got worse. It got so bad that, out in the fifth row, the director shuddered and longed for the show to be over. How, he wondered, could he have misjudged a thing so badly? Was he so out of touch with the public mood so far as the wretched war was concerned? It didn't help, of course, that von Metzer was making no effort whatsoever to be entertaining or even villainous in the role of Captain Hook. The man was a dummy. A dummy with a face as cold as yesterday's pudding, and a voice like Adolf Hitler's—no comedy in it at all.

Some of the patients, sensing the mood, but not understanding it, were getting agitated—cheering wildly whenever Peter Pan appeared, and the atmosphere lightened, and then rocking and mumbling whenever von Metzer spoke.

The near-fatal poisoning of Tinker Bell came as something of a relief, and the collective clapping and riotous belief in fairies nearly raised the roof. It didn't seem to matter that Tink's light wasn't fading prettily, only clicking jerkily on and off. Everyone called, at the tops of their voices, for it to stay . . . to grow . . . to light up the whole stage.

And Rowan, leaning forward and begging as loudly as anyone, for Tinker Bell to hang on, found himself hoping—really hoping—that Nurse Sarah Jane Springfield was out there after all, watching him do just as good a job of pretending to care about a torch beam as he had when he'd been stupid enough to swoon over her.

And then the curtain went down again, everyone scurried around with bits of pirate ship, two hefty male nurses pushed the crocodile into place, and it was time for Captain Hook to die.

They had rehearsed this scene very carefully, Rowan and Doctor Von.

'*Back, back, you mewling spawn*!' Hook was supposed to shout at the Darling children and the Lost Boys. '*And prepare, all of you, to die! A holocaust of children. There is something grand in the idea!'* That was the cue for Peter Pan to appear on the raised platform and for Hook to spot him and come after him, with a cutlass and his hook.

The Lost Boys, along with Wendy, John, and Michael, were huddled like chickens on the pretend-deck of the *Jolly Roger*—Wendy in her nightdress, the boys in striped pyjamas.

'Back! Back!' von Metzer began—and then he faltered. They weren't children, not really. But some of them, some of the low-risks cringing away from him like that, were so child-like in their minds, and the way they behaved, that he couldn't help but compare them to . . .

'Back!' he repeated, the word slicing the air, like a whip. *'You mewling spawn!'* And out in the audience someone, finally, hissed.

'And prepare, all of you, to . . . to . . . '

He couldn't say it. He couldn't bear to even think it.

They go in droves, the children, to a special house in the woods.

Those words, and those alone, were suddenly all there was. They filled the space between his ears like an explosion . . . like gas . . . like feathers being shaken by the old woman of the sky.

They go in droves . . . they go in droves . . .

Apart from that one long hiss, nobody in the hall made a sound as the silence grew and the Lost Boys cowered, and Captain Hook just stood there, speechless. The pause grew desperate. *'Get on with it!'* someone called.

Then: *'A holocaust . . . '* came Nurse Bradley's prompt, low and urgent, from the side of the stage. *'A holocaust of children . . . '*

And von Metzer looked up at Rowan, hovering anxiously above him, and then out into the audience—a blur of unforgiving English faces—and then back at little Wendy and the Lost Boys, their eyes round with genuine fright now, as they wondered what on earth this doctor was about to say—or do—to them all.

And all he could see were the flawed children of his homeland—the lost boys and girls of Germany—moving trustingly . . . so trustingly . . . through that open door.

And so, he removed the flower pot from his right hand, set it carefully down with the hook sticking up like a strange, curved root, turned on the heels of his villain's boots and walked right off the stage.

A murmur went through the audience, as they waited to see if he was coming back . . . planning to throw streamers . . . or what. And the Lost Boys looked at Wendy and Wendy looked at Peter Pan, and then the whole cast looked at Nurse Bradley, standing furious-faced in the wings, and it seemed pretty clear to all concerned that Doctor von Metzer had thrown in the towel and would not be finishing the show.

'Good riddance to Captain Hook!' Rowan improvised, quickly. 'He's gone for ever!' And he began to clap, harder than for believing in fairies, harder, even, than if he'd heard the war was over, and after a moment or two so did one or two members of the audience—tentatively at first (they'd wanted that Jerry in the jaws of the crocodile, preferably head first and from a great height) but, at last, with more conviction. And then the rest of the audience joined in and Nurse Bradley gave a frantic, waving, signal for the curtain to come down.

'Final scene!' she hissed. 'Pirate ship off! Nursery on!'

'Perhaps he's ill,' Rowan called down from the platform, under cover of the stage-people's clatter as they dismantled the *Jolly Roger*. 'Perhaps he was going to be sick, and didn't want to do it on stage. Perhaps—'

'Perhaps nothing,' Nurse Bradley growled. 'He's ruined my pantomime. Ruined it completely! Sick? I'll give him something to be sick about . . . '

The last scene passed in a rush. Wendy was too flustered to even pretend that she was going to miss Peter Pan, or Neverland, or any of the Lost Boys; and Michael and John kept edging closer and closer to one side of the stage in their eagerness to get off.

Only Rowan continued to do his best. And when it was all over, and he took his bow, the audience cheered him so wildly that, had he been in a different show, in another place entirely, he might actually have felt like a star.

Afterwards, wearing a dressing gown over his cobwebs and leaves, he was allowed to go into the hall to speak to his relatives before they left. He wouldn't be seeing them again for a while. More snow had been forecast, turning to blizzards over the next few days, so they had decided to be sensible and head back to London first thing in the morning.

'You were *wonderful*, pet,' his mother said. 'I was so proud!'

'Marvellous!' his nana agreed. 'Although, tell me—did Captain Hook mean to leave the stage the way he did? Was it in the script or did he simply lose his nerve?'

'Bad form if you ask me,' Eddie Dobbs declared. 'Putting on a Jerry accent like that. Not funny—not funny at all. Were you expecting it, like, or did he do it at the last minute? One of the more serious cases, is he? Unpredictable?'

'You did a good job, son,' his father remarked, before Rowan could answer Eddie Dobbs. 'Well done.'

Out of the corner of his eye, Rowan noticed John Wallace making his way towards the back of the hall. Sid and Donald had already gone, distressed over the way Doctor Von's performance had been received and wanting to get back to the ward. A male nurse, sitting right next to Sid, had muttered *'Bloody Nazi spy,'* halfway through the show, loud enough for everyone sitting around him to hear. And if Sid hadn't been such a terrible coward, he would have thumped that nurse into the middle of next week.

'John!' Rowan called out. 'Over here!'

John Wallace froze. Then he turned and, with obvious reluctance, began walking back across the hall, his feet moving slowly, as if through mud. *I should have left him alone,* Rowan realized. *But it's too late now . . .*

'John,' he said, as his friend drew closer. 'This is my father, Lawrence Scrivener. Dad—this is John Wallace.'

The two men shook hands, while Rowan watched, greedily. *Could his father tell? Could he look into John Wallace's eyes, just as John had looked into his, on the tray, and know that they were both poor souls from the last war—from the front?*

'You have the same cigarette cases,' he was going to say, just to help things along. But before he could speak a peculiar hush descended on the rest of the room and he turned to find that Doctor Von had come in and was whispering something, urgently, in the director's ear.

'Oh look,' said old Rosa, loudly. 'It's Captain Hook.

He's nowhere near as handsome without his curly wig, is he, Ive?'

'Hush, Rosa,' pleaded Daphne. 'Tell her, Mum.' And she moved behind the comforting solidity of Eddie Dobbs's body, just in case the crazy actor with the Jerry accent was about to cause trouble.

But as quickly as he'd arrived in the hall, Doctor Von left. The director clapped his hands for everyone's attention and cleared his throat. 'Thank you all so much for coming,' he said in his most amiable voice. 'But I've just been told that it's snowing quite heavily out there, and that visitors would be wise to leave now—straightaway—while the hill is still negotiable.'

'Right,' said Eddie Dobbs, for whom the prospect of being snowed in at a lunatic asylum made imprisonment in the van with the blue cross seem like a joy and a privilege. 'Best we make a move then.'

'Yes,' Rowan's mother agreed. 'Best we do. Goodbye, Rowan, pet. I can't tell you how lovely it's been to see you. And you'll be home very soon, the director says—by Easter, he thinks. And goodbye, Mister . . . ?'

'Wallace,' said John.

'Goodbye, Mister Wallace. I'm sorry it's all such a mad—I mean huge—rush.'

And in a flurry of hugs which unsettled Rowan's cobwebs, and back-pats which dislodged a few of his leaves, and reminders to wear his vests and eat everything he was given, particularly if it ended up being rationed, they were gone.

'You have a very interesting family,' John said. 'You're lucky.'

'Yes,' Rowan replied, and it seemed to him that they could both have been on stage just then, reading from a script.

A male nurse hurried over. 'Come on,' he ordered them both. 'Beddy-byes.'

Rowan frowned. 'Where's Doctor von Metzer?' he said. 'He told me he'd be on duty until midnight. Is he sick? I told Nurse Bradley he was probably sick.'

The nurse jerked his head towards the door. 'Save the talk,' he said. 'Move.'

Rowan stood his ground, John Wallace too. Something was wrong, they could sense it. Beyond the hustle to get visitors out, and return patients to the wards, something was very wrong.

'What's happening?' Rowan demanded to know. 'What's going on?'

The male nurse raised his eyes to the ceiling. *If this is what that new treatment does,* he thought, *if it makes every loony this lippy, I preferred it when we just tied the buggers to bath chairs and left 'em alone.*

'There's a patient missing,' he said, impatiently. 'Your Jerry's organizing a search party. Now *move,* or there'll be trouble.'

'FORGIVE ME'

One of the gardeners found her at first light, hanging from a tree. She had walked a long way, barefoot across the frozen lawn, and the tree was one of the closest to the high, iron gates as if she had tried to get as near as possible to the outside world before leaving it.

The first thing the director said, before thumping the top of his desk in a mixture of fury and regret, was, 'Thank God none of the visitors picked her out in their headlights.'

The gardener did not reply. He just stood there, with his cap in his hands like a strangled bird, and his boots dripping slush on the carpet.

'Thank you,' the director said to him after a while, his voice straining towards sympathy. 'You can go now. Take the rest of the day off.' The director wanted to tell that gardener to keep his mouth shut, but knew enough about the village, and the unstoppable way tongues wagged down there, not to bother.

It was eight o'clock in the morning. The search for Dorothea had been called off at one a.m., once every nook and cranny of the hospital, every broom cupboard and stairwell, every bathtub and bed, had been checked and checked again.

They could, the director knew, have combed the grounds more thoroughly (small torches, used with discretion, were allowed during the blackout, after all, just as a tiger's eye of light could be left between the bands of tape covering a car's headlamps). But the weather had got worse, so after checking the nearest outhouses himself, and tripping, twice, in the watery beam of a ridiculous torch, he had banned everyone from searching any further afield.

'We'll go out again at first light,' he had said, and so they had. Von Metzer was still out there somewhere, wading thigh-deep through snow, calling the girl's name.

The director moved, heavily, to the window. It was like a Christmas card out there, now that the snow had stopped falling: everything iced and larded; so bright it hurt his eyes.

The girl's family would be told the truth. No reason why not. She'd tried to do away with herself before. They'd all known she was a risk, and Sir Edward and Lady de Vere had washed their hands of her years ago. What was it he'd said to von Metzer, right here in this office, not so long ago? *'Nine times out of ten, a patient's rapid and irreversible deterioration is the best thing that could happen.'* Well this was irreversible all right.

Through the window he saw the German doctor moving jerkily over the lawn, plodding through snow like Good King Wenceslas. His head was lowered and his spine bowed, as if an invisible sack weighed him down. He wore no gloves or hat and, even from this distance, the director could see that his fingers and ears were red-raw from the cold.

After he'd passed, leaving a turmoil of marks in the perfect white, the director waited, counting the seconds it took a person to walk up the slippery stone steps, through the hospital's front entrance, and along the only corridor in the building that began, and ended, with carpet.

'Come in,' he said, when the knock came.

Von Metzer entered the room gasping, his nose beginning to drip from the relative warmth of being indoors. 'There is no sign of her,' he panted. 'No sign . . . I have searched the walk of the rhododendrons . . . the glasshouses also . . . and the sheds where the tools for gardening are kept . . . I am wondering, maybe she managed to slip unseen through the gates—early last night, while people were leaving in their cars and on their bicycles. I am thinking, perhaps she has walked as far as the village and that . . . '

'Sit down,' the director said to him. 'Sit down, Doctor von Metzer, and listen.'

Rowan couldn't—wouldn't—believe it. For many days and nights he kept expecting Dorothea to walk back into Ward Five with a look on her face that said 'Fooled you!' She would be cold and thin from hiding somewhere—somewhere brilliant where no one had thought to look—and the first thing she would want would be a nice hot bath behind the duck-and-frog screen,

After that, she would ask for her looking glass and spend a while fussing with her hair. It would have grown a bit, that hair, and she would be pleased about that. Then: 'Joan's back, everyone!' she would call, in her parroty voice, and they would all cheer. He and John Wallace, Sid and Donald and Doctor Von would all cheer themselves hoarse.

Eventually—the next day maybe, after she'd slept—Dorothea would lay the shadow across his bed, and admit to having taken it from his pillow case while his back had been turned. 'It was just a joke, stupid,' she would say. 'I was bored, all right? Bored, bored, bored . . . '

When it finally sank in that Dorothea would not be coming back—not that day, not the next, not ever—Rowan went to Doctor Von and demanded a treatment.

'I want to forget what she did,' he said. 'I can't bear knowing.'

Von Metzer said he understood, but that sometimes the things that hurt the most in life were the things you most needed to face. Head on. No running away. Sorrow shaped a person, he said. However much it hurt, it made you stronger, in the end.

Rowan thought that was the biggest load of tosh he'd ever heard in his life. 'I can't sleep,' he said. 'I think about her all the time. I go over and over it all until I feel sick. I keep thinking . . . if only I'd tightened those straps properly, or told you they were loose . . . I keep thinking it's all my fault. I helped her. If it wasn't for me, she'd still be alive.'

'Rowan.' Von Metzer took both the boy's hands, held him steady. 'Listen to me. Dorothea took her own life.

You are not responsible for that and you must not blame yourself.'

Rowan hung his head. Deep down, he had sort-of known that he wasn't really to blame; that Dorothea had already made up her mind. He had just needed to hear it said. To be absolved.

There was something else though: 'She used my shadow,' he whispered, 'didn't she?'

Von Metzer flinched. He had let all of them know, here on Ward Five, what Dorothea had done, for he would not lie and have them find out later, from a nurse or one of the low-risks. He had kept it simple though. Just the one sad fact—'Dorothea has committed suicide.'

How? they had wanted to know, not for ghoulish reasons but because they did not want the lifelong torment of wondering. 'She hanged herself,' von Metzer had told them. 'Outside, in the hospital grounds.'

How stark it had sounded, but enough . . . enough. The real heartbreak was in the details, as it always was, and he had meant to spare them those.

'She did, didn't she?' Rowan persisted. 'She used my shadow, instead of a rope.'

'Yes,' von Metzer admitted. 'She did.'

Later, towards evening, John Wallace pointed out that since it was Twelfth Night, the Christmas decorations really ought to come down. Packing the paper chains away in a cardboard box, von Metzer took the opportunity to remove Dorothea's looking glass, comb, and snowstorm from his desk and pack them away too. Her clothes, and few other possessions, had been parcelled up already and posted back to her family. Dorothea herself, they had not wanted, although her father had sent a generous donation for the upkeep of her grave.

Sadly, von Metzer placed the looking glass, the comb, and the snowstorm in among the decorations. He simply didn't know what else to do with them.

From close by the window, Rowan watched. They were snowed in—drifts five feet high had cut the hospital off from the rest of the world and it seemed, to him, that everything and everyone was being buried . . . stifled . . . put away for good.

'Don't,' he called, sharply, as the lid went down on the cardboard box. 'Don't do that.'

Von Metzer looked up tentatively, then removed the lid as Rowan came towards him. 'If you would like these things, Rowan,' he said, 'then please have them. Dorothea, I am certain, would have been happy about that.'

The snowstorm, being heavy, had gone right to the bottom of the box. Groping through paper chains Rowan found it and lifted it out. 'She said this was rubbish,' he told von Metzer.

'She would,' von Metzer replied, with the tremor of a smile. 'That is exactly what Dorothea would have said.'

Rowan gave the snowstorm a swift, hard shake. 'I'm angry with her now,' he said. 'I'm so furious with her I could . . . I could *kill* her. That's wicked, isn't it? That's a wicked thing to say about someone who's already killed themselves.'

'It is normal, Rowan,' von Metzer told him. 'It is perfectly normal to think that way. And she tricked you don't forget—made you a part of what she did, against your knowledge and your will. You must forgive her for that.'

For a moment they watched as the snowstorm settled.

'Why did she do it, Doctor Von? Was it because of the pantomime? Or because she heard a voice? Did a voice in her head tell her to do that to herself?'

Von Metzer switched his gaze from the snowstorm to the boy's troubled face. 'It is impossible for me—for anyone—to understand, for certain, why,' he replied. 'All I know for sure—and you must remember this, Rowan—is that if Dorothea had only waited . . . allowed some time to pass . . . all that she felt to be unbearable in her life would have altered. Like your kaleidoscope, yes? One shift and all is changed. You see things a different way.'

Rowan nodded. He could sort of understand that. Only: 'She might never have got her angel back,' he said, 'however long she'd waited. Maybe that's the thing she couldn't bear—the thing that made her want to die. She couldn't go on without Joan.'

Von Metzer swallowed, hard. He couldn't look at Rowan any more. 'Do you wish for the looking glass as well?' he said. 'Or the comb?'

'No,' Rowan replied. 'Only this. I'll keep this. You don't usually get a rainbow do you, after it snows, only after rain. And there are two colours missing—orange and blue. It's all wrong, like Dorothea was, which is probably why I like it.'

Much later, alone in his room, von Metzer took his Christmas card from Professor E. out of the drawer and looked at the picture, one last time. Then he placed the card in the box, along with the paper chains, the comb, and the looking glass, taped down the lid and put the box beneath his bed.

He had expected to weep, as he stowed the box away. For Dorothea. For himself. For the children on the card . . . for the epileptic, the retarded boy, the cripple, the blind girl, the deaf and dumb girl, and the schizophrenic. For John Wallace and the ghost of his carol singer. For the whole of mankind.

Instead, he remained on his knees, his forehead pressed against the iron rim of his bed. *I am a good man,* he reminded whoever, or whatever, might be listening. *But I have been a very poor doctor. I should, it is true, have stayed in my homeland. But I made my decision and that is that. My patients are here, my work is here, yet all has been neglected—despised, at times—while I wallowed in guilt and remorse. I failed Dorothea just as surely as I failed the damaged children of Germany. Forgive me.*

THE MOAT AWASH WITH CABBAGES

Dear Rowan,

At last the big freeze appears to be over. The snowdrops are out, and the top of your nana's Anderson shelter is an absolute riot of yellow and purple crocuses (at least until Clark Gable digs them up!). Today, what with the sun shining and a blackbird singing in the courtyard, it really does feel as if spring is in the air even though we are not quite into March.

We are all so pleased to hear that you will be coming home in April. Your father and I will spend Easter weekend in Weymouth, visiting Laurel, then that will give me a couple of weeks to make your room nice, and bake a chocolate cake or two (with real chocolate and real eggs—only don't tell the Ministry of Food!) before we come and collect you.

We will see about school. Don't worry for now. Your father thinks a private tutor, coming here to the house, might be the best option for a while. Everything is so topsy-turvy still, with so many children away and the 'situation' dragging on and on.

I'm writing yet another 'Dig for Victory' article, encouraging people to grow their own veg now that so much of our food is either rationed, or in short supply. Apparently, the moat around the Tower of London has been given over to cabbages and there are even plans to turn the centre court at Wimbledon into an allotment. Imagine that!

Keep well, pet. The director tells me you are listening regularly to the wireless and that as soon as it's a bit warmer you will be given jobs to do in the hospital grounds. We are all so happy that you are well, and so close to coming home.

With all our love for now

Your mother

Rowan folded his mother's letter back into its envelope and set it aside. He didn't want to think about going home. It scared him—he didn't feel ready, whatever his mother thought and the director said. Picturing the Tower of London, though, lapped around by cabbages, and the country's most famous tennis court given over to runner beans or carrots made him smile. Surreal. That was the word for it. Surreal, like his father's paintings.

'Hey, Rowan.' Donald called out. 'Time for *ITMA*—quick, or you'll miss the start.'

ITMA stood for *It's That Man Again*, a comedy show on the wireless which the whole nation was hooked on. Eddie Dobbs, according to Rowan's mother, had joked that if Hitler was ever going to invade Britain, half past eight on a Thursday evening would be the ideal time to do it since no one would even notice—they'd be glued by their ears to *ITMA*.

Rowan liked it that he and Donald, John Wallace and Sid, had *ITMA* in common with the rest of the nation. He just wished, every time, that Dorothea was there, to listen to the programme as well. She would, he told John Wallace, have loved the bumbling Colonel Chinstrap, and the man in the Office of Twerps who was Minister of Aggravation and Mysteries. And she would have done a perfect take-off of Mrs Mopp, the char: *'Can I do you now, sir?'*

John Wallace had disagreed. 'Isn't it more likely,' he'd said, 'that she would have stayed in bed, shouting things out to spoil our enjoyment?'

At first, Rowan had been shocked by that. It was speaking ill of the dead. Perhaps, he'd reflected, when you'd killed as many people as John Wallace had, it made you less respectful of the recently-deceased. Later though, after he'd thought about it some more, he had to admit John had probably been right. Dorothea had been a pain, a lot of the time, and would have carried on being one had she chosen to stay alive.

Still, as he took his chair across to where the wireless was (Doctor Von had brought proper chairs onto the ward—chairs you could pick up and shift around) Rowan wouldn't have cared if Dorothea had ranted and screeched from the start of the show to the final credits. She was lodged in his mind, as prickly as a conker case, and he missed her so much that it hurt.

That night, as on every night, she haunted his dreams, stealing his things and laughing in his face. Then one of the dreams shifted its focus and he found himself outside, following Dorothea across the hospital lawn. It was summer, the sun just setting, and Dorothea's nightgown glimmered, as she disappeared between some trees. When he reached the gates Rowan saw her again, hurrying away down the hill—hurrying so fast that her nightgown billowed and it seemed she was about to take flight. 'Wait for me!' he shouted, rattling the bars of the gate. 'Wait—I'll come with you. Don't leave me behind.'

Rowan talked, every day, to Doctor Von, particularly about his dreams. Doctor Von was very interested in those dreams—in their twists and turns and hidden meanings. 'Isn't it obvious what they mean?' Rowan said to him, tetchily. 'I miss her. I hate it that she killed herself. What else is there to know?'

Von Metzer was worried about Rowan. For although the boy spoke openly, and often, about Dorothea he had yet to shed a single tear over the loss of her. And when asked how he felt about returning to his family he looked puzzled, and then uncertain, as if he had reasons of his own to believe it would never actually happen.

In group chats, he spoke a great deal about death. Did

Donald believe in Heaven? Did John? And if there was a God, would He ever forgive Dorothea for killing herself, or would Dorothea end up in Hell or that place beginning with 'p' that was neither one thing nor the other?

'Purgatory,' said Donald, whose brain was ticking better by the day.

'Purgatory,' Rowan repeated, morosely. 'Dorothea would be bored there. But then, she'd be just as bored in Heaven too, I expect. Bored out of her skull. There ought to be another place, don't you think? For people who aren't wicked, or saintly, or anywhere in the middle—just strange. Maybe there is such a place, but we only find out about it after we're dead. Maybe it's a bit like this hospital, only holier, and with no need for lavatories.'

It was good, von Metzer knew, that Rowan felt able to talk like this but the boy was becoming morbid. Obsessive. And that dream he'd had, about wanting to follow Dorothea to wherever she was bound . . . you didn't have to be a devotee of the late Doctor Freud to understand, and be disturbed by, the implications of that.

'Fly that past me again,' the director said, with an exaggerated sigh. 'You want to take the test-cases to Canterbury? To visit the cathedral and have tea and cake in a shop?'

'That is correct,' von Metzer said. 'And to a beach next week, to look at the sea. And, later this month, to a cinema, to see a film. *The Wizard of Oz* is coming. They would all enjoy that, I think.'

The director shook his head, amused yet exasperated.

'But this is a hospital, doctor,' he said. 'A private asylum for the mentally deranged, not a country hotel. We are not obliged to organize day-trips—in fact I would advise, very strongly, against it.'

Von Metzer stood his ground. 'My test-cases have a pressing need to go beyond the gates,' he insisted. 'Rowan Scrivener, in particular, should mix with ordinary people as often as possible, before the time comes for him to return to his home. I am worried about that boy. He needs—how can I put this—taking out of his own head.'

The director frowned. 'What do you mean "taking out of his own head"?' he said. 'Don't tell me he's regressed. Don't tell me he's showing renewed signs of schizophrenic . . . '

'No,' von Metzer reassured him. 'Not that. But he is troubled. Deeply troubled—about the death of Dorothea, about death itself . . . about who he is, and his place, and worth, in this world.'

The director smiled, wryly. 'A perfectly normal adolescent boy, in other words,' he said.

'No,' von Metzer repeated, impatient to be understood. 'Please listen. You have read the studies, surely, on the frequency and timing of suicides in institutions such as this? You understand, I am sure, the risk of "clustering"—the copying of both the act, and the method, by patients who were close to the original suicide victim?'

The director shifted, uncomfortably, on the seat of his chair. 'I've read something along those lines,' he agreed. 'So, you honestly think Rowan Scrivener might . . . ?'

'I hope not,' von Metzer said, gravely. 'I most sincerely hope not, Doctor Thomas. But the possibility plays on my mind.'

'Yes, of course . . . it would do.' The director wasn't smiling now. He was seeing the trials spiralling towards disaster as test-case after test-case developed suicidal tendencies. He was imagining a scandal as opposed to a triumph . . . a hasty cover-up instead of glowing reports in *The Lancet*.

One suicide was just about sustainable—inevitable, you could argue, given the acutely disturbed natures of patients involved in the trials. One you could explain away without it detracting too much from the treatment's overall success. But more than one . . .

'By all means, take your test-cases to Canterbury,' the director told von Metzer. 'If you think it will keep them on an even keel, I will even pay for the cakes.'

THE WINDOW ABLAZE WITH PEOPLE

It was the strangest sensation, being on a bus; so strange that Rowan feared he might be sick. It wasn't the motion of the vehicle, though, churning up his innards, it was the fact of being a passenger—a person out in public, a boy with somewhere to go—that was getting to him.

The bus was crowded and after a couple of stops both von Metzer and John Wallace rose from their seats so that two elderly women could sit down.

One of those women settled herself next to Rowan, taking up most of the space. Her coat smelled of mothballs and her hat had a spray of artificial cherries pinned to it, and once the sick-feeling in his stomach had passed, Rowan found he was longing to talk to her: to ask her where she was going; how many grandchildren she had; whether she listened to *ITMA* on Thursday nights; what she was having for her tea . . .

If I start a conversation, will she guess where I'm from? he wondered. *Will she want to swap seats—or even jump off the bus—rather than be next to a loony from the house up on the hill?*

In front of him, Sid and Donald were sitting very quietly, gazing at the passing scenery as if the trees and the hedges, the houses and the barns were good things to eat or drink. Sid was nervous, Rowan could tell, and Donald was doubtless thinking much too hard about everything—but they looked normal enough, at least from the back.

Glancing up, Rowan caught John Wallace's eye, and John nodded at him: *you're doing fine.* Of the four of them—the four patients—John was the one most used to being out in the world. He would have been back in it too, just as soon as Christmas was over, had he not volunteered as a test-case. He wasn't having treatments any more—none of them were—but being eased back to normality, according to Doctor Von, was an important part of the process.

'We are soon to arrive in Canterbury,' von Metzer announced as the bus slowed down. 'And it is straight to the cathedral we will be going.' His voice was loud, he was so used to calling across wards, and, as he spoke, Rowan felt the woman sitting next to him stiffen inside her mothball coat. A conversation, further down the bus, trailed away into silence and a young mother tightened her hold on a little boy on her lap, bending her body forward as if to shield the child from danger.

It was a relief to get off that bus.

'Now . . . ' said von Metzer. 'The cathedral . . . is that it over there? I am supposing it must be.'

You couldn't really miss Canterbury Cathedral, or mistake it for anything else and Rowan couldn't help smiling as he imagined what Dorothea might have said just then.

(*'What did you think it was, Doctor Von? A rabbit hutch? The local chippie?'*) Yet it wasn't the cathedral's imposing arches and pinnacles that grabbed Rowan's attention as he and the others stepped into its shadow; it was the people milling all around: the soldiers, the men in smart suits, the women pushing prams or carrying bags of shopping, the old folk sitting on benches, resting their bones. Such ordinary people . . . not a nurse or a helpless feeble in sight.

Donald and Sid were walking so close together that they could have been joined at the hip. It was months—years—since either of them had been out in public. In fact the last time Sid had gone anywhere—to buy shoes in London's Bond Street—it had ended, disastrously, with him cursing and lashing out because nobody was calling him 'Your Majesty' or bowing as he passed by.

'All right, Sid?' said John Wallace.

'I am, John, thank you,' Sid replied. 'Surprisingly, I am.'

'Donald?'

'A lot to think about, John . . . a very great deal for the brain to take in. But I'm fine . . . fine.'

And so they entered the cathedral. Wide-eyed and reverent. And 'Oh, my,' breathed Rowan. 'Look at all the people in the windows.'

They stood in a row—Rowan, Doctor Von, John Wallace, Sid and Donald—and tipped their heads back, the better to study the expanse of stained glass stretching so high and far above their faces that the figures in the topmost panels could have been angels or devils, saints or mortals—it was impossible to tell.

The beauty of it all though . . . the blaze and the glow

of it . . . After the blandness of hospital walls and the ugliness of barred windows, it was intoxicating. It made them dizzy.

'I will lay thy stones with fair colours, and lay their foundations with sapphires,' said Donald, dreamily. 'And I will make thy windows of agates, and thy gates of carbuncles, and all thy borders of pleasant stones.'

A middle-aged man standing just in front of them turned round, impressed. 'Is that from the Bible?' he asked. 'Or have you just made it up?'

Donald squinted, thoughtfully, while the others waited, willing him to know, and to answer for himself.

'Isaiah fifty-four,' Donald said, after just a moment's pause. 'Verses eleven to twelve.'

'Thank you,' the man replied. 'I'll remember that. Might even look it up. It's rather nice, isn't it, apart from the mention of carbuncles.'

He turned away—or half-turned, anyway, before Donald's right hand shot out and stopped him. 'No,' Donald said, his voice rising in sudden alarm. 'You're thinking, aren't you, of an infected mass, filled with fluid, pus and dead tissue? But no . . . no . . . that's not it. That's not it at all. A carbuncle, within the specific context of Isaiah fifty-four, verses eleven to twelve, is a red garnet—either pyrope or almandine, but definitely from a group of isometric aluminosilicate minerals that form twelve or twenty-four faced crystals in metamorphic rocks, and glitter quite beautifully in the dark.'

'All right,' the man answered, tugging nervously and uselessly, to free his left arm. 'All right, old pal . . . I get it. But I have to go now. I'm meeting my wife at the pulpit.'

'Donald,' von Metzer said, 'let go, please, of the gentleman's arm.'

Surprised, his eyes still shining with visions of a jewel-encrusted Jerusalem, Donald did as he'd been told.

'Sorry,' he called out, as the man scuttled away. 'Sorry about that.'

Tea and cake, von Metzer said, heartily. Tea and cake might be just the ticket next, for he, personally, had a parched throat, and was longing to try an English tart.

Rowan said no. There were other windows to look at, he said, and he, personally, wanted to see every one. 'I'm trying to find Saint Joan,' he explained. 'I know I might not recognize her, unless they've done her in a stained-glass fire, but Dorothea wouldn't have left this place until she'd looked among all the people, in all the windows, so I'm going to do it for her. She'd want me to. She'd want us all to look, to try and find Joan of Arc.'

He was gabbling. He was sweating. What Donald had just done . . . it would have been all right, back on Ward Five. No one would have shied away from him there, or tried to cover up for his strangeness with talk of tea and cake. They didn't belong here, that was the problem. They were loonies and test-cases and the sooner they got back to the hospital the better. Only . . . Dorothea would have stayed so, for her sake, so would he.

'That's a good idea of yours, kid,' Sid volunteered. And John Wallace and Donald agreed, and so off they all trooped, in search of Dorothea's angel.

It took a long time, that fruitless search. In the end, Doctor Von had to ask one of the building's official tour guides whether Joan of Arc was in a window anywhere.

She wasn't, the guide said. Definitely not. And Rowan couldn't help noticing that he kept a sharp eye on them, after that, as if *'Is Joan of Arc in a window?'* was not an innocent question, but some kind of coded message, and Doctor Von a bumbling Jerry spy who had come in and delivered his information to the wrong person.

'We must go now,' von Metzer said, eventually. 'I am glad that we stayed. You were right, Rowan, to suggest it and I am sorry for my hastiness, earlier, in saying that we should leave. But now we really must go, or we will be missing the final bus.'

'What about our cakes?' asked Rowan.

'There is no longer the time,' von Metzer replied. 'We have feasted our eyes instead, yes? On saints and kings and prophets. In some ways that is better. Food for the soul.'

Back at the hospital, von Metzer sat with each test-case in turn, to discuss the trip to Canterbury before writing his reports.

Rowan, he discovered, was in two minds about the outing: uncertain whether it had been worthwhile, overall, or too full of anxieties to be remembered as a pleasure.

'I'm sorry about the cakes,' Rowan said. 'But I'm glad we looked for Joan. It's what Dorothea would have wanted.'

'Never mind, for now, about Dorothea,' von Metzer replied, gently. 'How did you feel, Rowan, about being away from the hospital?'

'Scared,' Rowan admitted.

Von Metzer waited which, Rowan knew by now, meant *go on*.

'I was scared,' he continued, 'in case one of us—in case I—got into a panic. Mostly I was worried about someone getting hurt, like when Donald grabbed that man's arm, I thought *Oh, no, here we go . . .* I thought: if anyone guessed we were from the hospital, we might have been laughed at or . . . I don't know . . . spat at. Attacked even. And I felt . . . useless.'

'Useless?'

'Yes.'

Again the waiting.

Rowan sighed. 'I don't like going out,' he said. 'Being in the real world, among ordinary people . . . I'm no good at it. I'm like . . . I'm like a dot out there. Small and insignificant.'

'We are all small and insignificant, Rowan,' von Metzer said, with the hint of a smile. 'Particularly in a cathedral.'

Glumly, Rowan shook his head. 'I'm insignificant everywhere,' he said. 'I might as well not exist.'

Von Metzer looked startled. He couldn't stop himself.

'Oh, it's all right,' Rowan added, quickly. 'I'm not about to do anything stupid, not like Dorothea. I'm just scared about going home, that's all. My mother says she can't wait for us all to return to normal but . . . what if it's impossible? For me, I mean. What if all the worry about not being normal, and interesting, and able to fit in, makes me panic again—*what if the Voice comes back?*'

Von Metzer thought very hard before answering. 'One day at a time, Rowan,' he said. 'You will take it one day at a time and try, always, to have faith in yourself.' It was not a satisfactory answer, he knew that. But then, he was not a god, or a prophet, he knew that too.

'HE'S A LOONY. WHO WOULD LISTEN?'

The following day, von Metzer passed Sarah Jane Springfield in a corridor. He had known she was back at work but this was the first time, since her terrible clash with Dorothea, that they had actually crossed paths.

She passed him with her nose in the air and it was as much as he could do not to curse her.

'Wait,' he said, before she could disappear around a corner and into Ward One.

She stopped, her face defiant, as if daring him to blame her for Dorothea's death. And although he longed to do precisely that—if only to shift a pile of guilt from his own soul—von Metzer knew it would not be fair, or even necessary. This girl knew what she had done, just as surely as he knew, and would always know, the part he himself had played in driving Dorothea across that frozen lawn.

One thing, though, needed saying:

'You are to come nowhere near Ward Five,' he told her. 'Do not approach my ward or have anything to do with my test-cases. Rowan Scrivener, in particular, would be greatly disturbed by your presence.'

Sarah Jane turned very pink. 'I don't know what you're talking about,' she said, haughtily.

'I think you do,' von Metzer insisted. 'I think you know exactly what I am talking about. You may not know—more likely you do not care—but Rowan Scrivener heard every word you said to Dorothea, that time on the pantomime stage. Every word.'

'Pah!'

Such a short exclamation . . . but so full of contempt that von Metzer could tell that Nurse Springfield had not lost any sleep, and nor would she, ever, over what Rowan Scrivener may or may not have overheard. *It's his word against mine,* said that 'pah!'. *He's a loony. Who would listen?*

He should, he thought afterwards, have left the conversation right there. He should have turned and gone about his business, leaving the girl to stew—was that the right expression? To stew, and to ponder, and to maybe see herself, eventually, as a person of poor quality. Inferior. Insignificant. Aspiring, one might even say, to the grandeur of being a dot.

The anger, though, that came roaring out of him, wasn't just for Rowan Scrivener. It was for all the so-called loonies he had ever known, and treated. It was for the sadness in John Wallace's eyes, and the hunger in the faces of Donald and Sid as they had watched the world go by, through the rain-streaked window of a bus. It was for the ones reduced to oily smoke in the secret silence of a forest. It was for the way a young girl had smarmed wisps of her hair across the scorch marks on her temples.

'Young woman!' he raged. 'You are not fit to hold a candle to most of the patients here. Get out of my sight—go . . . go!'

Nurse Springfield backed away so quickly that she banged against a wall. Male nurses appeared within seconds, running from the wards, bulldog faced and with the muscles in their arms already clenched. Realizing that this was not, after all, a patient going berserk, but the Jerry doctor having a rant, they hung back. Reluctantly.

Knowing that those nurses would just love to thump a Jerry, and guessing, quite correctly, that given a bit more provocation they might hammer von Metzer into the linoleum, Nurse Springfield took a deep and daring breath:

'Keep your filthy hands to yourself,' she yelled. 'I've told you before—I'm not interested. I wouldn't touch a Jerry for anything. I'd sooner *die*.'

And for a girl who couldn't usually act for toffee she was good. Very good. And her audience believed every word.

For once, the director did not need to weigh up his options, or have anything flown past him a second time.

'You're lucky those boys didn't break both your arms,' he said after the male nurses, having shoved von Metzer into the office and spat out their accusations, had gone stomping from the room. 'They've been turned down for active service—flat feet and a stutter—so there's a lot of pent-up aggression there.'

'The girl lied,' von Metzer told him. 'I swear to you, on my life, that I did not lay my fingers on her.'

'You know what?' the director replied. 'I believe you. Unfortunately, I'm in a minority of one.'

Von Metzer saw some hope in that. 'One is a start,' he said. 'One person can become two, and then three, and then four . . . it should not be impossible to clear my name.'

The director shook his head. He had already reached a decision. 'Nurse Bradley was right,' he said. 'With things the way they are, this is not a good time for a German to be here at this hospital, in charge of an important trial. Some of the nurses think you're a spy—did you know that?'

Von Metzer shrugged. He wasn't surprised.

'So if it gets rumoured around the village that you're a sexual deviant into the bargain . . . well, I can't afford the scandal, doctor. You do see, don't you, what a difficult position this puts me in?'

The sun was shining into the room, pooling on the director's desk and soothing the back of von Metzer's head. There was real warmth in that sun, von Metzer noticed. A promise, at last, of spring. And it was good to see it splashed on the desk in one big block of light, not cut into stripes by bars on the window, the way it was on the wards.

And as he stared at that square of brightness it dawned on von Metzer that within this unjust and unsavoury situation lay an unexpected, yet surely God-given, means of escape. Back to Germany. To Munich, where he would seek out Professor E. and work—in secret and without rest—to prevent as many more children as possible from following the ones whose lives—whose very names—had already been wiped out and forgotten.

'I will leave this place,' he said. 'Just as soon as Rowan Scrivener has been reunited with his family, I will go from here.'

The director looked hugely relieved.

'It is for the best,' he agreed. 'At least for the time being.'

'So, you will release me from my contract?'

'I will. Yes.'

'And the trials? If I go, I cannot promise to return. Anything could happen—with the war, with me . . . '

The director told him not to worry about the trials. 'I think we can safely say,' he said, 'that they have already proved a resounding success. Rowan Scrivener, John Wallace, Donald Granger, Sid Eccles . . . the shocks have worked wonders on all four of them, wouldn't you agree?'

'Perhaps,' von Metzer answered him. 'Perhaps not. Sometimes, doctor, I wonder . . . did the electricity banish the voice in Rowan Scrivener's head or was it something else—his faith in the treatment? . . . his own willpower? . . . some click or twist in his brain that might have happened anyway, whether he had come to us or not?

'John Wallace, it is true, is a less tormented soul but, then, it is no longer the time of year for carol singers. Donald's mind is sharper now. Sid Eccles is no longer the great big coward. But they have helped each other, in that respect, and been assisted, also, by the comradeship and understanding of Rowan and John.

'So you see, Doctor Thomas, electroconvulsive therapy may not be the great and wonderful cure we have all imagined it to be. And I, certainly, will not administer it to the brain of a patient again. Ever.'

The director took up his golden pen. He was beyond fed-up. Listening to von Metzer unpick months of research—unravelling the whole trial with one sentence after another—he was sinking and wallowing in gloom. And as his visions of glory . . . of articles in *The Lancet* . . . of patients coming in droves to the hospital for this new and wonderful treatment . . . faded away to nothing he began to doodle on a sheet of blotting paper in front of him on the desk.

Von Metzer was still talking. 'Compassion . . . human kindness . . . the effects of these, far more than the shocks, I have seen and can measure with confidence. Cruelty too. And just recently I have come to a startling thought: is a person's strangeness always to be seen as such a terrible thing? A thing to be altered, hidden away or even, in extreme cases—'

'Enough,' the director interrupted him. 'I understand. You've made your point; a totally unscientific one, but a point nonetheless. I'll give you three weeks to complete your reports and present your conclusions. And if I can cobble together a report out of them for *The Lancet* I will—although after listening to that load of waffle I'm not holding my breath.'

Von Metzer stood up. He felt full of energy all of a sudden; flooded through with new ambition.

'Thank you,' he said. 'For your understanding. For giving me another chance.'

Left alone, the director continued to doodle on the blotter, until his golden pen ran out of ink. *My 'understanding'?*

he thought, as he contemplated the brain he had drawn—a brain with flower-doodles in the temporal lobe, zigzags and hearts in the cerebellum, and a game of noughts and crosses where the spinal cortex should have gone. *I swear, the more I learn here, about the workings of the human mind, the less I truly understand.*

THE RAT ON A SACKFUL OF SECRETS

'So you're leaving the hospital too?'

'I am, Rowan, yes, but not straightaway. I have my reports to finish. Some loose strings to tie up.'

'So what will happen to Ward Five?'

'It will return to the way it was before, a ward for epileptics, I believe, and the general paralytics.' *And suicide risks*, von Metzer thought, but didn't say.

'Back to normal then,' said Rowan, meaning it as a joke.

'Indeed,' von Metzer replied, not getting it.

Sid and Donald agreed they would return to Ward One as happier men. John Wallace said he was ready to go home—back to his lodgings in Maidstone. 'I might get a dog,' he said, 'if my landlady doesn't object. Just a small one; a rescue dog perhaps.'

'You should talk to my nana,' Rowan told him. 'My nana will find you a dog. Or you could come to London, on the train, and choose one for yourself, from her rescue centre.'

'I might do that, Rowan,' John said. 'Thank you.'

They were sitting above Dover beach—sitting in a row, on the very edge of the promenade, dangling their legs and eating jam sandwiches. Behind them, most of the grand hotels were shuttered and closed. Even with Easter coming, no one wanted to holiday here. Not with the war raging just across the channel.

'It's very peaceful,' Sid observed. 'Very good for the nerves, sitting here above the beach. I could listen to the sea all day. I could live by it, I think, and never be anxious again with the sound of waves in my ears.'

'It's a shame we can't paddle,' said Rowan. 'Although it's probably freezing cold in there, and those stones would hurt our feet.'

Apart from a few seagulls hoping, nastily, for crusts, the beach was deserted. Great rolls of barbed wire had been stretched across the shingle—more to stop the enemy wading ashore, Rowan supposed, than to prevent a boy from paddling. All the same . . .

Peering through and beyond the loops of wire he could see the boats at anchor in the harbour. Not fishing boats or pleasure cruisers but the Royal Navy's torpedo and gunboats, all floating quietly on the grey-green water.

'It is getting chilly,' von Metzer said, after a while. 'We should go now, to wait for our bus.'

The seagulls rose with them, hovering and shrieking; getting ready to dive-bomb for crumbs.

Turning away from the sea, Rowan was struck by the sight of the cliffs—the white cliffs of Dover—too far away to touch or try to climb, but as surprising to look upon as a perfect smile. And they were strangely familiar, although he was sure he had never been to this part of England before.

Father's painting, he remembered, after racking his brains. *The one with the girl's head in it—the girl with the sea-weed hair. These cliffs are in father's painting.*

'They're your last glimpse of England,' John Wallace said, for he too was staring at the whiteness of the cliffs. 'When you cross the channel to France, I mean. And then, they're the first things you see coming back. If you come back.'

'They're grubbier, close to,' said Sid. 'The closer you get, the dirtier they are.'

'Formations of calcium carbonate,' said Donald. 'Accentuated by streaks of black flint. Not a true white at all, you're quite right about that, Sid.'

The bus stop was in the middle of town, outside a post office. Their bus was late, so they had plenty of time to study the various posters and advertisements in the post office window.

The biggest poster of all was right in the centre. It showed a rat—a huge black thing with its teeth bared and a Nazi swastika emblazoned on its flanks. It was about to rip into a sackful of grain. Only the sack had the words 'War Secrets' on it and the title of the poster, in big letters across the top, blared 'STARVE HIM WITH SILENCE'.

Upset, Rowan turned away from the window and looked up at the sky . . . then across at a blank stone wall . . . then up at the sky again—anywhere but at the rat, and the words, and the big bag of secrets.

He didn't properly understand that poster. He just

knew it was the ugliest thing he had seen for a very long time, and that it had spoiled his afternoon.

Behind him, in the queue, a couple of women began talking about other posters they'd seen, and it didn't take long for Rowan to work out, from what they said, that there was a big campaign going on, here in the outside world, to stop people giving information to the enemy, through gossip and careless talk.

'They're all over the place,' one of the women said, meaning the posters, not the enemy. 'You must have seen the "Walls Have Ears" one, Gert—two women talking about the war, with Hitler's face behind them, all over the blessed wallpaper. Have you seen that one?'

Her friend made a dismissive sound. 'I've seen it,' she said. 'And the "Keep it under your Hat" one, and the one that says "Be like Dad—Keep Mum"! Seems to me they're all a blinking waste of paper . . . Do you know any secrets, Beryl, that could lose us the war if the Nazis got wind of them?'

The woman called Beryl gave a wicked chuckle.

'Oh, I know plenty of secrets, Gert,' she said. 'I know secrets that would make Hitler blush red as a cherry. But they're none of 'em a threat to national security . . . '

It was a long time, Rowan realized, since he had listened to women laugh.

When the bus arrived, he sat next to Doctor Von, willing the man to stay quiet. Gert and Beryl were right in front of them and, dismissive though they had been about the posters, he instinctively knew they wouldn't want a Jerry listening in behind their backs.

Listening in himself, Rowan couldn't help hoping that

Beryl would get onto the secrets that would make Hitler blush. But their talk was of meat rationing, the better weather, and the pattern on Gert's new curtains. *'Not quite peonies, Beryl, but not quite roses either——do you know what I mean?'*

This was normal talk, Rowan realized. Normal women's talk, anyway. And he found himself picturing, and even looking forward to, being back in the kitchen at Spitalfields while Daff made a pot of tea, and his nana and his mother discussed dogs and knitting patterns and recipes for stews, their voices as soothing as a song known by heart.

It was still light when the bus reached the village and stopped at the foot of the hill. But as Doctor Von led his test-cases up a track that wound, steeply, up to the hospital, the sun began to set, and the bright marigold-glow of it turned the way ahead a magical yellow-gold.

Rowan could hear blackbirds singing as the track joined the road, with its border of apple trees, that led the final few yards to the hospital. And it struck him, as they approached the gates, that he hadn't thought of Dorothea for quite a long time.

That was a good day we've just had, he told her in his head. *Apart from the poster with the rat on it, you missed a good day, stupid.*

'BECAUSE, BECAUSE, BECAUSE, BECAUSE, BECAUSE . . .'

Rowan had yet to read the story of *The Wizard of Oz* and John, Sid, and Donald had never even heard of it. Doctor Von said he understood it was a fairy tale, of sorts, and that he was surprised it was out as a film, not a cartoon. He was also surprised that Shirley Temple wasn't in it, since she was in just about everything else.

They went to a matinee performance, but the queue outside the cinema was so long that they didn't get in.

'We will wait,' Doctor Von said, 'and go to the later show.'

Sid began to scratch at his arms, realized what he was doing and stopped. 'Won't it be dark?' he wondered, doing his best to sound unafraid. 'When we get back to the village? Won't it be too dark to be out, and climbing the hill?'

'I have a torch,' von Metzer reassured him. 'All will be fine.'

They didn't mind staying put, towards the front of a

new queue, for even though the wait was a long one there was plenty to look at and Rowan, John, Sid, and Donald had grown used to remaining still, sifting quietly through their own thoughts.

At last the cinema doors opened and the matinee audience streamed out. From the comments people were making, as they hurried down the steps, Rowan could tell it had been a film worth seeing and he shuffled his feet, eager to get a move on and find a good seat.

He saw Sarah Jane before she saw him, and could have kicked himself for the blush that rose, uncontrollably, from his neck right up to his forehead. Her hair was longer and blonder than he remembered and she looked just like a film star herself, in a hat and coat the exact same red as her lipstick.

She was clinging to someone's arm, as she came clacking down the steps in her going-out shoes, and Rowan's face flushed even hotter as he recognized the young man who had once been such a frequent visitor to Ward Five's bathroom.

I'm sorry, he told Dorothea, in his head. *I know I shouldn't let her get to me like this, after what she did to you . . . but I can't help it.*

Hoping, yet dreading, that Sarah Jane would speak to him he fixed his gaze on the cinema doors. And if Sid had done his best, earlier, to appear casual about the dark, that was nothing compared to the effort Rowan was making now, to seem like a nice, normal boy who went to the cinema all the time, with his nice, normal chums.

When he dared to look back, Sarah Jane and her friend

had gone. *She must have spotted us,* he fretted, wishing, now, that he'd tried to catch her eye. *I wonder if she smiled?*

In fact, Sarah Jane had not smiled; not at Rowan, or anyone else in the queue. Instead, she had glared daggers at Doctor von Metzer before nudging her friend and hissing in his ear: 'That's him. That's the one.'

'Right,' the young man had replied. 'And out for a spot of entertainment, is he? Well, we'll have to see what we can organize for him, won't we—for later.'

If von Metzer caught Nurse Springfield's look, or sensed her friend's hostility, he did not allow either to darken his mood. All seemed well, to him, as he accompanied his test-cases into the cinema and settled them all in a row.

The name of the girl was the first thing to startle Rowan about the film, *The Wizard of Oz.*

Dorothy . . .

And when she leaned back against that cornstack and wished to go to a place where there was no trouble . . . a place behind the moon . . . beyond the rain . . . he did not have to turn to Doctor Von, or to any of the others, to know that they, too, were remembering that moment, at the pantomime auditions, when Dorothea had stretched towards an imaginary window, yearning to go . . . to fly . . .

Then the girl began to sing, her voice spilling, deliciously, into the cinema's smoky dark. And: *That's it,* Rowan thought. *That's the kind of place Dorothea wanted to go to. Not to Neverland with those stupid lost boys but somewhere over the rainbow . . .*

He swallowed, hard, determined not to blub, even though his throat hurt and he was seeing Kansas through a film of tears.

Only . . . you should have waited, Dorothea. Waited, and then stayed . . . stayed right here, until it was your proper time to go. Your hair would have grown. You'd have seen the saints in the windows, and the white cliffs of Dover, and been the first one, I bet, to sit near the wireless on Thursday nights. Now you'll never know what good things might have happened to you, on this side of the rainbow, and neither will we.

And then he forgot about not wanting to blub—forgot, and no longer cared—as the tears spilled over, his shoulders heaved and he wept, at last, for his friend.

Sid was crying too, and so was Donald. Gasping and blubbering, and mopping their faces with the big hospital handkerchiefs that had the initials of long-forgotten patients embroidered in the corners. Even John Wallace felt a tear roll down his face, and he licked at the saltiness in wonder.

Von Metzer simply sat, drinking in the song. Later, after the film had ended, John Wallace would quietly thank him for not getting dismayed and trying to hustle them out of the cinema for tea and cakes.

'Why?' von Metzer would reply, in genuine surprise. 'I did not notice. I was lost in the voice of that girl. That Judy Garland. And I was thinking . . . had Dorothea been required to sing, while playing the part of Wendy, that is exactly—precisely—the way she would have sounded.'

Luckily, nobody else in the cinema so much as tutted to hear grown men and a boy sobbing their hearts out over a song. Maybe that's what war did to people, Rowan thought, as he began, at last, to calm down. Even a war in which no one's house had been bombed yet might be making people kinder towards each other—here in the outside world.

Up on the screen a tornado was causing havoc. Had they filmed a real disaster? Rowan wondered, for it looked astonishingly real. And then—crikey—Dorothy's house! The house was actually flying through the air! Spinning out of control with Dorothy and her little dog still inside it.

It was all incredibly clever . . . so with a final, juddery sigh, he allowed himself to stop grieving for Dorothea, and be whirled from his seat to the magical land of Oz.

Dorothy killed someone although she didn't mean to. The house she was flying in squashed a person flat when it came smack-down to land. This didn't bode well for Dorothy. Yet who in their right mind, Rowan wondered, was ever going to blame her? It wasn't as if she'd meant to kill anyone. It had all been beyond her control. Nobody did blame Dorothy, at first, for the dead person had been wicked, which seemed to make it all right, Rowan noticed, like when his father and John Wallace shot the Germans.

A good and beautiful witch gave Dorothy a pair of magic slippers and some very odd-looking people called Munchkins danced and sang a high-pitched little song. It was all very peculiar, and poor Dorothy just wanted to go home and get back to normal—understandably enough, Rowan thought.

She met a scarecrow who said he was not so bright about doing things any more. Then she met a tin man who had no heart so could not love. Then a cowardly lion turned up—a bumbling bag of nerves, that lion, although he yearned to be King of the Forest.

(Oh, my, thought Rowan, as Donald and John and Sid leaned so far forward in their seats it seemed they might leap, at any moment, into the film themselves. Oh my, oh my. Oh my . . .)

The Wizard would help each one of them, Dorothy decided. They would follow the yellow brick road until they got to the Emerald City, where the all-powerful Wizard of Oz would make everything all right.

Only . . . the wizard turned out to be a great big phoney. 'I'm a very good man,' he cried out, as the trappings of his splendour and so-called expertise came tumbling down around his ears. 'I'm just a very bad wizard.'

They forgave him though because, really, they didn't need him any more. The lion had already been brave, the scarecrow wise, and the tin man all heart. Somewhere along the yellow brick road, or while standing up for themselves against the wicked witch of the west, they had found for themselves all the qualities they thought they lacked, but had really possessed all along.

And Dorothy did get back to Kansas. She could have gone any time, apparently. She just needed to understand how much she was loved and missed at home. She needed to discover there was no place like it.

They emerged, blinking, into the remains of daylight. John Wallace was the first to speak. 'You wouldn't think,' he said, 'that all I've been doing is sitting tight in a chair, watching a film. I feel like I walked to that Oz place myself, and then all the way back again. I'm dead beat!'

'I know exactly what you mean,' said Donald.

'Me too,' Sid agreed.

Von Metzer raised an arm and chuckled, happily, as the bus to the village—a bus that passed only once every two hours, and not always on the dot—slowed down and then stopped. 'How about that?' he said. 'A big coincidence, yes? This world is full of them.'

'KEEP RIGHT ON WALKING, SONNY'

The mob was waiting at the bottom of the hill. Some of the men carried pitchforks and crowbars. The women were hanging back, like the gulls on Dover beach.

'No one's to touch the loonies,' ordered Sarah Jane's friend. 'We've no argument with them.'

Von Metzer and his test-cases were not quite close enough to hear, only to see. It was dark, as Sid had sort-of-feared it would be, but the moon provided just enough light for Rowan to pick out one or two faces and to wonder why they looked so fierce. Then he caught the glint of metal, in somebody's hands, and his stomach did a somersault.

'What's going on?' Sid wondered. 'Who are all those people, and what are they doing, blocking the stile? They'll move, won't they, when we get to it? They'll move if we ask them?'

Von Metzer flung wide both his arms, bringing everyone to a halt.

'Trouble,' said John Wallace—a statement, not a question.

'John,' von Metzer said, quietly, 'whatever happens, do not interfere. It is me they have come for.'

'It's not on,' John replied, swiftly. 'A pack of pea-brained bullies armed to the teeth and lying in wait for a defenceless man? It's not on at all, I tell you.'

'Nevertheless, you will stay back, keeping the others, also, out of harm's way. If possible you will slip past these people, without attracting their attention, and take Rowan, Donald, and Sid straight back to the hospital. That is an order, John Wallace. I expect you to obey.'

Rowan's stomach was still somersaulting. Why was this happening? What had Doctor Von done?

'Von Metzer?' It was Sarah Jane's friend calling out. He was a big, strapping lad—Rowan had never noticed before quite how big and strapping he was—and if running his father's farm hadn't kept him from joining up, he would have been a dab hand by now with a bayonet.

And the way he'd said 'Von Metzer', spitting out the name like rotten fruit . . . *He loathes him,* Rowan realized, in mounting horror. *He hates his guts.*

'What is it you want with me?' Von Metzer was trying to sound neutral—pleasant, even—but just the sound of his voice, guttural in the soft English air, was enough to make the women shiver and the men clench their fists. Von Metzer could have grovelled or threatened; promised them retribution or his whole life's savings, and still they would have wanted his blood.

This is all because he's a Jerry, Rowan agonized. *They don't know, or care, how kind he is. All they see is a rat.*

A filthy Nazi rat, listening to gossip on buses, and gobbling up secrets.

'Your patients can keep going,' Sarah Jane's friend shouted. 'On to the hospital—send them through.'

'Hang on!' It was one of the women from the village speaking. 'What if they get lost? They'll just wander around all over the place, won't they? And there'll be hell to pay with the director if they go falling into ditches, or dying of exposure.'

'They won't get lost.'

Rowan flinched.

'They're not that stupid. And if the boy—that one in the middle—can follow directions on stage I'm pretty sure he can follow the path to the hospital.'

She means me, Rowan realized. *Sarah Jane's talking about me. I'm 'the boy in the middle', the one she reckons has just about enough sense to walk up a hill by himself.*

An older man raised a pitchfork and jabbed it towards von Metzer. 'Give the boy your torch,' he yelled across the space between the two groups. 'Now!' He looked like a devil, standing there with his face all twisted and the prongs of the fork shedding bits of old muck as he jabbed the air a second time.

'No,' Rowan muttered. 'I'm not going anywhere. None of us are, are we?'

'No,' Sid agreed, with only a hint of a tremble. 'We're on your side, doc. We'll see those bullies off. Like John just said, it's not on.'

'We could try reasoning with them,' Donald added.

Von Metzer grabbed Rowan's hand, and clamped his fingers around the torch.

'Thank you,' he said. 'All of you. But if you stay, you will only make the matter worse. Go. I want you to go . . . John? Will you please . . . '

John Wallace thought for a moment, then took hold of Rowan's elbow, forcing him to move. 'Come on, lad,' he urged, in a low whisper. 'If we get a move on we can raise the alarm—send someone down sharpish from the hospital, to break up this little spat.'

But this isn't just a 'little spat', stupid, Rowan wanted to shout. *Don't make out that it is, just to make me feel better about abandoning Doctor Von. And don't pretend we can do anything about it, either, once we're over that stile. Because by the time we reach the hospital it's going to be TOO LATE. Even if we ran all the way, even if we could FLY, Doctor Von is going to be badly hurt here—maybe even killed—before anyone can stop it happening.*

The mob parted as Rowan, John, Donald, and Sid shuffled forward, towards the stile. And although people stared as they passed, there was neither malice nor compassion in their glances—just a dull and fleeting curiosity.

We are insignificant, Rowan realized. *We are like ghosts or cattle, plodding along. We are less than dots.*

'Hurry along there, idiot-boy.'

He had one foot on the stile. John Wallace and the others were right behind him. The beam of the torch was lighting up the track, turning it yellow the way the setting sun had done, just a week or so earlier.

I am not an idiot-boy.

The stile was narrow. Too narrow to be a stage. But then, Rowan wasn't acting as he leapt onto it and spun round to face the mob.

'You have no right, any of you, to judge Doctor Von or to hurt him.'

Heads turned and eyes blinked. He had their attention now all right.

'Keep right on walking, sonny,' Sarah Jane's friend called out. 'Go on—over the big stile, and up the big hill like you've been told.' He sounded affable, as if he was enjoying an unexpected joke; as if Rowan was a small child wanting to do his party piece at an inappropriate time. A ripple of amusement ran through the mob. The loony defending the Jerry . . . it was really rather sweet. But only for a moment.

'I said get going,' Sarah Jane's friend yelled, not so pleasantly this time. 'Or do you need a bit of a push?'

A push?

I don't need a push.

Little kids on swings need pushes.

I am not a little kid.

Rowan aimed the torch. Not at Sarah Jane's friend—not yet—but at the woman who had been concerned, a few minutes ago, about ditches and exposure. 'Doctor Von would never hurt a fly,' he appealed to her, as she cringed away from the spotlight. 'He's not a spy. He's not even interested in the war. Not really. His mission in life is to keep people alive and happy in their minds. He is a good man. Please tell the others to leave him alone.'

'He's a filthy pervert!' one of the men shouted. 'And what would you know about it anyway? How old are you—ten?'

Rowan frowned. 'I'm thirteen,' he answered. 'And a lot smarter than you think.' *Brighter than you any day,* he wanted to add, but was smart enough not to.

The mob began to shift and mutter. As a distraction, Rowan set about swinging the torch in wide, crazy arcs. Meanwhile, he noticed, John Wallace, Sid, and Donald had fallen into line in front of him, shoulder to shoulder, facing the crowd; each man ready to chip in if necessary but allowing Rowan his moment. *I cannot . . . I must not . . . mess this up*. Peering easily over his friends' heads (for the stile was quite a high one, and set on a slope) Rowan aimed the torch at random—and caught Sarah Jane's face, full-on.

For a second the light wavered, on the point of sliding away. Then: '*You* know Doctor Von's a good man, don't you?' Rowan called out, sternly. 'Tell them, Nurse Springfield. Get your man-friend, and all these others, to leave him alone.'

'That's enough, frazzle-brain. Shut up and get down. Right this second, before I lose my temper.'

The torchlight flew, unerringly, into the reddening face of Sarah Jane's friend.

'And switch that sodding thing off before I whack it clean out of your hands and shove it up your . . . '

'Steady on, Jim,' someone called out. 'He's just a kid.'

Jim, is it? thought Rowan. *Well then, Jim*: 'You're the only filthy pervert around here,' he shouted. 'A filthy pervert *and* a trespasser. I saw you, and I heard you—behind the screen with Nurse Springfield when she was supposed to be on duty.'

Immediately, he felt bad. That was private stuff he'd listened to, night after night after night. Private stuff between two adults who, for all he knew, were very much in love. If anyone was a filthy pervert, it was probably him for listening . . .

Then: 'Sarah—is this true?'

Rowan didn't have to move the torch very far to see betrayal written all over the face of a fair-haired young man, standing just to the right of Nurse Springfield.

Out of respect, he lowered the light to the man's knees.

'I'm asking you: IS THIS TRUE? Have you been having it off with Jimmy Simmonds?'

'I . . . I . . . '

Uh-oh . . . . Sarah Jane, Rowan knew, didn't have a leg to stand on. Nor was she a good enough actress to lie—not out here, anyway, with no chance to prepare some good lines. He didn't dare move the torch, although it seemed bizarre and more than a little cruel to be lighting up a pair of knees that were probably trembling with shock and disappointment. For this man was clearly very fond of Sarah Jane, and devastated by what she'd been getting up to with the Jimmy-one.

'It's true, isn't it? *Isn't it?* I *knew* something was up. And you were with him this afternoon, weren't you? Not out shopping with your sister, like you told me you were. Well go on then—were you with Jimmy Simmonds today or not?'

Rowan moved the torch instinctively, the way he would have moved his head, had it not been so dark, to catch Sarah Jane's response. But the light didn't go to her face—it was a movement across, not up. It fixed upon her hand. Her left hand.

'Yes, Robbie, all right—I was with Jimmy. It's all true and I don't care who knows it.'

There you are. Didn't I tell you? She's as common as muck, that Miss Clacton-on-Sea.

Not 'Miss', Dorothea. 'Mrs'. Sarah Jane Springfield is a married woman! How come I never noticed that gold ring before? Right there on her wedding finger? I suppose I just didn't think to look.

Or maybe she took it off when she went to work, stupid.

You're enjoying this, aren't you?

Only entirely, Superboy. Only entirely . . .

All hell was breaking loose. Robbie Springfield had jumped on Jimmy Simmonds's back, threatening to break his neck. Another farmer had grabbed Robbie by the scruff, and was attempting to haul him off, even though his own wife was telling him to stay out of it, because of his groin; and the other men were either dithering, or thumping their fists in the air, shouting: 'Go on, Robbie lad,' and, 'Smash his face in!' and 'That's it, son—teach the randy blighter a lesson he won't forget.'

'For pity's sake!' one of the women cried out, followed by: 'This is all your fault, you little tart.'

'My fault?' shrieked Sarah Jane. 'Talk about the pot calling the kettle black! What's the name of that butcher again? The one with a shop over Margate way? I bet he's slipping you a few extra sausages, Betty Ruddle, rationing or no rationing.'

'Why you little . . . '

It was like being back in the cinema. It was like turning on the wireless in Ward Five. It was completely and utterly bonkers, and all Rowan could do was stand open-mouthed up on the stile, watching it all unfold.

Then: 'Quick, lad, now's our chance. Run for it.'

'John . . . ?'

'Now, I said. Only switch the torch off first. Go!'

'Where's Doctor . . . '

'I'm here, Rowan. I'm right here. We're all here—now run!'

Rowan didn't need telling four times. Leaping from the stile he set off up the hill as if his socks had wings. The others followed, John as silent on his feet as an Indian brave, the others panting like dogs from a lack of strenuous physical exercise in their lives, up until that point.

It was tough going, in the dark. But if one of them stumbled, or tripped over a stone, one of the others hauled him up. Somewhere, away among the apple trees, a barn owl hooted and Rowan thrilled to the sound as he jumped over a pothole he could only just see and forced his aching legs to keep going . . . and going . . .

'We're safe,' gasped John Wallace, as, at long last, the track joined the road and the hospital loomed into view. 'We can . . . slow down . . . '

'Are you . . . sure?' panted Sid.

'Yes. There's no one . . . behind us. We made it. Stop awhile . . . all of you . . . grab a breath. And Rowan . . . you can switch the torch . . . back on . . . now.'

'All right,' said Rowan. 'I wouldn't mind . . . sitting down . . . for a minute. Just over . . . here.'

'Hey, kid!' Donald called after him. 'That was some . . . story . . . you spun back there. About the nurse and the . . . bully. Pure genius, turning the pack . . . upon itself. You deserve . . . a medal . . . for quick thinking.'

Rowan couldn't help smiling. Later he would explain, but not now.

'And for . . . bravery,' gasped Sid, shaking sweat from

his brow. 'Because for a boy to stand up to . . . an ugly mob . . . like that takes a whole heap . . . of courage.'

Von Metzer remained silent. In agony from a stitch in his side, but not about to complain, he bent almost double and clutched both his knees while he breathed, and breathed . . . Then, just as soon as his heart rate had slowed to something approaching normal, he straightened up and walked over to Rowan Scrivener.

Rowan was sitting on the grass at the side of the road, his head resting against the trunk of an apple tree. The grass was wet—his mother and his nana would have made him get up—but he wasn't bothered. It was refreshing. And anyway, his mother and his nana weren't here. They were at home.

Home . . . Rowan's thoughts spooled back to the way the girl, Dorothy, had tapped her feet together in *The Wizard of Oz* and wished with all her might to be in Kansas.

There is no place like home.

Was that true? Rowan couldn't say. Not yet. Not while 'home' still meant a place lit by stripes of sunlight through a barred window and where the bath was screened by ducks and frogs and where everyone knew why the snowstorm beside his bed was more precious to him than gold. But as he thought about the old house in Spitalfields he found himself looking forward, imagining his welcome-home party . . . the drawing room lit by all thirty-four candles . . . his bedroom with the Superboy portrait, vibrant on a wall. He could smile, now, to think of that portrait . . .

There would be lessons to catch up on. Latin, mathematics, history and art—subjects to enjoy sharpening his mind against. Laurel would come back from Weymouth and he would do his best not to scrap with her, however annoying she got. And if Daff and Eddie hadn't seen *The Wizard of Oz* yet he would tell them it was not to be missed.

He was shining the torch upwards, through and beyond the branches of the apple tree, and didn't realize anyone else was there until von Metzer cleared his throat.

'Oh!' he said then, turning the torch briefly, to look, and then away towards the hospital gates, so it wouldn't dazzle von Metzer's eyes. 'It's you, Doctor Von. Are you all right?'

There was just enough moonlight for them both to see by as von Metzer hunkered down on the wet grass and held out his right hand. 'You don't have to thank me,' Rowan said, quickly. 'We had a lucky escape, that's all. It could just as easily have gone the other way. I could have made things worse for you—for all of us—by speaking out like that . . . don't you think?'

'Rowan,' von Metzer said, 'what you did tonight was . . . heroic. I owe you my life, perhaps, and would be glad if you would shake my hand.'

'Really?'

'Really.'

And so they shook hands, the Jerry doctor and Ro-the-Strange. And in that moment, sitting under an apple tree, a stone's throw from a lunatic asylum, six months and twenty-seven days into the war, they felt, both of them, wholly blessed.

Touched by angels, Dorothea would have said.